Pocket Rough Guide

ROME

written and researched by

MARTIN DUNFORD

with additional contributions by

NATASHA FOGES

Contents

<< DOME OF SANTA MARIA DI LORETO
< VIEW OVER ST PETERS SQUARE

INTRODUCTION TO

ROME

When most people think of Rome they imagine sights and monuments: the Colosseum, Forum, the Vatican and St Peter's. Yet it is much more than an open-air museum: the city has constantly reinvented itself over the years, and with its unpretentious outlook, vibrant people, culture and food it has a modern and irresistible edge. As an historic place, it is special enough, but as a contemporary European capital, it is unique.

TREVI FOUNTAIN

Best places for the perfect Roman pizza

There are loads of great pizzerias in Rome that serve up traditional thin, crispy pizzas with the usual accompaniments of *baccalà* and *fiori di zucca*. Most are open evenings only; if you want a lunchtime slice of pizza – *pizza al taglio* – try *Lo Zozzone* (see p.46) or *Il Forno* (see p.57). **THESE ARE OUR OTHER FAVOURITES** > Da Francesco p.47 > La Montecarlo p.48 > Alle Carette p.100 > Da Remo p.120

Rome's eras crowd in on top of one another to a remarkable degree: there are medieval churches atop ancient basilicas and palaces, houses and apartment blocks that incorporate fragments of Roman columns and inscriptions, and roads and piazzas that follow the lines of ancient amphitheatres and stadiums. It's not an easy place to absorb on one visit, and you need to take things slowly, even if you only have a couple of days here. Most of the sights can be approached from a number of directions, and part of the allure of Rome is stumbling across things by accident, gradually piecing the city together, rather than marching around to a timetable. It's best to decide

on a few key attractions (check out our ideas in "Best of…") and see where your feet take you. Above all, don't be afraid to just wander.

You'd certainly be mad to risk your blood pressure in any kind of vehicle, and the best way of getting around the city centre is to walk. The same goes for the ancient sites, and probably the Vatican and Trastevere quarter too – although for these last two you might want to jump on a bus or a tram going across the river. Keep public transport for longer hops – down to Testaccio, Ostiense or EUR, or to the catacombs and the Via Appia Antica, and of course for trips outside the city: to Ostia Antica, Tivoli or nearby beaches.

However you get around, the atmosphere is like no other city – a monumental, busy capital and yet an appealingly relaxed one, with a centre that has yet to be consumed by chainstores and multinational hotels. Above all, there has perhaps never been a better time to visit. Rome has recently been hauled into the twenty-first century: museums, churches and other buildings that had been "in restoration" as long as anyone can remember have reopened, and some of the city's historic collections have been re-housed. Plus, the city's cultural life has been enhanced, with frequent open-air concerts and a flourishing film festival in October. Transport, too, is being tackled, with the construction of a third metro line, although it may be some time before this is finished.

Whether all this will irrevocably alter the character of the city remains to be seen – the enhanced crowds of visitors, spurred on by the growth of cheap flights in recent years, are certainly having a go. But it's a resilient place, with a character like no other, and for now at least there's definitely no place like Rome.

When to visit

You can enjoy Rome at any time of year. However, you should, if you can, avoid coming in July and especially August, when it can be uncomfortably hot and most Romans are on holiday – indeed in August you may find many of the restaurants recommended in this book closed. May, June and September are the most comfortable months weather-wise – warm but not unbearably so, and not too humid. April and October can be nice too – the city is less crowded, outside Easter, and days can still be warm and sunny. The winter months can be a good time to visit, but bear in mind that the weather is unpredictable and while you'll find everything pleasantly uncrowded, a lot of attractions will have reduced opening hours.

ROME AT A GLANCE

>>EATING

Food is one of the highlights of any trip to Rome. You won't really eat badly anywhere: there are lots of good choices in the centro storico; the **Ghetto** and **Testaccio** have a large number of places serving traditional Roman food, while the densest concentration of restaurants of all kinds can be found in **Trastevere**. There's also an abundance of good, honest **pizzerias**, churning out thin, crispy pizza from wood-fired ovens. Be wary of restaurants adjacent to some major monuments. Note that many places are closed during August.

>>DRINKING

Many Roman bars are traditionally daytime haunts, but nowadays there are also plenty of bars and pubs conducive to an evening's drinking, and the city's old-fashioned wine bars or *enoteche* have also become more popular in recent years. The Milanese tradition of *aperitivi* has taken off in bars throughout the city; many places put on a free buffet at around 6–7pm to attract pre-dinner drinkers. Wherever you are, you can drink late – most places are open until at least 1am – but **Campo de' Fiori** and the **centro storico** near Piazza Navona, and the nightlife districts of **Trastevere** and **Testaccio**, are the liveliest areas in the city centre.

>>SHOPPING

Fashion straight from the catwalk is well represented on the streets close to the Spanish Steps – Via Condotti, Via Frattina and Via del Babuino – where you'll find the flagship stores of Prada, Valentino and the like. **Via del Corso** caters to young fashion and cheap clothing. There are lots of small, independent boutiques around the **Campo de' Fiori** and in Monti, and antique shops line **Via dei Coronari** and the streets around. Food is freshest and best in the markets on Campo de' Fiori and Testaccio. The **Porta Portese** flea market every Sunday morning is a quintessentially Roman experience.

>>NIGHTLIFE

There's a concentration of clubs in **Ostiense** and **Testaccio** (especially lively in summer), while **Trastevere**, and the **centro storico** from the Jewish Ghetto to the Pantheon, are good for bars, with the odd backstreet club. The **San Lorenzo** area near Termini has plenty of laid-back, studenty hangouts, often with live music. More alternative places are run as private clubs – usually known as *centri sociali*, a device that means you may be stung for a membership fee, but entry will be free. Festivals take place throughout the summer featuring concerts of every sort, many of them free.

OUR RECOMMENDATIONS FOR WHERE TO EAT, DRINK AND SHOP ARE LISTED AT THE END OF EACH PLACES CHAPTER

Day One in Rome

1 Capitoline Hill > p.42. Rome began here, and the two museums that flank the elegant square are among the city's key sights.

2 Roman Forum > p.70. Some of the most ruined ruins you'll see, but also the most atmospheric.

3 Colosseum > p.68. The most recognizable and perhaps the greatest ancient Roman monument of them all.

Lunch > p.109. Enjoying the good, traditional Roman food at *Taverna dei Quaranta*, it's hard to believe you're just five minutes from the Colosseum.

4 Fontana di Trevi > p.81. No trip to the city could be complete without a visit to this fountain.

5 Piazza di Spagna > p.74. The Spanish Steps, Keats-Shelley House and the square itself are among the city's most compelling attractions.

6 Ara Pacis > p.80. Enclosed in an impressive purpose-built structure, this amazing frieze displays the imperial family during the time of Augustus.

7 Galleria Borghese > p.133. The Bernini sculptures here are the pure essence of Rome (be sure to book in advance).

Dinner > p.129. A meal in lively Trastevere is a must – and you can't go wrong with a slap-up dinner at *La Gensola*.

Ice cream > p.86. *San Crispino* serves arguably the city's best ice cream.

Day Two in Rome

1 **St Peter's** > p.144. It would be a pity to leave Rome without seeing the city's greatest Baroque attraction.

 Coffee > p.152. *Gran Caffe Borgo* is the best place for coffee and a pastry within easy reach of the Vatican.

2 **Vatican Museums** > p.146. So much more than the Sistine Chapel – this staggering complex of museums is not to be missed.

Lunch > p.153. *Dal Toscano*, a long-established Tuscan restaurant close by the Vatican walls, is a good place to recover from museum fatigue.

3 **Piazza Navona** > p.40. One of the centro storico's loveliest open spaces, and close to the church of San Luigi dei Francesi and Palazzo Altemps.

4 **The Pantheon** > p.38. Rome's most intact ancient sight, and near one of the city's great churches, Santa Maria sopra Minerva.

5 **The Ghetto** > p.55. Stroll through the crumbling old Jewish quarter, an ancient part of the city centre.

Dinner > p.58. *Piperno* is the best of the Ghetto's restaurants, with fantastic Roman-Jewish cooking served in lovely surroundings.

Ice cream > p.57. *Alberto Pica* is one of the longest running and best of Rome's many *gelaterie*.

Budget Rome

Rome's piazzas, fountains and other public structures are a fantastic free spectacle, and many of its churches are packed with sumptuous art. Here are some suggestions for how to spend a great day in Rome without spending a penny on anything, apart from food and drink.

1 Vittoriano > p.61. Free to clamber up the steps and enjoy the views – though you pay for the lifts to the very top.

2 Fontana di Trevi > p.81. The only cost is the coins you decide to chuck in.

3 Spanish Steps > p.75. All you need is energy to climb to the top and enjoy the views.

Lunch > p.57. *Il Forno* on Campo de' Fiori is renowned for its pizza by the slice.

4 Palazzo Farnese > p.54. Viewings of the fantastic Carracci ceiling are free, if you can time it right and book in advance.

5 St Peter's > p.144. There's no entry fee for this or any other Roman church.

6 Vatican Museums > p.146. Free on the last Sunday of the month – perhaps the world's greatest sightseeing bargain.

Dinner > p.152. Head up to *Mondo Arancina* for some of the city's best *arancini* –just €2 a pop.

Ice cream > p.152 *Fatamorgana* serves huge portions of delicious ice cream.

Secret Rome

You could spend several days seeing Rome's most obvious sights, and you'd have a wonderful time – mostly with lots of other people. Here are some suggestions for having a great day out in the city, while avoiding the crowds.

1 Largo di Torre Argentina > p.50. The temple ruins of the square are rarely open but animal lovers can visit the rooms and shop of the volunteers who look after a large cat colony here.

2 Rooms of St Ignatius > p.51. Take in the small museum next door to the Gesù; it incorporates the rooms where St Ignatius stayed and a fantastic trompe l'oeil painting by Andrea Pozzo.

3 Galleria Colonna > p.81. Only open on a Saturday morning, and partly because of this an undiscovered treasure among the city's great family palace-galleries.

🍴 **Lunch** > p.87. Tucked away around the corner from the Trevi Fountain, *Colline Emiliane* does delicious Emilian food.

4 Casa di Chirico > p.75. Don't miss this "house" museum, left just as it was when the artist lived and worked here.

5 Santi Quattro Coronati > p.105. The frescoes in the chapel of St Sylvester here are really something special.

6 Museo Storico della Liberazione > p.108. Housed in the wartime headquarters of the Gestapo, this is one of Rome's most moving museums.

🍴 **Dinner** > p.109. Close by San Giovanni, *Charley's Sauciere* is a long-established French food outpost that is little known by tourists.

Museums
and galleries

1 Vatican Museums Home to the largest, richest, most diverse and most dazzling collections in the world. **> p.146**

2 Capitoline Museums Two amazing galleries – one displaying Roman sculpture, the other Roman sculpture and Italian art. > **p.62**

3 Galleria Borghese Fabulous Bernini sculpture and one of Rome's best picture galleries, housed in the Borghese family villa. > **p.133**

4 Museo Nazionale Romano You'll find the finest art collection in this museum's two main locations: Palazzo Altemps and Palazzo Massimo. > **p.44 & p.97**

5 Galleria Doria Pamphilj Private art collection that's intimately exhibited. > **p.34**

Viewpoints

 **St Peter's** It's worth the climb up the dome to see this classic panorama.
> p.144

2 Il Vittoriano Many people's favourite view of Rome, because you can't see the Vittoriano monument itself. > **p.61**

3 Janiculum Hill Of all Rome's hills, this one, to the west of the city centre, gives the fullest panorama of Rome. > **p.127**

4 Spanish Steps Tourist Central, but ignore the crowds – the whole of Rome's centre is spread out before you. > **p.75**

5 Aventine Hill The best views of the Vatican are from the top of Aventine Hill on the other side of the river. > **p.110**

Eating out

1 Roman specialities Sample traditional "poor" cuisine at *Checchino dal 1887*; the oxtail stew is a classic. **> p.120**

2 Eating alfresco Dining outdoors at *Dar Filettaro da Santa Barbara* gives you a great view of the evening *passeggiata*. **> p.57**

3 Pizza With a thin, crispy base and the freshest of toppings, the pizza at *Da Remo* is irresistible. **> p.120**

4 Backstreet trattorias Unassuming, tucked-away trattorias can be full of surprises; old-timer *Da Tonino* is a gem. **> p.48**

5 Roman-Jewish cuisine A meal in the Ghetto is a quintessentially Roman experience – and *Piperno* is the place to indulge. **> p.58**

Shopping

1 Campo de' Fiori This long-standing fruit and veg market takes place every morning; in the surrounding streets you'll find countless independent boutiques. > **p.52**

2 Via del Corso This narrow street, lined with all the mid-range chains, is jam-packed with shoppers at weekends. **> p.34**

3 Via Condotti Lined with eye-wateringly expensive boutiques, this is the main spine of Rome's designer shopping quarter. **> p.74**

4 Via dei Coronari Rome's antiques alley, lined with shops selling everything from Renaissance chests to 1960s Italian coffeepots. **> p.43**

5 Castroni Among the city's best gourmet food stores, great for treats to take home. **> p.152**

Palaces

1 Palazzo Farnese Perhaps the city's most elegant palace, now the French embassy, whose Carracci murals are one of the city's must-sees. **> p.54**

2 Villa Farnesina This Trastevere mansion was home to the banker Agostino Chigi, who employed Raphael to do the decorating. > **p.126**

3 Palazzo Spada The home of one Cardinal Spada is perhaps best known for its ingenious Borromini trompe l'oeil tunnel. > **p.53**

4 Palazzo Barberini The Barberini family's palace is one of the most sumptuous in Rome, and it also houses remarkable collections of art. > **p.83**

5 Palazzo del Quirinale The residence of the Italian president, today open once a week. > **p.84**

Churches

1 Santa Maria Maggiore One of the great Roman basilicas, and a treasure trove of art and history. > **p.91**

2 Santa Maria sopra Minerva The city's only Gothic church, although it's a treasure-house of Renaissance art too. > **p.35**

4 San Pietro in Vincoli A beautifully plain church, home to one of Michelangelo's greatest sculptures. > **p.94**

3 Santa Prassede The chapel of St Zeno here has amazing ninth-century mosaics, which reflect the daylight beautifully. > **p.94**

5 San Clemente This ancient Roman church is the best place to appreciate the city's multi layered history. > **p.106**

Ancient Rome

1 Colosseum The most photographed of Rome's monuments – it has provided the blueprint for virtually all sports stadiums since. **> p.68**

2 The Pantheon An amazing building even in its time, but all the more incredible now, given how completely it has survived. > **p.38**

3 Trajan's Markets Quite simply, an ancient Roman shopping mall, fantastically preserved and newly excavated. > **p.67**

4 Ostia Antica The ruins of Rome's ancient port are some of the most atmospheric you will find anywhere. > **p.160**

5 Ara Pacis The gleaming marble walls were sculpted in 13 BC to celebrate the subjugation of Spain and Gaul. > **p.80**

Baroque

1 Palazzo Barberini Check out Pietro da Cortona's ceiling, gushingly appropriate for the main patrons of the Baroque movement. **> p.83**

2 Santa Maria della Vittoria The daring statue of the *Ecstasy of St Theresa* by Bernini is perhaps the city's most dramatic piece of Baroque art. > **p.84**

3 San Carlo alle Quattro Fontane With four lovely fountains outside, this church is a masterpiece in Baroque design. > **p.83**

4 The Gesù As the centre of the Jesuit movement, this church set the benchmark for all Baroque churches to come. > **p.50**

5 Piazza San Pietro Bernini's colonnaded piazza is pure, theatrical Baroque – as is the church itself. > **p.141**

Outdoor Rome

1 **Villa Borghese** Rome's largest and most central open space, and by any standards a beautiful and diverse city park. **> p.132**

3 Janiculum Hill Some of the best views of the city are from this hill just above Trastevere. > **p.127**

2 Tivoli Tivoli's two Renaissance gardens are among the region's most compelling sights, and are just forty-five minutes from the city centre. > **p.154**

4 Via Appia Antica Though relatively close to the city centre, the Via Appia Antica feels like real countryside and is full of intriguing sights from ancient times. > **p.116**

5 Villa Celimontana Just above the Colosseum, this little park is a good venue for both shady picnics and regular summer jazz concerts. > **p.104**

PLACES

The centro storico

The heart of Rome is the centro storico ("historic centre"), which makes up most of the triangular knob of land that bulges into a bend in the Tiber. This area, known in ancient Roman times as the Campus Martius, was outside the ancient city centre and mostly given over to barracks and sporting arenas, together with several temples, including the Pantheon. Later it became the heart of the Renaissance city, and nowadays it's the part of the town that is densest in interest, a knot of narrow streets and alleys that hold some of the best of Rome's churches and monuments and its most vivacious street- and nightlife. Whichever direction you wander in there's something to see; indeed its appeal is that even the most aimless ambling leads you past some memorably beautiful and historic spots.

VIA DEL CORSO

MAP P.36–37, POCKET MAP F13–15

Running north–south from Piazza del Popolo to Piazza Venezia, **Via del Corso** divides the city centre in two: the western side gives onto the dense streets of the centro storico and to the east, the swish shopping streets that converge on Piazza di Spagna. Named after the races that used to take place along here during Renaissance times, it is also Rome's main shopping street – the stretch beyond Via Condotti, right up as far as Piazza del Popolo, is pedestrianized each evening and hosts a busy *passeggiata* during summer.

GALLERIA DORIA PAMPHILJ

Via del Corso 305. Daily 10am–5pm; €10.50, including audio guide in English; ☏ 06.679.7323, ✆ www.doriapamphilj.it. MAP P.36–37, POCKET MAP F15

The Palazzo Doria Pamphilj is among the city's finest Rococo palaces; the Doria-Pamphilj have long been one of Rome's most illustrious families, and still own the building and live in part of it. They were also prodigious collectors of art, and, inside, the **Galleria Doria Pamphilj** constitutes one of Rome's best late Renaissance art collections, its paintings mounted in the style of the time, crammed in floor-to-ceiling, around the palace's main courtyard. There are many highlights: a rare Italian work by Bruegel the Elder, a highly realistic portrait of an old man, the fabulously ugly *Moneylenders and their Clients* by Quentin Matsys, and a Hans Memling *Deposition*, as well as several paintings by Caravaggio – the magnificent *Rest on the Flight into Egypt*, *John the Baptist* and *Repentant Magdalene* – in the series of rooms on the right, alongside *Salome with the head of St John*, by Titian. Across the courtyard look out also for the gallery's most famous works: a badly cracked bust of Innocent X by Bernini, which the sculptor apparently replaced in a week with the more famous version

GALLERIA DORIA PAMPHILJ

down the hall, next door to Velázquez's famous painting of the same man. Beyond here are a small shop and a series of private apartments, furnished in the style of the original palace and with more paintings. All in all, it's a marvellous collection of work, displayed in a wonderfully appropriate setting.

SANT'IGNAZIO

Mon–Sat 7.30am–7pm, Sun 9am–7pm. MAP P.36–37, POCKET MAP F15

The Jesuit church of **Sant'Ignazio** was dedicated to the founder of the Society of Jesus after his death and canonization. It's worth visiting for its marvellous Baroque ceiling by Andrea Pozzo, showing St Ignatius being welcomed into paradise by Christ and the Virgin, a spectacular work that creates the illusion of looking at the sky through open colonnades. Pozzo also painted the ingenious false dome in the crossing (a real dome was planned but was deemed too expensive). Stand on the disc in the centre of the nave to get the full effect of this trompe l'oeil masterpiece.

SANTA MARIA SOPRA MINERVA

Mon–Fri 7am–7pm, Sat & Sun 8am–12.30pm & 3–7pm. MAP P.36–37, POCKET MAP E15

Piazza della Minerva is home to the medieval church of **Santa Maria sopra Minerva**, Rome's only Gothic church, and one of the city's art-treasure churches, with the Carafa chapel, in the south transept, home to Filippino Lippi's fresco of the *Assumption*. The children visible in the foreground here are portraits of the future Medici popes, Leo X and Clement VII – both of whose tombs lie either side of the main altar. Look also at the figure of *Christ Bearing the Cross*, just in front, a serene work that Michelangelo completed for the church in 1521. Outside, the diminutive **Elephant Statue** is Bernini's most endearing piece of work: a cheery elephant trumpeting under the weight of the obelisk he carries on his back – a reference to Pope Alexander VII and supposed to illustrate the fact that strength should support wisdom.

centro storico

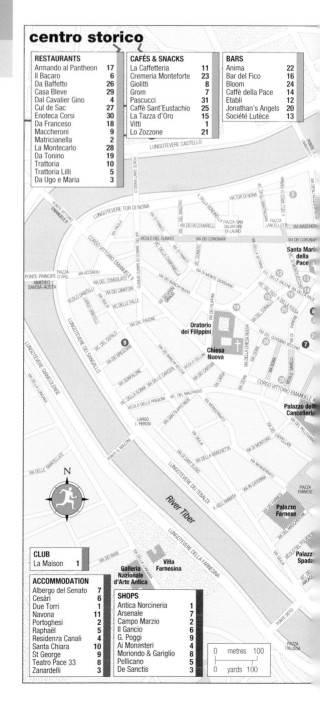

RESTAURANTS

Armando al Pantheon	17
Il Bacaro	6
Da Baffetto	26
Casa Bleve	29
Dal Cavalier Gino	4
Cul de Sac	27
Enoteca Corsi	30
Da Francesco	18
Maccheroni	9
Matricianella	2
La Montecarlo	28
Da Tonino	19
Trattoria	10
Trattoria Lilli	5
Da Ugo e Maria	3

CAFÉS & SNACKS

La Caffetteria	11
Cremeria Monteforte	23
Giolitti	8
Grom	7
Pascucci	31
Caffè Sant'Eustachio	25
La Tazza d'Oro	15
Vitti	1
Lo Zozzone	21

BARS

Anima	22
Bar del Fico	16
Bloom	24
Caffè della Pace	14
Etabli	12
Jonathan's Angels	20
Société Lutèce	13

LUNGOTEVERE CASTELLO

Santa Maria della Pace

Oratorio dei Filippini

Chiesa Nuova

CORSO VITTORIO EMANUELE

Palazzo della Cancelleria

River Tiber

Palazzo Farnese

Palazzo Spada

N

CLUB

La Maison	1

Villa Farnesina

Galleria Nazionale d'Arte Antica

ACCOMMODATION

Albergo del Senato	7
Cesàri	6
Due Torri	1
Navona	11
Portoghesi	2
Raphaël	5
Residenza Canali	4
Santa Chiara	10
St George	9
Teatro Pace 33	8
Zanardelli	3

SHOPS

Antica Norcineria	1
Arsenale	7
Campo Marzio	2
Il Gancio	6
G. Poggi	9
Ai Monasteri	8
Moriondo & Gariglio	4
Pellicano	5
De Sanctis	3

0	metres	100
0	yards	100

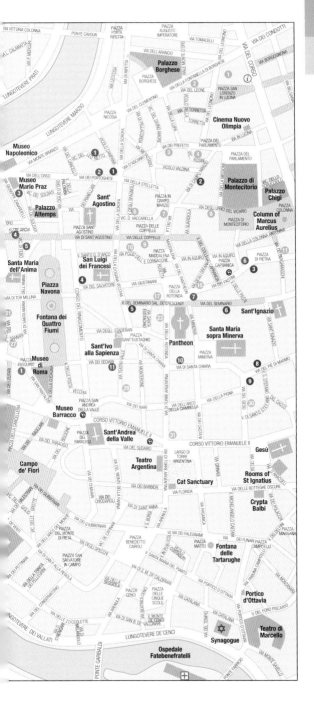

THE PANTHEON

Mon–Sat 8.30am–7.30pm, Sun 9am–6pm; free. MAP P.36–37, POCKET MAP F15

One of the centro storico's busiest sights, the **Pantheon** is the most complete ancient Roman structure in the city, and along with the Colosseum, visually the most impressive. Though originally a temple that formed part of Marcus Agrippa's redesign of the Campus Martius in around 27 BC – hence the inscription – the building was rebuilt by the emperor Hadrian and finished around the year 125 AD. Since consecrated as a church, it's a formidable architectural achievement even now, and inside you get the best impression of the engineering expertise of the time: the diameter is precisely equal to its height (43m), the hole in the centre of the dome – from which shafts of sunlight descend to illuminate the musty interior – a full 9m across. Most impressively, there are no visible arches or vaults to hold the whole thing up; instead they're sunk into the concrete of the walls of the building.

It would have been richly decorated, the coffered ceiling heavily stuccoed and the niches filled with the statues of gods. Now, apart from the sheer size of the place, the main object of interest is the tomb of Raphael, between the second and third chapel on the left, with an inscription by the humanist cardinal Pietro Bembo: "Living, great Nature feared he might outvie Her works, and dying, fears herself may die." The same kind of sentiments might well have been reserved for the Pantheon itself.

SAN LUIGI DEI FRANCESI

Daily except Thurs pm 8.30am–12.30pm & 4–7pm. MAP P.36–37, POCKET MAP E14

The French national church of **San Luigi dei Francesi** is worth a visit, mainly for the works by Caravaggio it numbers amongst its collection. In the last chapel on the left are three paintings: *The Calling of St Matthew*, in which Christ points to Matthew, who is illuminated by a shaft of sunlight; *St Matthew and the Angel*, showing the visit of an angel as the apostle writes his Gospel; and *The Martyrdom*

of St Matthew. Caravaggio's first public commission, these paintings were actually rejected at first, partly on grounds of indecorum, and it took considerable reworking by the artist before they were finally accepted. These days they are considered to be among the artist's greatest ever works, especially *The Calling of St Matthew*, which manifests the simple, taut drama, as well as the low-life subject matter, for which Caravaggio became so well known.

SANT'AGOSTINO

Daily 7.45am–noon & 4–7.30pm. MAP P.36–37, POCKET MAP D14

The Renaissance facade of the church of **Sant'Agostino** is not much to look at from the outside, but a handful of art treasures might draw you in – this was the church of Rome's creative community in the sixteenth century and as such drew wealthy patrons and well-connected artists. Just inside the door, the serene statue of the *Madonna del Parto*, by Sansovino is traditionally invoked during pregnancy, and is accordingly surrounded by photos of newborn babes and their blissful parents. Further into the church, Raphael's vibrant fresco of *Isaiah* is on the third pillar on the left, beneath which is another work by Sansovino – a craggy *St Anne, Virgin and Child*. But the biggest crowds gather around the first chapel on the left, where the *Madonna di Loreto*, painted in 1605 by Caravaggio, is a characteristic work of what was at the time almost revolutionary realism, scruffy clothes contrasting with the pale, delicate feet and skin of Mary.

MARCUS AURELIUS COLUMN

PIAZZA DI MONTECITORIO AND PIAZZA COLONNA

MAP P.36–37, POCKET MAP E14–15

On the northern edge of the centro storico, **Piazza Montecitorio** takes its name from the bulky Palazzo di Montecitorio on its northern side, home since 1871 to the lower house of the Italian parliament (open first Sun of each month 10am–6pm; free). Just beyond, Piazza Colonna, flanked on its north side by the late sixteenth-century Palazzo Chigi, official residence of the prime minister, hosts the **Column of Marcus Aurelius**, erected between 180 and 190 AD to commemorate military victories in northern Europe, and – like the column of Trajan which inspired it – decorated with reliefs depicting scenes from the campaigns.

SANT'IVO ALLA SAPIENZA

Sun 9am–noon. MAP P.36–37, POCKET MAP E15

Between the Pantheon and Piazza Navona, the Palazzo della Sapienza cradles the church of **Sant'Ivo alla Sapienza** – from the outside at least, one of Rome's most impressive churches, with a playful facade designed by Carlo Borromini. Each of the two small towers is topped with the weird, blancmange-like groupings that are the symbol of the Chigi family and the central cupola spirals helter-skelter fashion to its zenith, crowned with flames that are supposed to represent the sting of the Barberini bee, their family symbol. Inside, too, it's very cleverly designed, impressively light and spacious given the small space the church is squeezed into, rising to the tall parabolic cupola.

PIAZZA NAVONA

MAP P.36–37, POCKET MAP D14–15

The western half of the centro storico focuses on **Piazza Navona**, Rome's most famous square. Lined with cafés and restaurants and often thronged with tourists, street artists and pigeons, the best time to come is at night, when the flavour of the place is at its most vibrant, with crowds hanging out around the fountains watching the buskers and street artists or enjoying the scene while nursing a pricey drink at a table outside one of the bars. The square takes its shape from the first-century AD Stadium of Domitian, the principal venue of the athletic events and later chariot races that took place in the Campus Martius, and until the mid-fifteenth century the ruins of the arena were still here, overgrown and disused. It was given a facelift in the mid-seventeenth century

PIAZZA NAVONA

by Pope Innocent X, who built most of the grandiose palaces that surround it and commissioned Borromini to redesign the church of **Sant'Agnese in Agone** (daily 9.30am–12.30pm & 4–7pm) on the piazza's western side. One of three fountains that punctuate Piazza Navona, the **Fontana dei Quattro Fiumi** is a masterpiece by Bernini, built in 1651. Each figure represents one of what were considered at the time to be the four great rivers of the world – the Nile, Danube, Ganges and Plate – though only the horse, symbolizing the Danube, was actually carved by Bernini himself. The fountain is topped with an Egyptian obelisk, brought here by Pope Innocent X from the Circus of Maxentius.

PIAZZA PASQUINO

MAP P.36–37, POCKET MAP D15

Just off Piazza Navona, it's easy to miss the battered marble torso of Pasquino, in the corner of the small triangular space of Piazza Pasquino. This is perhaps the best known of Rome's "talking statues" of the Middle Ages and the Renaissance, upon which anonymous comments on the affairs of the day would be attached. These comments had a serious as well as a humorous intent, and gave us the word "pasquinade", and the statue is still normally covered with rants, poems and pontifications of all kinds.

MUSEO DI ROMA

Piazza San Pantaleo 10. Tues–Sun 10am–8pm; €9, €11.50 with Museo Barracco ☎ 060608, Ⓦ www.museodiroma.it. MAP P.36–37, POCKET MAP D15

The eighteenth-century Palazzo Braschi is the home of the **Museo di Roma**, which has a permanent collection relating to the history of the city from the Middle Ages to the present day. It's a large museum, and to be honest only sporadically interesting; the building is probably the main event, particularly the magnificent Sala Nobile where you go in, the main staircase and one or two of the renovated rooms. But some of the paintings are absorbing, showing the city during different eras. Frescoes from demolished palaces are also highlights.

MUSEO BARRACCO

Corso Vittorio Emanuele II 166. Tues–Sun 9am–7pm. €5.50, €11.50 with Museo di Roma. MAP P.36–37, POCKET MAP D15

The Piccola Farnesina palace, built by Antonio Sangallo the Younger, holds the **Museo Barracco**, a high-quality collection of ancient sculpture that was donated to the city in 1904 by one Baron Barracco. It contains ancient Egyptian and Hellenistic pieces, ceramics and statuary from the Greek classical period and later Roman items, most notably a small figure of Neptune from the first century BC and an odd column-sculpture of a very graphically depicted hermaphrodite. The two charming busts of young Roman boys date from the first century AD.

SANT'ANDREA DELLA VALLE

Mon–Sat 7.30am–noon & 4.30–7.30pm, Sun 7.30am–12.45pm & 4.30–7.45pm. MAP P.36–37, POCKET MAP E16

This church sports the city's second-tallest dome (after St Peter's) built by Carlo Maderno, and of being the setting for the first scene of Puccini's *Tosca*. Inside, it's one of the most Baroque of Rome's churches and your attention is drawn not only to the dome, decorated with paintings of the *Glory of Paradise* by Giovanni Lanfranco, but also to a marvellous set of frescoes in the apse by his contemporary, Domenichino, illustrating the life of St Andrew. In a side chapel on the right, you may, if you've been in Rome a while, recognize some copies of not only Michelangelo's *Pietà* (the original is in St Peter's), but also of his figures of *Leah* and *Rachel*, from the tomb of his patron, Julius II, in the church of San Pietro in Vincoli (see p.94).

PALAZZO DELLA CANCELLERIA

MAP P.36-37, POCKET MAP D15

The grand **Palazzo della Cancelleria** was the seat of the papal government that once ran the city. The Renaissance architect Bramante is thought to have had a hand in its design and it is a well-proportioned edifice, exuding a cool poise quite at odds with the rather grimy nature of its location. You can't get in to see the interior, but you can stroll into the marvellously proportioned, multi-tiered courtyard, which is a treat enough in itself, although **San Lorenzo in Damaso** (daily 7.30am–12.30pm & 4.30–8pm), one of the oldest churches in Rome, also forms part of the complex. It was rebuilt with the palace and has since been greatly restored, most recently at the end of the nineteenth century, and has a painting by Federico Zuccaro, *The Coronation of the Virgin*, over the altar, and a twelfth-century icon of the Virgin Mary in a chapel.

VIA DEL GOVERNO VECCHIO

MAP P.36-37, POCKET MAP D15

Via del Governo Vecchio leads west from Piazza Pasquino through one of Rome's liveliest quarters, the narrow streets noisy at night and holding some of the city's most vigorous restaurants and bars. A little way down on the left, the delightfully small **Piazza del Orologio** is named after the quaint clocktower that is its main feature – part of the Oratorio dei Filippini, designed by Borromini, which is part of the Chiesa Nuova complex (see below). The followers of St Philip Neri attended musical gatherings here as part of their worship, gifting the language forever with the musical term "oratorio".

CHIESA NUOVA

Mon-Sat 7.30am–noon & 4.30–7.30pm, Sun 8am–1pm & 4.30–8pm. MAP P.36-37, POCKET MAP C15

The **Chiesa Nuova** was founded by St Philip Neri, who tended the poor and sick in the streets around here for most of his life, and commissioned this church in 1577. Neri died in 1595 and was canonized in 1622, and this large church, as well as being his last resting-place (he lies in the chapel to the left of the apse), is his principal memorial. Inside, its main features include three

paintings by Rubens hung at the high altar, centring on the *Virgin with Angels*, and Pietro da Cortona's ceiling paintings, showing the *Ascension of the Virgin* in the apse and, above the nave, the construction of the church and Neri's famous "vision of fire" of 1544, when a globe of fire entered his mouth and dilated his heart – a physical event which apparently affected his health thereafter.

VIA DEI CORONARI

MAP P.36–37, POCKET MAP F13–15

Running from the Tiber to the top end of Piazza Navona, this is the fulcrum of Rome's **antiques** trade. Although the prices are as high as you might expect in such a location, there is a huge number of shops (Via dei Coronari itself consists of virtually nothing else), selling a large variety of stuff. A browse makes for one of the city's most absorbing bits of sightseeing.

SANTA MARIA DELL'ANIMA

Daily 9am–12.45pm & 3–7pm. MAP P.36–37, POCKET MAP O14

Just off Via dei Coronari, this church takes its name from the statue of the Virgin on its facade, between two pleading souls in purgatory. It's another darkly cosy Roman church, wide and squat and crammed into an impossibly small space. Nowadays it's the German national church in Rome, a richly decorated affair, almost square in shape, with a protruding main sanctuary flanked by Renaissance tombs. The one on the right, a beautiful, rather sad concoction, is that of the last non-Italian pope before John Paul II, the Dutchman Hadrian VI, who died in 1523, while at the

far end, above the altar, you can just make out a dark and glowing *Virgin with Saints* by Giulio Romano.

SANTA MARIA DELLA PACE

Mon, Wed, Sat 9am–noon; cloister open daily 10am–11pm. MAP P.36–37, POCKET MAP O14

The church of **Santa Maria della Pace** dates from the late fifteenth century, although its facade and portico were added a couple of hundred years later by Pietro da Cortona. Inside, you can see Raphael's frescoes of various sibyls above the Chigi chapel (first on the right), executed in the early sixteenth century, although the opening times are decidedly erratic. If the church is closed, look in instead on the attached **chiostro del Bramante**, finished in 1504, a beautifully proportioned two-tiered cloister that is nowadays given over to temporary art exhibitions and a small café where you can grab a coffee and a spot of lunch (entry ticket to exhibition not required).

ANTIQUES SHOP ON VIA DEI CORONARI

PALAZZO ALTEMPS

Tues–Sun 9am–7.45pm. €7, includes Palazzo Massimo, Terme di Diocleziano, Crypta Balbi, valid 3 days. MAP P.36–37, POCKET MAP D14

Just across the street from the north end of Piazza Navona, the beautifully restored fifteenth-century Palazzo Altemps now houses the cream of the **Museo Nazionale Romano**'s aristocratic collections of Roman statues. Among treasures too many to mention, there are two, almost identical renderings of Apollo the Lyrist, a magnificent statue of Athena taming a serpent, and, in the far corner of the courtyard, a shameless Dionysus with a satyr and panther. Upstairs, the **Painted Views Room**, so-called for the bucolic scenes on its walls, has a fine statue of Hermes; the Cupboard Room, next door, named for its fresco of a display of wedding gifts against a floral background, has a wonderful statue of a warrior at rest, the *Ludovisi Ares*, restored by Bernini in 1622, and a sensitive portrayal of *Orestes and Electra*, from the first century AD by a sculptor called Menelaus – his name is carved at the base of one of the figures. Beyond, one room retains a frieze telling the story of Moses as a cartoon strip, with each scene enacted by nude figures as if on an unfurled tapestry, while in the room itself there is a colossal head of Hera, and – what some consider the highlight of the entire collection – the famous Ludovisi throne: an original fifth-century BC Greek work embellished with a delicate relief portraying the birth of Aphrodite. There's also the Fireplace Salon, whose huge fireplace, embellished with caryatids and lurking ibex – the symbol of the Altemps family – looks onto the *Suicide of Galatian*, apparently commissioned by Julius Caesar to adorn his Quirinal estate and an incredible sarcophagus depicting a battle in graphic, almost visceral sculptural detail. Without question, one of Rome's best collections of classical art.

Shops

ANTICA NORCINERIA

Via della Scrofa 100. Mon–Sat 9am–8pm.
MAP P.36–37, POCKET MAP E14

This deli and butcher is a great place to stock up on Italian treats, such as home-cured *guanciale* and *pecorino*.

ARSENALE

Via del Governo Vecchio 64. Mon 3.30–7.30pm, Tues–Sat 10am–7.30pm. MAP P.36–37, POCKET MAP D15

This large store is one of many boutiques along this funky stretch, with great dresses by owner Patrizia Pieroni and other stuff by independent designers.

CAMPO MARZIO

Via Campo Marzio 41. Daily 10am–1pm & 2–7pm. MAP P.36–37, POCKET MAP E14

Small shop, part of a chain, dedicated to ultra-cool pens and writing accessories, briefcases and pencil cases.

IL GANCIO

Via del Seminario 82/83. Mon 3.30–7.30pm, Tues–Sat 10am–1pm & 3.30–7.30pm. MAP P.36–37, POCKET MAP E15

High-quality leather bags, purses and shoes, all made right here on the premises.

G. POGGI

Via del Gesù 74/75. Mon–Sat 10am–1pm & 4–7.30pm. MAP P.36–37, POCKET MAP F15

This long-established store in the heart of centro storico, caters to all your artistic needs, with paper, paint, brushes and more basic stationery items. Another branch in Trastevere.

AI MONASTERI

Piazza delle Cinque Lune. Mon–Sat 10am–1pm & 3–7.30pm, closed Thurs pm. MAP P.36–37, POCKET MAP D14

Cakes, spirits, toiletries and other items, all made by monks.

MORIONDO & GARIGLIO

Via Pie di Marmo 21/22. Mon–Sat 9.30am–1pm & 3.30–7.30pm. MAP P.36–37, POCKET MAP F15

A short walk from the Pantheon, this is the city centre's most sumptuous and refined hand-made chocolate shop – great for exquisitely wrapped gifts.

PELLICANO

PELLICANO

Via del Seminario 93. Daily 10am–7pm, except Mon am. MAP P.36–37, POCKET MAP E15

Ezio Pellicano only sells one thing: ties, made by Ezio himself or his daughter. You can buy any of the hundreds you see on display, or you can choose from one of the many rolls of material and have your own made up in about a week.

DE SANCTIS

Piazza di Pietra 24. Mon–Sat 10am–1.30pm & 3–7.30pm. MAP P.36–37, POCKET MAP F14

Upmarket gift shop with fun and often kitsch souvenirs of Rome.

Cafés and snacks

LA CAFFETTERIA

Piazza di Pietra 65. Tues–Sun 8.30am–
midnight. MAP P.36–37, POCKET MAP F14

Bureaucrats flock to this
Neapolitan café from
the nearby parliament: the
pastries are imported from
Naples daily, and the espresso
is among Rome's best. Good
for lunch too.

CREMERIA MONTEFORTE

Via della Rotonda 22. Tues–Sun
11am–11pm. MAP P.36–37, POCKET MAP E15

This award-winning *gelateria*
is a tiny treasure right in the
shadow of the Pantheon. Their
speciality, a Sicilian slush called
cremolato, comes in ten flavours.

GIOLITTI

Via Uffici del Vicario 40. MAP P.36–37, POCKET MAP E14

This *gelateria* is an Italian
institution, and once had a
reputation – now lost – for the
country's top ice cream. It's still
pretty good, however, with a
choice of seventy flavours.

GROM

Via della Maddalena 30/A. Daily 11am–
midnight. MAP P.36–37, POCKET MAP E14

The top Torino ice-cream
maker now has a home in
Rome, and its ice cream is
undeniably delicious. Second
branch at Piazza Navona 1.

PASCUCCI

Via di Torre Argentina 20. Mon–Sat 6am–midnight.
MAP P.36–37, POCKET MAP E16

This café specializes in *frullati* –
fresh fruit whipped up with ice
and milk. The ultimate Roman
refreshment on a hot day.

CAFFÈ SANT'EUSTACHIO

Piazza Sant'Eustachio. Sun–Thurs
8.30am–1pm, Fri 8.30–1.30am, Sat 8.30–2am.
MAP P.36–37, POCKET MAP E15

Fantastic coffee, as well as
coffee-based sweets and cakes.

LA TAZZA D'ORO

Via degli Orfani 84/86. Daily 7.30am–1am. MAP
P.36–37, POCKET MAP E15

This place is well named, since
it is by common consent the
home of one of Rome's best
cups of coffee, and sinfully rich
granita di caffè, with dollops of
whipped cream.

VITTI

Piazza San Lorenzo in Lucina 3. Daily 8am–
midnight. MAP P.36–37, POCKET MAP E13

A wide selection of pastries and
sandwiches, along with delicious
coffee; there are tables inside and
on the square. A lunch menu,
too, served from 12.30pm.

LO ZOZZONE

Via del Teatro Pace 32. Mon–Fri 9am–9pm, Sat
10am–11pm. MAP P.36–37, POCKET MAP D15

This Rome legend, just around
the corner from Piazza Navona
and with outside seating, serves
the best *pizza bianca* in town,
filled with whatever you want, as
well as lots of delicious *pizza al
taglio* choices.

Restaurants

ARMANDO AL PANTHEON

Salita de' Crescenzi 30 ☎ 06.6880.3034.
Mon–Fri 12.30–3pm & 7–11pm, Sat
12.30–3pm. MAP P.36–37, POCKET MAP E15

Unpretentious surroundings
and moderately priced food in
this long-standing staple close
by the Pantheon.

IL BACARO

Via degli Spagnoli 27 ☎ 06.686.4110.
Mon–Fri 12.30–3pm & 7.30–11.30pm, Sat
7.30–11pm. MAP P.36–37, POCKET MAP E14

This little restaurant has a small
menu featuring a good and
interesting selection of antipasti
and *primi*, and main courses
focusing on meat, particularly
beef.

DA BAFFETTO

Via del Governo Vecchio 114 ☎ 06.686.1617.
Daily 6pm–midnight. MAP P.36–37, POCKET
MAP D15

Tiny pizzeria that has long
been a Rome institution,
though it now tends to be
swamped by tourists. But it's
still good value, and has tables
outside in summer.

MAKING PIZZAS AT DA BAFFETTO

CASA BLEVE

Via del Teatro Valle 48/49. Tues–Sat
12.30–3pm & 7.30–11.30pm. MAP P.36–37,
POCKET MAP E15

Rome's beautiful folk come
to enjoy great wine and food
in this bright hall in the heart
of the centro storico. There's
a huge wine list, and a menu
of six or so hot dishes plus
cheese plates and other cold
specialities. Not cheap, but the
food is great and the service
ultra-attentive.

DAL CAVALIER GINO

Vicolo Rosini 4 ☎ 06.687.3434. Mon–Sat
1–3pm & 8–10.30pm. MAP P.36–37, POCKET MAP E14

Down a small alley by the
parliament building, Gino
presides over his constantly
bustling restaurant with
unhurried authority. The menu
is traditionally Roman, and
prices on the cheap side –
mains for around €10.

CUL DE SAC

Piazza Pasquino 73 ☎ 06.6880.1094. Daily
noon–4pm & 7pm–12.30am. MAP P.36–37,
POCKET MAP D15

Busy, long-running wine bar
with an excellent wine list, a
great city-centre location with
outside seating, and decent
food. A good choice if you
don't want a full meal.

ENOTECA CORSI

Via del Gesù 87/88 ☎ 06.679.0821. Mon–Sat
noon–3pm. MAP P.36–37, POCKET MAP F15

Tucked away between Piazza
Venezia and the Pantheon, this
is an old-fashioned Roman
trattoria and wine shop where
you eat what they've cooked
that morning. Inexpensive, and
a real taste of old Rome.

DA FRANCESCO

Piazza del Fico 29 ☎ 06.686.4009. Mon &
Wed–Sun 12.30–3.30pm & 7pm–1am. MAP
P.36–37, POCKET MAP D15

Not just pizzas in this full-on
place in the heart of trendy
Rome – though they're tasty
enough – but good *antipasti*,
primi and *secondi* too. The
service can be slapdash, but the
food and atmosphere are second
to none.

MACCHERONI

Piazza delle Coppelle ☎ 06.6830.7895. Mon–Sat 12.30–3pm & 8pm–midnight. MAP P.36–37, POCKET MAP E14

A friendly restaurant that enjoys a wonderful location in the heart of the centro storico. Inside is spartan yet comfy, while the outside tables make the most of the pretty square-cum-intersection. The food is basic Italian fare, affordably priced and cheerfully served.

MATRICIANELLA

Via del Leone ☎ 06.683.2100. Mon–Sat 12.30–3pm & 7.30–11pm. MAP P.36–37, POCKET MAP E13

This old favourite is one of the best places to try real Roman food, with deep-fried dishes like *filetti di baccali* and various vegetable *fritti*, classic Roman pasta dishes such as *cacio e pepe*, and a great wine list.

ENOTECA CORSI

LA MONTECARLO

Vicolo Savelli 12 ☎ 06.686.1877. Daily noon–3pm & 7pm–1am. MAP P.36–37, POCKET MAP D15

This hectic pizzeria not far from Piazza Navona is owned by the daughter of the owner of Da Baffetto (see p.47) and serves similar crisp, blistered pizza, along with good pasta dishes. Tables outside in summer but be prepared to queue.

DA TONINO

Via del Governo Vecchio 18/19 ☎ 06.333.587.0779. Mon–Sat 12.30–3.30pm & 7–11pm. POCKET MAP C15

Basic Roman food, always freshly cooked and always delicious, at this unmarked centro storico favourite. The simple pasta dishes start at €6, while the *straccetti* (strips of beef with rocket) are a steal at €7. The few tables fill up quickly, so come early or be prepared to queue. No credit cards.

TRATTORIA

Via del Pozzo in Cornacchie 25 ☎ 06.6830.1427. Mon–Fri 12.30–3.30pm & 7.30–11.30pm, Sat 7.30–11.30pm. MAP P.36–37, POCKET MAP E14

You feel a million miles away from the bustling centre in the cool, contemporary upstairs dining room of this restaurant, which serves superb Sicilian food. Reckon on €15 for a pasta dish, €23 plus for a main.

TRATTORIA LILLI

Via Tor di Nona 73 ☎ 06.686.1916. Mon–Sat 12.30–2.30pm & 8–10pm. MAP P.36–37, POCKET MAP D14

One of the city centre's most untouristed trattorias, with a great menu of classic Roman staples, well prepared and served with gritty Roman directness. Starters go for €8, mains for €9–10, and litres of house wine for €9. Tables outside, though you may need to book.

DA UGO E MARIA

Via di Prefetti. Mon–Sat 1–3pm & 8–10pm. MAP P.36–37, POCKET MAP E14

One of the least pretentious restaurants in Rome, with a choice of four starters and mains. Very basic food, and no real ambience, unless you count the blaring radio, but that's the point, as well as the prices: €7 for pasta, €9 for a main dish.

Bars

ANIMA

Via Santa Maria dell' Anima 57
☎ 347.850.9256. Daily 7pm–3am. MAP P.36–37, POCKET MAP D15

This late-night bar-club is kitted out in postmodern-meets-*The Flintstones* chic and offers an assortment of elegant snacks to go with your cocktails, as DJs spin house, funk and drum'n'bass beats.

BAR DEL FICO

Piazza del Fico 26. Mon–Sat 9–2am, Sun noon–2am. MAP P.36–37, POCKET MAP D15

This super little place has a vibrant terrace on which you can sip your (rather expensive) drink and feel at the heart of Rome's urban buzz.

BLOOM

Via del Teatro Pace 29 ☎ 06.6880.2029. Mon, Tues, Thurs–Sat 7pm–3am. MAP P.36–37, POCKET MAP D15

Perhaps the most self-conciously cool bar in Rome. It serves food too, but you'd do better to fill up elsewhere and come on here afterwards, saving your money for an excellent cocktail.

CAFFÈ DELLA PACE

Via della Pace 5. Daily 10pm–2am. MAP P.36–37, POCKET MAP D15

The summer bar, with outside tables full of Rome's beautiful people. Quietest during the day, when you can enjoy the nineteenth-century interior – marble, mirrors, mahogany and plants – in peace.

ETABLI

Vicolo delle Vacche 9 ☎ 06.9761.6694. Daily 12.30–3pm & 6pm–2am. MAP P.36–37, POCKET MAP D14

Lounge-style bar-restaurant in the heart of the centro storico's drinking triangle. Comfy sofas and a laid-back vibe.

JONATHAN'S ANGELS

Via della Fossa 18. Daily 1pm–2am. MAP P.36–37, POCKET MAP D15

This quirky bar certainly wins the "most decorated" award. Every inch (even the toilet, which is worth a visit on its own) is plastered, painted or tricked out in outlandish style.

SOCIÉTÉ LUTÈCE

Piazza Montevecchio 17. Tues–Sat 6pm–2am. MAP P.36–37, POCKET MAP D14

One of the most self-consciously cool bars in the centre of Rome, where patrons sip cocktails late into the night in a whitewashed interior hung with abstract art. An *aperitivo* buffet is included in the drink price.

Clubs

LA MAISON

Vicolo dei Granari 4 ☎ 06.683.3312. Wed–Sun 11pm–3am, till 5am Fri & Sat. MAP P.36–37, POCKET MAP D15

Ritzy club whose chandeliers and glossy decor attracts Rome's gilded youth. Sunday – gay night – is the one to go for, although you'll need to book a table if you want to sit down.

SOCIÉTÉ LUTÈCE

Campo de' Fiori, the Ghetto and around

This southern slice of Rome's historic core lies between busy Corso Vittorio Emanuele II and the river. It's an appealing area for a wander, with cramped, cobbled streets opening out onto picturesque little piazzas. More of a working quarter than the neighbouring centro storico, it is less monumental, with more functional buildings and shops, as evidenced by its main square, Campo de' Fiori, whose fruit-and-veg stalls and down-to-earth bars form a marked contrast to the pavement artists and sleek cafés of Piazza Navona. To the east it merges into the narrow streets and scrabbly Roman ruins of the old Jewish Ghetto, an atmospheric neighbourhood that huddles up close to the city's giant synagogue, while just north of here lies the major traffic intersection and ancient Roman site of Largo di Torre Argentina.

LARGO DI TORRE ARGENTINA

MAP P.52–53, POCKET MAP E16

The busy traffic hub of **Largo di Torre Argentina** holds the ruins of four Republican-era temples, now home to a thriving colony of cats; down the steps on the southwestern corner you can visit the somewhat pungent **cat sanctuary** (daily noon–6pm; Ⓦ www.romancats.com), which tends to the 300 cats that live in the excavations. On the far side of the square, the Teatro Argentina was, in 1816, the venue for the first performance of Rossini's *Barber of Seville*, not a success at all on the night: Rossini was apparently booed into taking refuge in the Bernasconi pastry shop (see p.57). Built in 1731, it is today one of the city's most prestigious theatres, and is thought to stand over the spot in Pompey's theatre where Caesar was assassinated.

THE GESÙ

Piazza del Gesù. Daily 6.45am–12.45pm & 4–7.30pm. MAP P.52–53, POCKET MAP F16

The church of the **Gesù** was the first Jesuit church to be built in Rome, and has since served as the model for Jesuit churches everywhere – its wide single-aisled nave and short transepts edging out under a huge dome were ideal for the

large congregations the movement wanted to draw. Today it's still a well-patronized church, notable not only for its size (the glitzy tomb of the order's founder, St Ignatius, is topped by a huge globe of lapis lazuli – the largest piece in existence) but also for the staggering richness of its interior. Opposite, the tomb of the Jesuit missionary, St Francis Xavier, holds a reliquary containing the saint's severed arm (the rest of his body is in Goa), while the ceiling's ingenious trompe l'oeil, the *Triumph of the Name of Jesus* by Baciccia, oozes out of its frame in a tangle of writhing bodies, flowing drapery and stucco angels stuck like limpets – the Baroque at its most fervent.

Occupying part of the first floor of the Jesuit headquarters are the **Rooms of St Ignatius** (Mon–Sat 4–6pm, Sun 10am–noon; free), where the saint lived from 1544 until his death in 1556. There are bits and pieces of furniture and memorabilia, but the true draw is the corridor just outside, decorated by Andrea Pozzo in 1680 – a superb exercise in perspective, giving an illusion of a grand hall in what is a relatively small space.

ACCOMMODATION	
Argentina Residenza	3
Campo de' Fiori	2
Fortyseven	5
Residenza Farnese	4
Teatro di Pompeo	1

CAFÉS & SNACKS	
Alberto Pica	16
Barnum Café	2
Bernasconi	12
Il Forno Di Campo de' Fiori	5

RESTAURANTS	
Al Bric	3
Ar Galletto	6
Dar Filettaro a Santa Barbara	8
Grappolo d'Oro Zampanò	4
Nonna Betta	17
Piperno	18
Roscioli	11
Da Sergio	13

BARS	
L'Angolo Divino	10
Bartaruga	14
Il Goccetto	1
Open Baladin	15
Vinaietto	9
La Vineria	7

SHOPS	
Ibiz	2
Loco	1
Spazio Sette	3

CRYPTA BALBI

Via delle Botteghe Oscure 31
☎06.3996.7700. Tues–Sun 9am–7.45pm. €7.
MAP P.52–53, POCKET MAP F16

This corner plot is the site
of a **Roman theatre**, the
remains of which later became
incorporated in a number of
medieval houses. An exhibition
takes you through the
evolution of the site, with lots
of English explanation, but you
have to take one of the hourly
tours to see the site proper, and
try to glean what you can from
the various arches, latrines,
column bases and supporting
walls that make up the cellar
of the current building. The
real interest is in the close
dissection of one city block
over two thousand years. On
Sundays at 3pm there are visits
to parts of the site currently
under excavation.

CAMPO DE' FIORI

MAP P.52–53, POCKET MAP D16

In many ways Rome's most
appealing square, **Campo
de' Fiori** is home to a lively
fruit and vegetable market
(Mon–Sat 8am–2pm), flanked
by restaurants and cafés, and
busy pretty much all day and
night; it's one of the best places
in town for an early-evening
aperitivo, but a rough late-night
crowd means it's worth
avoiding later on, at weekends
especially.

No one really knows how
the square came by its name,
which means "field of flowers",
but one theory holds that it
was derived from the Roman
Campus Martius, which used to
cover most of this part of town;
another claims it is after Flora,
the mistress of Pompey, whose
theatre used to stand on what

Campo de' Fiori and the Ghetto

is now the northeast corner of the square – a huge complex by all accounts, which stretched right over to Largo Argentina, and where Julius Caesar was famously stabbed on the Ides of March, 44 BC. Later, Campo de' Fiori was the site of the city's cattle market and public executions, the most notorious of which is commemorated by the statue of a hooded Giordano Bruno in the middle of the square. Bruno was a late sixteenth-century freethinker who was denounced to the Inquisition; when he refused to renounce his philosophical beliefs, he was burned at the stake.

PALAZZO SPADA

Piazza Capo di Ferro 13 ☎ 06.683.2409,
🖳 www.galleriaborghese.it. Tues–Sun
8.30am–7.30pm. €5. MAP P52–53, POCKET MAP D16

The Renaissance **Palazzo Spada** houses a **gallery** of paintings collected by Cardinal Bernardino Spada and his brother Virgilio in the seventeenth century. However, the main feature is the building itself: its facade is frilled with stucco adornments, and off the small courtyard is a crafty trompe l'oeil by Borromini – a tunnel whose nine-metre length is multiplied about four times through the architect's tricks with perspective. Inside, the gallery's four rooms aren't spectacularly interesting unless you're a connoisseur of seventeenth- and eighteenth-century Italian painting; of special note, though, are two portraits of Cardinal Bernadino by Reni and Guercino.

PALAZZO FARNESE

Piazza Farnese. Mon & Thurs visits in French or Italian at 3pm, 4pm, 5pm; free; book in advance on 📧 visitefarnese@france-italia.it or 📞 06.686.011. MAP P.52–53, POCKET MAP D16

Just south of Campo de' Fiori, **Piazza Farnese** is a quite different square, with great fountains spurting out of carved lilies – the Farnese emblem – into marble tubs brought from the Baths of Caracalla, and the sober bulk of the Palazzo Farnese itself. Commissioned in 1514 by Alessandro Farnese – later Paul III – from Antonio di Sangallo the Younger, the building was worked on after the architect's death by Michelangelo, who added the top tier of windows and cornice. It now houses the French Embassy and holds what has been called the greatest of all Baroque ceiling paintings, Annibale Carracci's *Loves of the Gods*, completed in 1603. Centring on the *Marriage of Bacchus and Ariadne*, this is supposed to represent the binding of the Aldobrandini and Farnese families, and is an erotic hotchpotch of cavorting flesh. Carracci did the main plan and the central painting himself, but left the rest to his brother and cousin, Agostino and Ludovico, and various assistants such as Guido Reni and Guercino, who went on to become some of the most sought-after artists of the seventeenth century. It's a fantastic piece of work, perhaps only eclipsed in Rome by the Sistine Chapel itself; sadly, Carracci, disillusioned by the work, and bitter about the relative pittance that he was paid for it, didn't paint much afterwards, and died penniless a few years later.

VIA GIULIA

MAP P.52–53, POCKET MAP B14–D17

Via Giulia, running parallel to the Tiber, was built by Julius II to connect Ponte Sisto with the Vatican. The street was conceived as the centre of papal Rome, and Julius commissioned Bramante to line it with imposing palaces. Bramante didn't get very far, but the street became a popular residence for wealthier Roman families, and is still lined with elegant *palazzi*; it makes for a pleasant wander, with features like the playful Fontana del Mascherone to tickle your interest along the way.

VIA GIULIA

FONTANA DELLE TARTARUGHE

MAP P.52–53, POCKET MAP E16

A sheltered enclave between Via Portico d'Ottavia and Via delle Botteghe Oscure, Piazza Mattei might be recognizable from its role as a set in the 1990s film, *The Talented Mr Ripley*. But it's best known as the site of one of the city's most charming fountains, the **Fontana delle Tartarughe**, or Turtle Fountain, a late sixteenth-century creation restored by Bernini, who apparently added the turtles.

THE SYNAGOGUE

Lungotevere Cenci ☎ 06.6840.0661, ⚛ www.museoebraico.roma.it. Synagogue: Mon–Thurs 9am–6pm, Fri & Sun 9am–12.30pm. Museum: mid-June to mid-Sept Sun–Thurs 10am–6.15pm, Fri 10am–3.15pm; mid-Sept to mid-June Sun–Thurs 10am–4.15pm, Fri 9am–1.15pm; closed Jewish holidays. €7.50. MAP P.52–53, POCKET MAP E17

The Ghetto's principal Jewish sight is the huge **Synagogue**, built in 1904. There are hourly guided tours of the building in English, and you should also visit the **Museo Etraica**, which has a well-presented collection of artefacts relating to Jewish ritual, the history of the Jews in Rome and of course the war years. The interior of the building is impressive, rising to a high, rainbow-hued dome, and the tours (20min) are excellent, giving a good background on the building and the persecution of Rome's Jewish community through history. Hour-long tours of the Ghetto in English are also organized (book through the museum; €8).

VIA PORTICO D'OTTAVIA

MAP P.52–53, POCKET MAP E17

Cross Via Arenula into the Ghetto and the contrast with stately Via Giulia can be felt immediately: this crumbling area of narrow, confusing switchback streets and alleys with a lingering sense of age is one of Rome's most atmospheric. The city's Jewish population stretches as far back as the second century BC, though nowadays a handful of kosher restaurants, butchers and the like are pretty much all that remains to mark this out from any other quarter.

The Ghetto's main artery, **Via Portico d'Ottavia**, leads down to the **Portico d'Ottavia**, a second-century BC gate, rebuilt by Augustus and dedicated to his sister in 23 BC. There's a walkway (summer daily 9am–7pm, winter daily 9am–6pm) through the ancient fish market, leading to the adjacent **Teatro di Marcello** (see p.65).

ISOLA TIBERINA

MAP P.52–53, POCKET MAP E17

Almost opposite the Synagogue, the Ponte Fabricio crosses the Tiber to the Isola Tiberina. Built in 62 BC, it's the only classical bridge to remain intact without help from the restorers. As for the island, it's a calm respite from the city centre proper, and is mostly given over to Rome's oldest hospital, that of the **Fatebenefratelli**, founded in 1548 – appropriately, it would seem, as the island was originally home to a third-century BC temple of Aesculapius, the Roman god of healing. The tenth-century church of **San Bartolomeo** (Mon–Sat 10.30am–1pm & 3–5.30pm, Sun 9am–1pm & 6.30–8pm) stands on the temple's original site and is worth a peep inside for its ancient columns, probably

rescued from the temple, and an ancient wellhead on the altar steps, carved with figures relating to the founding of the church, including St Bartholomew himself. The saint also features in the painting above the altar, hands tied above his head, on the point of being skinned alive – his famous and gruesome mode of martyrdom.

PIAZZA BOCCA DELLA VERITÀ

MAP P.52–53, POCKET MAP F18

Piazza Bocca della Verità has as its focus two of the city's better-preserved Roman temples – the Temple of Portunus and the Temple of Hercules Victor, the latter long known as the Temple of Vesta because, like all vestal temples, it is circular. Both date from the end of the second century BC, and although you can't get inside, they're fine examples of republican-era places of worship. The feature that gives the square its name, however, is the **Bocca della Verità** (Mouth of Truth), an ancient Roman drain cover in the shape of an enormous face that in medieval times would apparently swallow the hand of anyone who hadn't told the truth. It was particularly popular with husbands anxious to test the fidelity of their wives; now it is one of the city's biggest tour-bus attractions.

The piazza's church, **Santa Maria in Cosmedin** (daily 9.30am–5.50pm, until 5pm in winter) is a typically Roman medieval basilica with a huge marble altar and a colourful Cosmati-work mosaic floor – one of the city's finest.

Shops

IBIZ

Via dei Chiavari 39. Mon–Sat 10am–7.30pm.
MAP P.52–53, POCKET MAP D16

Great leather bags, purses
and rucksacks in exciting
contemporary designs made on
the premises.

LOCO

Via dei Baullari 22. Mon 3.30–8pm, Tues–Sat
10.30am–8pm. MAP P.52–53, POCKET MAP D16

Pricey, eccentrically designed
shoes, the like of which you
won't find anywhere else.

SPAZIO SETTE

Via dei Barbieri 7. Mon 3.30–7.30pm, Tues–
Sat 9.30am–1pm & 3.30–7.30pm. MAP P.52–53,
POCKET MAP E16

This homewares emporium
stocks the very best of
Italian design, from quirky
Alessi egg-timers to curvy
Flos lamps. Don't miss the
magnificent fresco on the top
floor.

Cafés and snacks

ALBERTO PICA

Via della Seggiola 12. July–Sept Mon–Sat
8.30am–2am & Dec also open Sun
4.30pm–2am. MAP P.52–53, POCKET MAP E17

Gelato has been the Pica
family's stock in trade for
generations, and it shows: this
gelateria has a great choice of
flavours, and the ice cream is
sublime.

BARNUM CAFÉ

Via del Pellegrino 87. Mon–Fri 8.30am–
midnight, Sat & Sun 8.30am–2am. MAP P.52–53,
POCKET MAP D15

A welcome addition to the area,
this friendly circus-themed
café with free wi-fi is great

for breakfast, coffee and cake
or a light lunch. After dark,
it's a relaxing bar with great
cocktails, and there's a popular
aperitivo buffet with DJ set on
Sunday evenings.

BERNASCONI

Piazza Cairoli 16. Tues–Sun 7am–8.30pm.
MAP P.52–53, POCKET MAP E16

A great family-run *pasticceria*,
with *sfogliatelle* to die for. Good
coffee too.

IL FORNO DI CAMPO DE' FIORI

Campo de' Fiori 22. Mon–Sat 7.30am–2.30pm
& 5–8pm. MAP P.52–53, POCKET MAP D16

The *pizza bianca* here (just
drizzled with olive oil on top)
is a Roman legend, and their
pizza rossa (with a smear of
tomato sauce) follows close
behind.

Restaurants

AL BRIC

Via del Pellegrino 51/52 ☏ 06.686.8986. Daily
7.30–11.30pm, Sun 12.30–3pm. MAP P.52–53,
POCKET MAP D15

Al Bric takes its wine and food
very seriously – as evidenced
by the hushed atmosphere,
gigantic wine list and high
prices. The food is varied, with
influences from all over Italy.
Pastas €15, mains €20–25.

ALBERTO PICA

GRAPPOLO D'ORO ZAMPANÒ

AR GALLETTO

Piazza Farnese 102 ☎ 06.686.1714. Mon–Sat 12.30–3pm & 7.30–11pm. MAP P.52–53, POCKET MAP D16

Situated on one of Rome's stateliest piazzas, this restaurant manages to retain the feel of a provincial trattoria, specializing in traditional Roman cookery with a homely touch – try the beef *straccetti* with rocket. Very good value, too.

DAR FILETTARO A SANTA BARBARA

Largo dei Librari 88 ☎ 06.686.4018. Mon–Sat 6–11.30pm. MAP P.52–53, POCKET MAP D16

A fish-and-chip shop without the chips. Paper-covered Formica tables (outdoors in summer), cheap wine, beer and fried cod. A timeless Roman speciality, though the service can be offhand.

GRAPPOLO D'ORO ZAMPANÒ

Piazza della Cancelleria 80 ☎ 06.686.4118. Mon & Wed–Sat 12.30–2.30pm & 7.30–11pm, Tues & Sun 7.30–11pm. MAP P.52–53, POCKET MAP D16

Curiously untouched by the hordes in nearby Campo de' Fiori, this restaurant serves imaginative Roman cuisine in a traditional trattoria atmosphere.

NONNA BETTA

Via del Portico d'Ottavia ☎ 06.6880.6263. Mon–Thurs & Sun 12.30–3pm & 7.30–10pm, Fri 12.30–3pm, Sat 7.30–10.30pm. MAP P.52–53, POCKET MAP E17

The best kosher restaurant in the Ghetto serves all the classes of *cucina Romana*, including fantastic deep-fried artichokes.

PIPERNO

Monte de' Cenci 9 ☎ 06.6880.6629. Tues–Sat 12.45–2.30pm & 7.45–10.30pm, Sun 12.45–2.30pm. MAP P.52–53, POCKET MAP E17

Tucked away on a hard-to-find piazza, *Piperno* is the best of the area's Roman-Jewish restaurants. It's not cheap, but it's a lovely space and there's outside seating in the summer. *Antipasti* and *primi* go for around €14, and *secondi* for €25.

ROSCIOLI

Via dei Giubbonari 21–22 ☎ 06.687.5287. Mon–Sat 12.30–3pm & 6pm–midnight. MAP P.52–53, POCKET MAP E16

Is it a deli, a wine bar, or fully fledged restaurant? Actually it's all three, and you can either just have a glass of wine and some cheese or go for the full menu, which has great pasta dishes and *secondi* at lunch time and in the evening. It's pricey, and the service can be on the snooty side, but the food is terrific. *Roscioli* also has its own bakery nearby at Via dei Chiavari 34.

DA SERGIO

Vicolo delle Grotte 27 ☎ 06.686.4293. Mon–Sat 12.30am–3.30pm & 7pm–midnight. MAP P.52–53, POCKET MAP D16

Towards the river from Campo de' Fiori, this is an out-of-the-way, cosy trattoria with a limited menu and the deeply authentic feel of old Rome. Inexpensive, and with outdoor seating in summer.

Bars

L'ANGOLO DIVINO

Via dei Balestrari 12. Tues–Sat 11am–3pm & 5.30pm–1am. Mon & Sun 5pm–2am; closed Mon & Sun June–Aug. MAP P.52–53, POCKET MAP D16

Quite a peaceful haven after lively Campo de' Fiori, this wine bar has a large selection of wine, and a menu of simple, typical wine-bar food fare – bread, cheese and cold cuts – as well as more substantial dishes in the evening, such as smoked goose with mashed potato (€15).

BARTARUGA

Piazza Mattei 9. Tues–Sun 6pm–2am. MAP P.52–53, POCKET MAP E16

This theatrical bar's wonderfully camp interior, eclectically furnished with eighteenth-century knick-knacks, is a great spot both for pre-dinner *aperitivi* and for late-night drinks. It does a good line in exotic cocktails too.

IL GOCCETTO

Via dei Banchi Vecchi 14. Mon–Sat 12.30–3pm & 6.30pm–midnight. MAP P.36–37, POCKET MAP C15

This family-run wine bar and shop, patronized by devoted regulars, is an atmospheric place for a drink, with wood-clad walls and a cosy feel. There is an extensive menu of wines by the glass and a selection of light appetizers, deli meats and cheeses.

OPEN BALADIN

Via degli Specchi. Daily noon–2am. MAP P.36–37, POCKET MAP D16

Central Rome's ultimate *birreria*, opened by the Baladin brewing company in 2009, and with a stark, modern interior and literally hundreds of mainly artisanal Italian beers to choose from, forty of them on tap.

VINAIETTO

Via Monti della Farina 38. Mon–Sat 10.30am–3pm & 6.30–10pm. MAP P.52–53, POCKET MAP E16

This hole-in-the-wall *enoteca* has just a handful of tables, so most of its regulars drink their wine outside on the cobbles. Though mainly a wine shop, the enthusiastic owners offer a range of wines to drink by the glass – and it's far less expensive than nearby Campo de' Fiori.

LA VINERIA

Campo de' Fiori 15. Mon–Sat 9–2am. MAP P.52–53, POCKET MAP D16

Long-established bar/wine shop right on the Campo, patronized by a mix of devoted regulars and tourists. There's an extensive list of wines by the glass, starting at just €2, as well as a few snacks and light meals.

LA VINERIA

Piazza Venezia and the Capitoline Hill

For many people the modern centre of Rome is Piazza Venezia – not so much a square as a road junction, close to both the medieval and Renaissance centre of Rome and the city's ancient ruins, and the best landmarked space in Rome, the great white bulk of the Vittorio Emanuele monument marking it out from anywhere else in the city. Behind lie the Piazza del Campidoglio and the Capitoline Hill, one of the first settled of Rome's seven hills.

PALAZZO VENEZIA

Via del Plebiscito 118. Tues–Sun 8.30am–7.30pm. €4. MAP P.61, POCKET MAP F16

Forming the western side of the piazza, **Palazzo Venezia** was built for the Venetian Pope Paul II in the mid-fifteenth century and was for a long time the embassy of the Venetian Republic. More famously, Mussolini moved in here while in power, occupying the vast Sala del Mappamondo and making his declamatory speeches to the huge crowds below from the small balcony, although this is only viewable if you're attending one of the exhibitions held here. Most of the rest of the building is home to the **Museo Nazionale di Palazzo Venezia** – which has a lot of fifteenth-century devotional works from central and northern Italy, some beautifully displayed bronzes and rooms full of weapons and ceramic jars from an ancient monastic pharmacy. You can also walk out to the palace's upper **loggia** for a view over the palm-filled courtyard – the gardens are some of the prettiest in Rome.

SAN MARCO

Mon–Fri 4–8pm, Sat & Sun 9am–noon & 4–8pm. MAP P.61, POCKET MAP F16

Adjacent to the Palazzo Venezia on its southern side, the church of **San Marco** is one of the oldest basilicas in Rome. Originally founded in 336 AD on the spot where the apostle is said to have lived, it was rebuilt in 833 and added to by various Renaissance and eighteenth-century popes including Pope Paul II. The apse mosaic dates from the ninth century and shows Pope Gregory IV offering his church to Christ above a graceful semicircle of sheep.

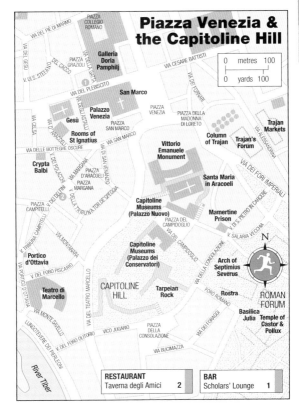

Piazza Venezia & the Capitoline Hill

RESTAURANT		BAR	
Taverna degli Amici	2	Scholars' Lounge	1

IL VITTORIANO

Daily 9.30am–6pm; free. Lifts to terrace: Mon–Thurs 9.30am–6.30pm, Fri–Sun 9.30am–7.30pm; museum daily 9.30am–6pm. €7. MAP P.61, POCKET MAP F16–G16

The rest of the buildings on Piazza Venezia pale into insignificance beside the marble monstrosity rearing up across the street– the **Vittorio Emanuele Monument** or **"Vittoriano"**, erected at the turn of the nineteenth century to commemorate Italian Unification. Variously likened in the past to a typewriter, and, by American GIs, to a wedding cake, there are things to see inside, not least the large **Museo di Risorgimento**, one of the best of many you will see in Italy. But it's the outside that's best, centring on the tomb of the unknown soldier and an enormous equestrian statue of Vittorio Emanuele II, on a plinth friezed with figures representing the major Italian cities. Clamber up and down the sweeping terraces and take the lifts from behind the monument to the top, which give perhaps the most fabulous views in Rome – partly because it's the one place in Rome from which you can't see the Vittoriano.

THE CAPITOLINE HILL

MAP P.61, POCKET MAP F17

The real pity about the Vittorio Emanuele Monument is that it obscures the view of the **Capitoline Hill** behind – once, in the days of imperial Rome, the spiritual and political centre of the Roman Empire. Its name derives from its position as the "caput mundi" or "head of the world", and its influence and importance resonates to this day – words like "capitol" and "capital" all derive from here, as does the word "money", which comes from the temple to Juno Moneta that once stood nearby and housed the Roman mint.

THE CAPITOLINE MUSEUMS

Tues–Sun 9am–8pm ☎ 060608, ⓦ www .museicapitolini.org. €12, €14 for joint ticket with Centrale Montemartini (see p.000); valid 7 days. MAP P.61, POCKET MAP F16–F17

If you see no other museums of ancient sculpture in Rome, try to at least see the **Capitoline Museums**, which are perhaps the most venerable of all the city's collections. They're divided into two parts – the Palazzo dei Conservatori and the Palazzo Nuovo – and you should try to see both rather than choosing one. Tickets are valid for a day so you can fit in each museum with a break inbetween, perhaps for a stroll around the Roman Forum.

The **Palazzo dei Conservatori** is the larger, more varied collection, with some ancient sculpture as well as later pieces and an art gallery. Inside, the centrepiece of the first floor, the Sala degli Orazi e Curiazi, is appropriately decorated with giant, late sixteenth-century frescoes depicting legendary tales from the early days of Rome. Check out the corner room, which contains the so-called

Spinario, a Roman statue of a
boy picking a thorn out of his
foot, and, next door, the sacred
symbol of Rome, the Etruscan
bronze she-wolf nursing the
mythic founders of the city.
Move on to the airy new wing,
where an equestrian statue
of Marcus Aurelius, formerly
in the square outside, takes
centre stage, alongside a giant
bronze statue of Constantine
– or at least its head, hand and
orb – and a rippling bronze of
Hercules.

The second-floor *pinacoteca*
holds Renaissance paintings
from the fourteenth to the
late seventeenth centuries –
highlights include a couple
of portraits by Van Dyck and
a *Portrait of a Crossbowman*
by Lorenzo Lotto, a pair of
paintings by Tintoretto – a
Flagellation and *Christ Crowned
with Thorns*, and a fine early
work by Ludovico Carracci,
Head of a Boy. There's also
a vast picture by Guercino,
depicting the *Burial of Santa

Petronilla (an early Roman
martyr who was the supposed
daughter of St Peter), and two
paintings by Caravaggio, one
a replica of the young *John the
Baptist,* which hangs in the
Palazzo Doria-Pamphilj (see
p.34), the other an early work
known as *The Fortune-Teller*.

The **Palazzo Nuovo** across
the square – also accessible
by way of an underpass – has
some of the best of the city's
Roman sculpture crammed
into half a dozen or so
rooms. Among them are the
remarkable statue of a *Dying
Gaul*, a *Satyr Resting*, the
inspiration for Hawthorne's
book *The Marble Faun*, and
the red marble *Laughing
Silenus* – along with busts of
Roman emperors and other
famous names: a young
Augustus, a cruel Caracalla,
and the centrepiece, a life-sized
portrait of Helena, the mother
of Constantine. Also, don't
miss the coy *Capitoline Venus*,
housed in a room on its own.

SANTA MARIA IN ARACOELI

Daily 9am–12.30pm & 2.30–5.30pm. MAP P.61, POCKET MAP G16

The church of **Santa Maria in Aracoeli** crowns the highest point on the Capitoline Hill and is built on the ruins of a temple to Juno. Reached by a flight of 124 steps up the steep **Aracoeli Staircase**, erected in 1348, or more easily from a side entrance accessible from the Vittoriano or Piazza del Campidoglio, the church is one of Rome's most ancient basilicas, known for its role as keeper of the so-called "Bambino", a small statue of the Christ Child, carved from the wood of a Gethsemane olive tree. The statue is said to have miraculous healing powers and was traditionally called out to the sickbeds of the ill and dying all over the city, its coach commanding instant right of way through the heavy Rome traffic. The Bambino was stolen in 1994, but a copy now stands in its place, in a small chapel to the left of the high altar. Take a look also at the frescoes by Pinturrichio in a chapel on the right, recording the life of St Bernardino.

PIAZZA DEL CAMPIDOGLIO

MAP P.61, POCKET MAP F16–G16

Next door to the Aracoeli Staircase, the smoothly rising ramp of the Cordonata leads to **Piazza del Campidoglio**, one of Rome's most perfectly proportioned squares, designed by Michelangelo in the last years of his life for Pope Paul III. Michelangelo died before his plan was completed, but his designs were faithfully executed – balancing the piazza, redesigning the facade of the Palazzo dei Conservatori and projecting an identical building across the way, the Palazzo Nuovo. These buildings are home to the Capitoline Museums (see p.62); both are angled slightly to focus on Palazzo Senatorio, Rome's town hall. In the centre of the square Michelangelo placed an equestrian statue of Emperor Marcus Aurelius (now a copy), which had previously stood outside San Giovanni in Laterano; early Christians had refrained from melting it down because they believed it to be of Constantine (the first Roman emperor to follow Christianity).

THE SHE-WOLF AND TARPEIAN ROCK

MAP P.61, POCKET MAP F17

Just off the Piazza del Campidoglio, the statue of Romulus and Remus suckling the she-wolf provides one of Rome's most enduring images. Beyond is the **Tarpeian Rock**, from which traitors were thrown in ancient times – and which now gives excellent views over the Forum.

THE MAMERTINE PRISON

Daily 9am–7.30pm. €10. MAP P.61, POCKET MAP G16

Steps lead down from the Tarpeian Rock to little **San Pietro in Carcere** – a low-vaulted church that lies above the ancient **Mamertine Prison**, where spies, vanquished soldiers and other enemies of the Roman state were incarcerated, and where St Peter himself was held. It's now part of a multimedia-assisted tour, taking in the murky depths of the jail, in which you can see the column to which St Peter was chained, along with the spring the saint is said to have used to baptize his guards and other prisoners. At the top of the staircase, hollowed out of the honeycomb of stone, is

an imprint claimed to be of St Peter's head as he tumbled down the stairs. Other parts of the tour take in further excavations and a film on the life and times of the saint, finishing up with a brief bit of evangelizing in the church.

TEATRO DI MARCELLO

Daily 9am–7pm; free. MAP P.61, POCKET MAP F17

Close to the Capitoline Hill, the **Teatro di Marcello** was begun by Julius Caesar and finished by Augustus. It became a fortified palace in Renaissance times, the property of the powerful Orsini family. Forming the backdrop for summer concerts, it also provides a neat cut-through to the Jewish Ghetto (see p.50) just beyond.

SAN PIETRO IN CARCERE

Restaurant

TAVERNA DEGLI AMICI

Piazza Margana 36/37 ☎ 06.6992.0637. Tues–Sat 12.30–3pm & 7.30–11pm. MAP P.61, POCKET MAP F16

On the edge of the Jewish Ghetto, this long-standing restaurant is great for lunch after the rigours of the Capitoline Hill, with tables outside on this atmospheric little square. Lots of Roman

classics, and moderate prices too – starters for around €12, mains for €15–20.

Bar

SCHOLARS' LOUNGE

Via del Plebiscito 101b. Daily 11am–3am. MAP P.61, POCKET MAP F15

A good city-centre Irish pub, with live music and screens showing football and other sports. Food all day.

Ancient Rome

There are remnants of ancient Rome all over the city, but the most famous and concentrated collection of sights – the Forum and Colosseum together with the Palatine Hill – stretches southeast from the Capitoline Hill. You can spend a good half-day, perhaps longer, picking your way through the rubble of what was once the core of the ancient world. The most obvious place to start is the original, Republican-period Forum, the political and commercial heart of the ancient city. You can then visit the later Imperial Forums that lie across Via dei Fori Imperiali before heading up the legendary Palatine Hill, once home to the city's most powerful citizens. Just beyond the Forum, the Colosseum is Rome's most iconic monument, a beautiful construction seemingly at odds with its violent past.

TRAJAN'S MARKETS

Visiting the Forum, Palatine and Colosseum

The **Forum**, **Palatine** and **Colosseum** are open daily (8.30am–1hr before sunset). A joint ticket to all three sights costs €12. **Queues**, to the Colosseum especially, can be a problem: while they do move quickly, they're rarely less than 100m long. To avoid them, buy your tickets at the Palatine ticket office on Via di San Gregorio, which generally has a shorter wait, buy an **Archeocard** or **Romapass** (see p.183), which allows you to use a different queue, or book online through Ⓦwww.ticketclic.it (€1.50 booking fee). There are guided tours of the Colosseum daily every 30min from 9.15am (€4) and of the Forum every day at 1pm (€4); audio guides for each site cost €4.50.

IMPERIAL FORUMS AND TRAJAN'S MARKETS

MAP P.68–69, POCKET MAP F5

The original Roman Forum was the centre of republican-era Rome but the rise of the empire, and Rome's increased importance as a world power, led to the extensions of the **Imperial Forums** nearby. Julius Caesar began the expansion in around 50 BC, and work was continued after his assassination by his nephew and successor Augustus, and later by the Flavian emperors – Vespasian, Nerva and finally Trajan. The remains litter the sides of Via dei Fori Imperiali, and are now in large part open to the public. **Trajan's Markets** (Tues–Sun 9am–7pm; Ⓦwww .mercatiditraiano.it; €11), are the most exciting city-centre ruins to be recently excavated, the result of years of restoration work. Entered from Via IV Novembre, the on-site museum starts with the airy Great Hall; beyond is the Great Hemicycle section, with displays of important finds from the various forums, as well as the Via Biberatica, an ancient street lined with the well-preserved remains of shops and bars.

Outside, the **Forum of Trajan** holds the **Column of Trajan**, erected to celebrate the emperor's victories in Dacia and covered top to bottom with reliefs commemorating the highlights of the campaign. The forums of Augustus (further along) and Caesar (on the other side of the road) might also detain you for a while.

THE COLUMN OF TRAJAN

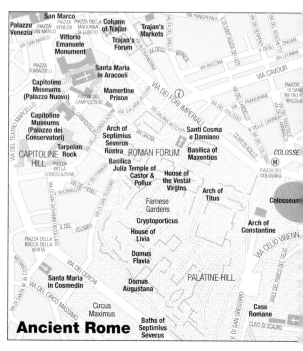

Ancient Rome

SANTI COSMA E DAMIANO

Via dei Fori Imperiali 1. Fri–Sun 10am–1pm & 3–6pm. MAP P.68–69, POCKET MAP F6

Across the road from the Forum of Augustus, the vestibule of the church of **Santi Cosma e Damiano** was originally created from the Temple of Romulus in the Forum, which you can look down into from the nave of the church. Turn around, and you'll see the mosaics in the apse, showing the naturalistic figures of the two saints being presented to Christ by St Peter and St Paul, flanked by St Felix on the left and St Theodore on the right. Outside, the cloister is wonderfully peaceful compared to the busy roads around. For a €1 donation you can also visit the massive eighteenth-century Neapolitan **presepio** or Christmas crib

(Fri–Sun 10am–1pm & 3–6pm), displayed in a room in the corner here, a huge piece of work with literally hundreds of figures spread amongst the ruins of ancient Rome.

THE COLOSSEUM

Piazza del Colosseo. Daily 8.30am–1hr before sunset ☎ 06.700.5469. €12 joint ticket with the Palatine and Roman Forum. MAP P.63–69, POCKET MAP G6

The **Colosseum** is perhaps Rome's most awe-inspiring ancient monument: an enormous amphitheatre that, despite the depredations of nearly 2000 years still stands relatively intact. You'll not be alone in appreciating it, and during summer visits can be a chore. But go late in the evening or early morning before the tour buses arrive,

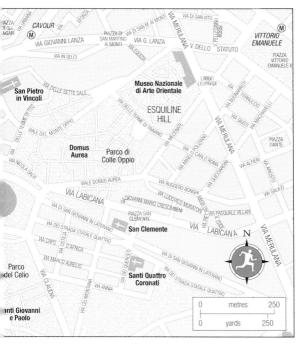

and the arena can seem more like the marvel it really is.

Originally known as the Flavian Amphitheatre (the name Colosseum is a much later invention), it was begun around 72 AD by the Emperor Vespasian, who was anxious to extinguish the memory of Nero, and so chose the site of Nero's Domus Aurea for the stadium. Inside, 60,000 people could be seated, with 10,000 or so standing. The seating was allocated on a strict basis, with the emperor and his attendants occupying the best seats in the house, and the social class of the spectators diminishing nearer the top. There was a labyrinth below that was covered with a wooden floor and punctuated at various places with trap doors and lifts to raise and lower the animals that were to take part in the games. The floor was covered with canvas to make it waterproof and the canvas was covered with several centimetres of sand to absorb blood; in fact, our word "arena" is derived from the Latin word for sand. Once inside, you can wander around most of the lower level, and a larger section of the upper level, though even here you are still only about halfway up the original structure. You can gaze down into the innards of the arena, but there's been no original arena floor since its excavation in the nineteenth century. The lower floor contains a decent bookshop and a space for regular temporary exhibitions; an area by the lifts is given over to a display of fragments of masonry from the Colosseum.

THE ROMAN FORUM

Largo della Salara Vecchia, 5/6
☏ 06.3996.7700. Daily 8.30am–1hr before
sunset. €12 joint ticket with Colosseum and
Palatine. MAP P70–71, POCKET MAP F6–G6

The two or so hectares that
make up the **Forum** were once
the heart of the Mediterranean
world, and although the glories
of ancient Rome are hard to
glimpse here now, there's a
symbolic allure to the place
that makes it one of the world's
most compelling (not to
mention most ruined) sets of
ruins anywhere in the world.
You need an imagination
and a little history to fully
appreciate the place, but the
public spaces are easy enough
to discern, especially the spinal
Via Sacra, the best-known
street of ancient Rome, along
which victorious emperors
and generals would ride in
procession to give thanks at
the Capitoline's Temple of
Juno. A little way beyond, the
large cube-shaped building is
the **Curia**, built on the orders
of Julius Caesar as part of his

programme for expanding the
Forum, although what you
see now is a third-century
AD reconstruction. The
Senate met here, and inside
three wide stairs rise to the
left and right, on which
about 300 senators could be
accommodated with their
folding chairs. In the centre
is the speaker's platform,
with a porphyry statue of a
togaed figure. Nearby, the
Arch of Septimius Severus
was constructed in the early
third century AD by his sons
Caracalla and Geta to mark
their father's victories in what
is now Iran. The friezes on it
recall Severus and in particular
Caracalla, who ruled Rome
with undisciplined terror for
seven years. To the left of the
arch, the low brown wall is the
Rostra, from which important
speeches were made (it was
from here that Mark Anthony
most likely spoke about Caesar
after his death). Left of the
Rostra are the long stairs of the
Basilica Julia, built by Julius

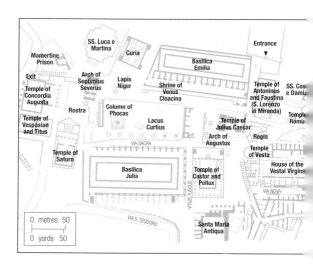

Caesar in the 50s BC after he returned from the Gallic wars, and, a bit further along, rails mark the site of the **Lacus Curtius** – the spot where, according to legend, a chasm opened during the earliest days and the soothsayers determined that it would only be closed once Rome had sacrificed its most valuable possession into it. Marcus Curtius, a Roman soldier who declared that Rome's most valuable possession was a loyal citizen, hurled himself and his horse into the void and it duly closed. Further on, to the right, the enormous pile of rubble topped by three graceful Corinthian columns is the **Temple of Castor and Pollux**, dedicated in 484 BC to the divine twins, or Dioscuri, who appeared miraculously to ensure victory for the Romans in a key battle. Beyond here, the **House of the Vestal Virgins** is a second-century AD reconstruction of a building originally built by

Nero: four floors of rooms around a central courtyard, still with its pool in the centre and fringed by the statues or inscribed pedestals of the women themselves, with the round Temple of Vesta at the near end.

Almost opposite, a shady walkway to the left leads up to the **Basilica of Maxentius** – in terms of size and ingenuity, probably the Forum's most impressive remains. Begun by Maxentius, it was continued by his co-emperor and rival, Constantine, after he had defeated Maxentius at the Battle of the Milvian Bridge in 312 AD. Back on the Via Sacra, the hill climbs more steeply to the **Arch of Titus**, built by Titus's brother, Domitian, after the emperor's death in 81 AD to commemorate his triumphant return after victories in Judea in 70 AD. It's a long-standing tradition that Jews don't pass under this arch.

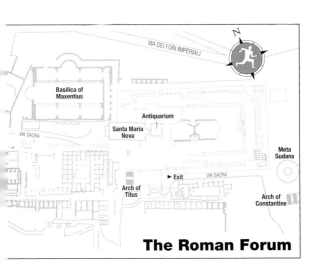

The Roman Forum

THE ARCH OF CONSTANTINE

Via di San Gregorio. MAP P.68–69, POCKET MAP G6

Just west of the Colosseum, the huge **Arch of Constantine** was placed here in the early decades of the fourth century AD after Constantine had consolidated his power as sole emperor. The arch demonstrates the deterioration of the arts during the late stages of the Roman Empire – most of the sculptural decoration here had to be removed from other monuments, and the builders were probably quite ignorant of the significance of the pieces they borrowed: the round medallions are taken from a temple dedicated to the Emperor Hadrian's lover, Antinous, and show Antinous and Hadrian engaged in a hunt. The other pieces, removed from the Forum of Trajan, show Dacian prisoners captured in Trajan's war there.

THE PALATINE HILL

Via di San Gregorio 30 ☎ 06.3996.7700. Daily 8.30am–1hr before sunset. €12 joint ticket with Colosseum and Roman Forum. MAP P.68–69, POCKET MAP G7

Rising above the Roman Forum, the **Palatine** is supposedly where the city of Rome was founded, and is home to some of its most ancient remnants. In a way it's a more pleasant site to tour than the Forum, a good place to have a picnic and relax after the rigours of the ruins below. In the days of the Republic, the Palatine was the most desirable address in Rome (the word "palace" is derived from Palatine), and the big names continued to colonize it during the imperial era, trying to outdo each other with ever larger and more magnificent dwellings.

Following the main path up from the Forum, the **Domus Flavia** was one of the most splendid residences, although it's now almost completely ruined. To the left, the top level of the gargantuan **Domus Augustana** spreads to the far brink of the hill – not the home of Augustus as its name suggests, but the private house of any emperor. You can look down from here on its vast central courtyard with fountains and wander to the brink of the deep trench of the Stadium, on the far side of which the ruins of the **Baths of Septimius Severus** cling to the side of the hill, the terrace giving good views over the Colosseum and the churches of the Celian Hill opposite. Nearby, the **Museo Palatino** (daily 9am–6pm) contains a vast assortment of statuary, pottery, terracotta antefixes and architectural fragments. Walking in the opposite direction from the Domus Flavia, steps lead down to the **Cryptoporticus**, a long passage built by Nero to link his Domus Aurea with the Palatine, and decorated along part of its length with well-preserved Roman stucco-work. You can go either way along the passage.

A left turn leads to the **Casa di Livia**, originally believed to have been the residence of Livia. West of here, the newly restored **Casa di Augusto** holds beautiful frescoes in striking shades of blue, red and ochre, dating back to 30 BC and considered to be among the most magnificent examples of Roman wall paintings anywhere; even the builders' ancient graffiti have been meticulously preserved. Further south, steps take you to the **Farnese Gardens**, among the first botanical gardens in Europe, laid out in the mid-sixteenth century and now a tidily planted, shady retreat from the exposed heat of the ruins. The terrace at the opposite end looks down on the excavations of an Iron Age village that perhaps marks the real centre of Rome's ancient beginnings.

THE PALATINE HILL

The Tridente, Trevi and Quirinale

The northern part of Rome's city centre is sometimes known as the Tridente, due to the shape of the roads leading down from the apex of Piazza del Popolo – Via del Corso in the centre, Via di Ripetta on the left and Via del Babuino on the right. This was historically the artistic quarter of the capital, to which artists and Grand Tourists would flock, in search of the colourful, exotic city. At the top of the Spanish Steps you can turn left for the Pincio and Villa Borghese, or right for Via Sistina and the Quirinale district, which holds some of the city's most compelling sights, including the enormous Palazzo Barberini, home of some of the best of Rome's art. West of here is the Fontana di Trevi, one of the city's most iconic and popular sights.

PIAZZA DI SPAGNA

MAP P.76–77, POCKET MAP F3

Piazza di Spagna underlines the area's international credentials, taking its name from the Spanish Embassy that has been standing here since the seventeenth century. It's a long, thin straggle of a square, almost entirely enclosed by buildings and centring on the distinctive boat-shaped Fontana della Barcaccia, the last work of Bernini's father, which remembers the great flood of Christmas Day 1598, when a barge from the Tiber was washed up on the slopes of Pincio Hill close by. The square itself is fringed by high-end clothes and jewellery shops and normally thronged with tourists, but for all that it is one of the city's most appealing open spaces and a fitting prelude to a spot of designer shopping on **Via Condotti**.

KEATS-SHELLEY MEMORIAL HOUSE

Piazza di Spagna 26 🚇 www
.keats-shelley-house.org. Mon–Fri 10am–1pm & 2–6pm, Sat 11am–2pm & 3–6pm, closed Sun. €4.50. MAP P.76–77, POCKET MAP F3

The English poet John Keats lived and died in a house on Piazza di Spagna in 1821 and it now serves as the **Keats-Shelley Memorial House**, an archive of English-language literary and historical works and a museum of manuscripts and mementos relating to the Keats circle of the early nineteenth century – namely Keats himself, Shelley

and Mary Shelley, and Byron (who at one time lived across the square). Keats came to Rome to recover his health but spent months in pain here before he finally died, at the age of just 25, confined to the house with his artist friend Joseph Severn. Among many bits of manuscript, letters and the like, you can see the poet's death mask, stored in the room where he died.

CASA DI CHIRICO

Piazza di Spagna 31 ☎ 06.679.6546. Tues–Sat & 1st Sun of the month 9am–1pm, tours hourly, only by appointment; €7. MAP P.76–77, POCKET MAP F3

Almost next door to the Keats-Shelley House, the fourth-floor **Casa di Chirico** was the home of the Greek-Italian artist Giorgio de Chirico for thirty years until his death in 1978. It's now a small museum that gives a glimpse into how De Chirico lived, and has a great many of his paintings on display: works from his classic surrealist period, and portraits of himself and his wife, who modelled for him. Upstairs, in keeping with the untouched nature of the

house, De Chirico's bedroom is left with his books and rather uncomfortable-looking single bed, while down the hall, the artist's studio, lit by a skylight in the terrace above, has his brushes and canvases.

THE SPANISH STEPS

MAP P.76–77, POCKET MAP F3

The **Spanish Steps** sweep down in a cascade of balustrades and balconies, the hangout of young hopefuls waiting to be chosen as artists' models during the nineteenth century, and nowadays not much changed in their role as a venue for international posing and flirting late into the summer nights. The Steps, like the square, could in fact just as easily be known as the "French Steps" because of the French church of Trinità dei Monti they lead up to, and because it was largely a French initiative to build them. After a few decades of haggling over the plans, they were finally laid in 1725, to a design by Francesco de Sanctis, and they now form one of the city's most distinctive and deliberately showy attractions.

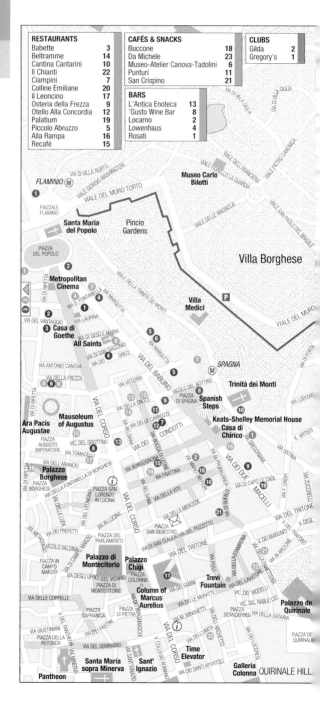

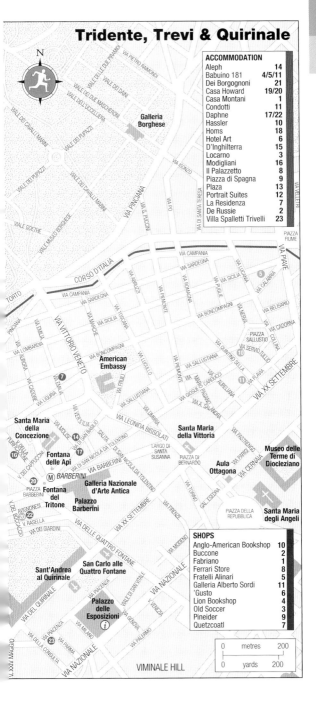

Tridente, Trevi & Quirinale

N

Galleria Borghese

ACCOMMODATION

Aleph	14
Babuino 181	4/5/11
Dei Borgognoni	21
Casa Howard	19/20
Casa Montani	1
Condotti	11
Daphne	17/22
Hassler	10
Homs	18
Hotel Art	6
D'Inghilterra	15
Locarno	3
Modigliani	16
Il Palazzetto	8
Piazza di Spagna	9
Plaza	13
Portrait Suites	12
La Residenza	7
De Russie	2
Villa Spalletti Trivelli	23

VIALE DELLE DUE PIRAMIDI
VIA PIETRO RAIMONDI
VIALE DEI DAINI
VIALE DELL'UCCELLIERA
VIALE DEI PUPAZZI
VIALE DEI CAVALLI MARINI
VIALE DEI CAVALLI MARINI
VIALE DEI PUPAZZI
VIALE GOETHE
VIALE MUSEO BORGHESE
VIA ISONZO
VIA PINCIANA
VIA G. PUCCINI
VIA DI SANTA TERESA
VIA PO
VIA VELLETRI

PIAZZA FIUME
VIA PIAVE

VIA CAMPANIA
VIA SARDEGNA
VIA LUCANIA
VIA SICILIA
VIA PUGLIE
VIA CALABRIA
VIA ABRUZZI
VIA PIEMONTE
VIA ROMAGNA
VIA BELISARIO

CORSO D'ITALIA
VIA CAMPANIA
VIA SARDEGNA
VIA BONCOMPAGNI
VIA NERVA
VIA CADORNA
VIA EMILIA
VIA MARCHE
VIA SICILIA
VIA TOSCANA
VIA LUCULLO
PIAZZA SALLUSTIO
VIA SERVIO TULLIO
VIA QUINTINO SELLA
VIA COLLINA
VIA VITTORIO VENETO
VIA BONCOMPAGNI
VIA PIEMONTE
VIA SALLUSTIANA
VIA FLAVIA
VIA XX SETTEMBRE
VIA LOMBARDIA
VIA AURORA
VIA FRIULI
VIA MARIO CAPUCCINI
VIA AURELIANA
VIA CADORE
VIA LIGURIA
VIA SALLUSTIANA
VIA GIOSUE PAGANINI
VIA A. SALANDRA
VIA A. SALANDRA

American Embassy
VALUMBRIA
VIA LEONIDA BISSOLATI

Santa Maria della Concezione
VIA TEST D'ILIA
VIA MOLISE
SALITA DI SAN BASILIO
VIA DI SAN NICOLA DA TOLENTINO
LARGO DI SANTA SUSANNA
PIAZZA DI BERNARDO
Santa Maria della Vittoria
VIA PASTRENGO
Museo delle Terme di Diocleziano

Fontana delle Api
VIA DI SAN NICOLA DA TOLENTINO
VIA BARBERINI
Aula Ottagona
VIA CERNAIA

(M) BARBERINI
Galleria Nazionale d'Arte Antica
PIAZZA BARBERINI
Fontana del Tritone
Palazzo Barberini
VIA TORINO
GIA. ESEDRA
PIAZZA DELLA REPUBBLICA
Santa Maria degli Angeli

PIAZZA BARBERINI
V. DEI CAPPUCCINI
V. DEL BOCCACCIO
V. RASELLA
VIA AVIGNONESI
VIA DEI GIARDINI
VIA DELLE QUATTRO FONTANE
VIA XX SETTEMBRE
VIA FIRENZE
VIA MODENA

Sant'Andrea al Quirinale
San Carlo alle Quattro Fontane
VIA PIACENZA
VIA DI SAN VITALE
VIA DEL QUIRINALE
Palazzo delle Esposizioni
(i)
VIA MILANO
VIA GENOVA
VIA PALERMO
VIA NAZIONALE

V. DEL QUIRINALE
VIA DELLA CONSULTA
V. PIACENZA
VIA PARMA
VIA XXIV MAGGIO
VIA NAZIONALE

VIMINALE HILL

SHOPS

Anglo-American Bookshop	10
Buccone	2
Fabriano	1
Ferrari Store	8
Fratelli Alinari	5
Galleria Alberto Sordi	11
'Gusto	6
Lion Bookshop	4
Old Soccer	3
Pineider	9
Quetzcoatl	7

0	metres	200
0	yards	200

TRINITÀ DEI MONTI

Piazza della Trinità dei Monti. Daily 10am–noon & 4–6pm. MAP P.76–77, POCKET MAP F3
Crowning the Spanish Steps, **Trinità dei Monti** is a largely sixteenth-century church designed by Carlo Maderno and paid for by the French. Its rose-coloured Baroque facade overlooks the rest of Rome from its hilltop site, and it's worth clambering up just for the views. While here you may as well pop your head around the door for a couple of impressive works by Daniele da Volterra, notably a soft, beautifully composed fresco of the *Assumption* in the third chapel on the right, whose array of finely realized figures includes a portrait of his teacher Michelangelo, and a superb, ingeniously composed *Deposition* across the nave. The French Baroque painter, Poussin, considered the latter – which was probably painted from a series of cartoons by Michelangelo (he's the greybeard on the right) – as the world's third greatest painting (Raphael's *Transfiguration* was, he thought, the best).

THE PINCIO GARDENS

MAP P.76–77, POCKET MAP E2
The terrace and gardens of the **Pincio**, a short walk from the top of the Spanish Steps, were laid out by Valadier in the early nineteenth century. Fringed with dilapidated busts of classical and Italian heroes, they give fine views over the roofs, domes and TV antennae of central Rome, right across to St Peter's and the Janiculum Hill. The view is the main event here, but there are also plenty of shady benches if you fancy a break, and the quirky nineteenth-century water clock at the back is worth a look. You can also hire bikes, rollerblades and odd little four-wheel carriages for getting around the gardens and the adjacent Villa Borghese (see p.132).

PIAZZA DEL POPOLO

MAP P.76–77, POCKET MAP E2
The oval-shaped expanse of **Piazza del Popolo** is a dignified meeting of roads laid out in 1538 by Pope Paul III to make an impressive entrance to the city; it owes its present symmetry to Valadier, who added the central fountain in

1814. The monumental Porta del Popolo went up in 1655 and was the work of Bernini; the Chigi family symbol of his patron, Alexander VII – a heap of hills surmounted by a star – can clearly be seen above the main gateway. During summer, the steps around the obelisk and fountain, and the cafés on either side of the square, are popular hangouts. But the square's real attraction is the unbroken view it gives all the way back down Via del Corso to the central columns of the Vittorio Emanuele Monument. If you get to choose your first view of the centre of Rome, make it this one.

SANTA MARIA DEL POPOLO

Piazza del Popolo. Mon–Sat 7.30am–noon & 4–7pm, Sun 8am–1.30pm & 4.30–7.30pm. MAP P.76–77, POCKET MAP E2

Santa Maria del Popolo holds some of the best Renaissance art of any Roman church, with frescoes by Pinturicchio in the first chapel of the south aisle, and fine sculpture and mosaics in the Raphael-designed Chigi chapel (second on the left). Designed for the banker Agostino Chigi in 1516, the chapel was not finished until the seventeenth century and most of the work was undertaken by other artists: Michelangelo's protégé, Sebastiano del Piombo, was responsible for the altarpiece, and two of the sculptures in the corner niches, of Daniel and Habakkuk, are by Bernini. The church's star attractions are perhaps the two pictures by Caravaggio in the left-hand chapel of the north transept: the *Conversion of St Paul* and the *Crucifixion of St Peter*, whose realism was considered extremely risqué in their time.

VIA DEL BABUINO

MAP P.76–77, POCKET MAP E3–F3

Leading south from Piazza del Popolo to the Piazza di Spagna, **Via del Babuino** and the narrow Via Margutta – where the film-maker Federico Fellini once lived – was, in the 1960s, the core of a thriving art community and home to the city's best galleries and a fair number of its artists. High rents forced out all but the most successful, and the neighbourhood now supports a prosperous trade in antiques and designer fashions. Via del Babuino – literally "Street of the Baboon" – derives its name from the statue of Silenus that reclines outside the Tadolini studio about halfway down on the right. In ancient times the wall behind was a focus for satirical graffiti, although it is now coated with graffiti-proof paint. Inside the studio, the **Museo-Atelier Canova-Tadolini** (see p.86) is a café-restaurant, but a highly original one, littered with the sculptural work of four generations of the Tadolini family.

VIA DEL BABUINO

CASA DI GOETHE

Via del Corso 18 ☎ 06.3265.0412, ⓦ www
.casadigoethe.it; Tues–Sun 10am–6pm. €4.
MAP P.76–77, POCKET MAP E3

A short way down Via del
Corso from Piazza del Popolo,
the **Casa di Goethe** is a small
and genuinely engaging
museum, housed in the
home the writer occupied
for two years when travelling
in Italy. He wrote much of
his classic travelogue *Italian
Journey* here – indeed, each
room is decorated with a
quote from the book – and
the house has been restored
as a modern exhibition space
and holds books, letters,
prints and drawings, plus a
reconstruction of his study in
Vienna. Among the objects
on display are Piranesi prints
of public spaces in Rome,
watercolours by Goethe himself
and drawings by the German
artist **Tischbein**, with whom he
shared the premises.

ARA PACIS

Lungotevere in Augusta. Tues–Sun 9am–7pm;
€9, audio guide €3.50. MAP P.76–77, POCKET
MAP E3

Forming the central core of the
largely modern square of Piazza
del Augusta Imperatore, just
off Via del Corso, the massive

Mausoleum of Augustus is the
burial place of the emperor and
his family, though these days it's
not much more than a peaceful
ring of cypresses, circled by
paths, flowering shrubs and
the debris of tramps. On the
far side of the square, the
Ara Pacis Augustae or "Altar
of Augustan Peace" is now
enclosed in a purpose-built
structure designed by the New
York-based architect Richard
Meier. A marble block enclosed
by sculpted walls, the altar
was built in 13 BC, probably
to celebrate Augustus' victory
over Spain and Gaul and the
peace it heralded. Much of it
had been dug up piecemeal
over the years, but the bulk
was uncovered in the middle of
the last century. It is a superb
example of imperial Roman
sculpture, with a frieze on one
side depicting the imperial
family at the height of its
power. It shows Augustus, his
great general Marcus Agrippa
and Augustus' wife Livia,
followed by a victory procession
containing her son (and
Augustus' eventual successor)
Tiberius and niece Antonia and
her husband, Drusus, among
others, while on the opposite
side, the veiled figure is believed
to be Julia, Augustus' daughter.

ARA PACIS AUGUSTAE

TREVI FOUNTAIN

MAP P.76–77, POCKET MAP G14

One of Rome's more surprising sights, the **Trevi Fountain** is a huge, Baroque gush of water over statues and rocks built onto the backside of a Renaissance palace. There was a Trevi fountain, designed by Alberti, around the corner in Via dei Crociferi, a smaller, more modest affair by all accounts, but Urban VIII decided to upgrade it in line with his other grandiose schemes of the time and employed Bernini, among others, to design an alternative nearby. Work didn't begin until 1732, when Niccolò Salvi won a competition held by Clement XII to design the fountain, and even then it took thirty years to finish the project. It's now, of course, the place you come to chuck in a coin if you want to guarantee your return to Rome, though you might remember Anita Ekberg throwing herself into it in *La Dolce Vita* (you're not encouraged to do the same).

TIME ELEVATOR

Via dei Santissimi Apostoli 20 ☎ 06.6992.1823, Ⓦ www.timeelevator.it. Daily 10.30am–7.30pm. €12, 5–12 years €9. MAP P.76–77, POCKET MAP F15

Flight-simulator seats and headphones (English audio available) set the stage for a 45min virtual tour of three thousand years of Roman history; one way of priming the kids for the sights they will be seeing, though it probably wouldn't suit toddlers. Shows every 30min.

GALLERIA COLONNA

Via della Pilotta 17 ☎ 06.678.4350, Ⓦ www.galleriacolonna.it. Sat 9am–1pm, closed Aug; €7; free guided tours in English at 11.45am. MAP P.76–77, POCKET MAP G15

The **Galleria Colonna** is well worth a visit if you can time it right, not least for its chandelier-decked Great Hall, which glorifies the achievements of the nobleman Marcantonio Colonna – notably his great victory against the Turks at the Battle of Lepanto in 1589. Of the paintings, highlights include two lascivious depictions of Venus and Cupid, facing each other across the room, by Bronzino and Ghirlandaio, a group of landscapes by Dughet (Poussin's brother-in-law), Carracci's early and unusually spontaneous *Bean Eater*, a *Portrait of a Venetian Gentleman*, caught in supremely confident pose by Veronese, and a Tintoretto portrait of an old man. All told, a great small collection, displayed in a sumptuous environment.

PIAZZA BARBERINI

MAP P.76–77, POCKET MAP F4–G4

At the top end of the busy shopping street of Via del Tritone, Piazza Barberini is centred around Bernini's **Fontana del Tritone**, whose god of the sea gushes a high jet of water from a conch shell. Traditionally, this was the Barberini family's quarter of the city, and works by Bernini in their honour – they were the sculptor's greatest patrons – are thick on the ground around here. He finished the Tritone fountain in 1644, going on shortly after to design the **Fontana delle Api** (Fountain of the Bees) across the road at the bottom end of Via Veneto – a smaller, quirkier work, with a broad scallop shell studded with bees, the symbol of the Barberinis.

SANTA MARIA DELLA CONCEZIONE

Via Veneto 27. Daily 9am–noon & 3–6pm. Donation expected for the cemetery. MAP P.76–77, POCKET MAP G3

The church of **Santa Maria della Concezione** was another Barberini-sponsored project, and although not particularly distinguished, it is worth a visit for its ghoulish Capuchin cemetery, erected in 1793 and home to the bones of 4000 monks, set into the walls of a series of chapels. The bones appear in abstract or Christian patterns or as fully clothed skeletons, their faces peering out of their cowls in various twisted expressions of agony – one of the more macabre and bizarre sights of Rome.

VIA VENETO

MAP P.76–77, POCKET MAP G3

The pricey bars and restaurants lining Via Veneto were once the haunt of Rome's beautiful people, made famous by Fellini's 1960 film *La Dolce Vita*. But they left a long time ago, and the street, despite being home to some of the city's fanciest hotels, has never quite recovered the cachet it had in the Sixties and Seventies. Nonetheless, its pretty tree-lined aspect, pavement cafés, swanky stores and uniformed hotel bellmen lend it an upmarket European air that is quite unlike anywhere else in the city.

PALAZZO BARBERINI

Via delle Quattro Fontane 13. Tues–Sun 9am–7pm; €5; apartment tours can be booked in advance. MAP P.76–77, POCKET MAP G4

The Palazzo Barberini is home to the **Galleria Nazionale d'Arte Antica** – a rich patchwork of mainly Italian art from the early Renaissance to the late Baroque period. It's a splendid collection, highlighted by works by Titian, El Greco and Caravaggio. But perhaps the most impressive feature of the gallery is the building itself, worked on at different times by the most favoured architects of the day – Bernini, Borromini and Maderno. The first-floor Gran Salone is dominated by Pietro da Cortona's manic fresco of *The Triumph of Divine Providence*, an exuberant Baroque work which almost crawls down the walls to meet you. Of the paintings, be sure to see Caravaggio's *Judith Beheading Holofernes*; Fra' Filippo Lippi's warmly maternal *Madonna and Child*; and Raphael's beguiling *Fornarina* – a painting of the daughter of a Trasteveran baker thought to have been his mistress (Raphael's name appears clearly on the woman's bracelet). Look out also for Bronzino's rendering of the marvellously erect *Stefano Colonna* and a portrait of *Henry VIII* by Hans Holbein.

SAN CARLO ALLE QUATTRO FONTANE

Via del Quirinale 23. Mon–Fri 10am–1pm & 3–6pm, Sat 10am–1pm, Sun noon–1pm. MAP P.76–77, POCKET MAP G4

The church of **San Carlo alle Quattro Fontane** – next door to the four fountains that give it its name – was Borromini's first real design commission. In it he displays all the ingenuity he later became known for, cramming the church elegantly into a tiny and awkwardly shaped site that apparently covers roughly the same surface area as one of the main piers of St Peter's. Tucked in beside the church, the cloister is also squeezed into a tight but elegant oblong, topped with a charming balustrade.

SANT'ANDREA AL QUIRINALE

Via del Quirinale 29. Mon–Sat 8.30am–noon & 3.30–7pm, Sun 9am–noon & 4–7pm. MAP P.76–77, POCKET MAP G4

A flamboyant building that Bernini planned as a kind of flat oval shape to fit into its wide but shallow site. Like San Carlo up the road, it's unusual and ingenious inside, its wide, elliptical nave cleverly made into a grand space despite its relatively small size. For a €1 fee you can also visit the sacristy, whose frescoes are similarly artful, with cherubs pulling aside painted drapery to let in light from mock windows, and the upstairs rooms of St Stanislaus Kostka, where the Polish saint lived (and died) in 1568. Paintings by Andrea Pozzo illustrate the life of the saint and culminate in a chapel that focuses on a disturbingly lifelike painted statue of Stanislaus on his deathbed.

FONTANA DEL TRITONE IN PIAZZA BARBERINI

PALAZZO DEL QUIRINALE

Piazza del Quirinale ⓦ www.quirinale.it. Sun 8.30am–noon. €5. MAP P.76–77, POCKET MAP F4

The sixteenth-century **Palazzo del Quirinale** was the official summer residence of the popes until Unification, when it became the royal palace. It's now the home of Italy's president. The main feature of the piazza outside is the huge statue of the Dioscuri, aka Castor and Pollux: massive five-metre-tall Roman copies of classical Greek statues, brought here by Pope Sixtus V in the early sixteenth century. Inside, the palace is well worth a visit if you're in town on a Sunday, with some spectacular rooms glorifying Pope Paul V among others, and a fragment of Melozzo da Forlì's fifteenth-century fresco of Christ, painted for the apse of Santi Apostoli (the rest is in the Vatican; see p.150).

VIA XX SETTEMBRE

MAP P.76–77, POCKET MAP G4–H3

Via XX Settembre spears out to the Aurelian Wall from Via del Quirinale and was the route by which troops entered the city on September 20, 1870 – the place where they breached the wall is marked with a column. It's not Rome's most appealing thoroughfare by any means, flanked by the deliberately faceless bureaucracies of the national government. However, halfway down, the Fontana dell'Acqua Felice is worth a look: it focuses on a massive, bearded figure of Moses playfully fronted by four basking lions, and marks the end of the Acqua Felice aqueduct.

SANTA MARIA DELLA VITTORIA

Via XX Settembre 17. Daily 6.30am–noon & 4.30–6pm. MAP P.76–77, POCKET MAP G3

Santa Maria della Vittoria's best-known feature is Bernini's sculpture the *Ecstasy of St Theresa of Avila*, the centrepiece of the sepulchral chapel of Cardinal Cornaro. St Theresa is one of the Catholic Church's most enduring mystics, and Bernini's sculpture records the moment when, in 1537, she had a vision of an angel piercing her heart with a dart. It's a very Baroque piece of work in the most populist sense – not only is the event quite literally staged, but St Theresa's ecstasy verges on the worldly as she lies back in groaning submission beneath a mass of dishevelled garments and drapery. The Cornaro cardinals are depicted murmuring and nudging each other as they watch the spectacle from theatre boxes.

Shops

ANGLO-AMERICAN BOOKSHOP

Via della Vite 102. Mon 3.30–7.30pm, Tues–Sat 10.30am–7.30pm. MAP P.76–77, POCKET MAP F13

One of the best selections of new English books in Rome, especially good on history and academic books.

BUCCONE

Via di Ripetta 19. Mon–Thurs 9am–8.30pm, Fri & Sat 9am–11.30pm. MAP P.76–77, POCKET MAP E3

The centre's best wine shop, with a large selection of wines, spirits and especially grappa.

FABRIANO

Via del Babuino 172. Mon–Sat 10am–7.30pm. MAP P.76–77, POCKET MAP E3

Tridente branch of this chain, specializing in lovely contemporary stationery, wallets and bags.

FRATELLI ALINARI

Via Alibert 16a. Mon–Sat 3.30–7.30pm. MAP P.76–77, POCKET MAP F3

If you want to know what Rome's piazzas looked like before *McDonald's* came to town, come here for a fine selection of black-and-white photographs of Rome.

GALLERIA ALBERTO SORDI

Via del Corso. Daily 10am–10pm. MAP P.76–77, POCKET MAP F14

This nineteenth-century shopping arcade is home to some great shops and provides a cool escape from the Via del Corso crowds on hot days.

'GUSTO

Piazza Augusto Imperatore 7. Daily 10.30am–2am. MAP P.76–77, POCKET MAP E3

Everything for the aspirant gourmet: wines, decanters, glasses and all the top-of-the-line kitchen gadgets you could ever hope to find. Also a large selection of cookbooks in English.

LION BOOKSHOP

Via dei Greci 33. Mon 9.45am–2pm & 3–7.15pm, Tues–Sun 10am–7.30pm. MAP P.76–77, POCKET MAP E3

Veteran English bookshop with a great selection and helpful service.

OLD SOCCER

Via di Ripetta 30. Daily 10am–8pm. MAP P.76–77, POCKET MAP E3

Old-fashioned Italian football shirts – ironically enough, made in England.

PINEIDER

Via Due Macelli 68. Mon 3.30–7.30pm, Tues–Sat 10am–1.30pm & 3.30–7.30pm. MAP P.76–77, POCKET MAP G13

This exclusive store has been selling beautiful hand-made stationery, briefcases and bags since 1774.

QUETZALCOATL

Via delle Carrozze 26. Mon–Sat 10am–noon & 2.45–7.30pm. MAP P.76–77, POCKET MAP E3

Chocolates here are presented as if they were art; once you taste them, you'll probably feel that they are. Gift boxes of all sizes available.

GALLERIA ALBERTO SORDI

THE TRIDENTE, TREVI AND QUIRINALE

Cafés and snacks

BUCCONE

Via di Ripetta 19. Mon–Fri noon–2pm.
MAP P.76–77, POCKET MAP E13

One of the best places for lunch in the Piazza del Popolo area, with lots of tables laid out amid its bottle-lined shelves, and a separate room out the back and a menu that changes daily. You can eat as much or as little as you like, with salads or cold cut platters (€8–10) as well as a few hot daily specials for €7–10.

SAN CRISPINO

DA MICHELE

Via dell' Umilta 31. Sun & Mon–Thurs 9am–7.30pm, Fri 9am–2pm, closed Sat.
MAP P.76–77, POCKET MAP F15

This classic Roman snack joint used to be in the Jewish Ghetto (when it was known as *Zi Fenizia*) but was replaced by a burger bar, and the Ghetto's loss is very much the Trevi area's gain. Under its changed name it still does kosher pizza to go – the house speciality is pizza with fresh anchovies and *indivia* (endives) – roast chicken and *suppli* (fried rice balls).

MUSEO-ATELIER CANOVA-TADOLINI

Via del Babuino 150a. Mon–Sat 9am–7.30pm.
MAP P.76–77, POCKET MAP E3

It's a bit odd eating here amongst the grand sculptures of this café-cum-museum, and certainly not cheap. But this is one of the few places to sit down along this busy street, serving decent sandwiches, salads and simple pasta dishes. There are a few outside tables, too, to watch the designer bags bustle by.

PUNTURI

Via Flavia 48. Mon–Fri 7.30am–8pm, Sat 7.30am–2pm. MAP P.76–77, POCKET MAP H3

One of the city's most historic *gastronomie*, with superb pizza by the slice and a handful of hot dishes – lasagne, *arancini* – at lunch time, and a couple of tables out the back to eat at.

SAN CRISPINO

Via della Panetteria 42. Mon–Thurs & Sun noon–12.30am, Fri & Sat noon–11.30am, closed Tues in winter. MAP P.76–77, POCKET MAP G14

Considered by many to be the best ice cream in Rome. Wonderful flavours – all natural – will make the other *gelato* you've known pale by comparison.

Restaurants

BABETTE

Via Margutta 1–3 ☎ 06.321.1559. Mon 8–11.15pm, Tues–Sun 1–3pm & 8–11pm.
MAP P.76–77, POCKET MAP E2

Yes, the name is derived from the Danish foodie film, *Babette's Feast*, but food here is Italian with a few twists rather than Danish, with a great-value lunch buffet on weekdays (€15) and a lovely courtyard to eat it in. Dinner is good value too.

BELTRAMME

Via della Croce 39. No phone. Daily 12.30–3pm & 7–11pm. MAP P.76–77, POCKET MAP E3

Originally this place sold only wine, by the *fiasco* or flask. Now, a few blocks from the Spanish Steps, it is a full-blown restaurant and just about always packed. But if you want authentic Roman food and atmosphere at affordable prices – €10 for a *primo*, €15 for a *secondo* – then this is the place. Service can be a bit slow. No credit cards.

CANTINA CANTARINI

Piazza Sallustio 12 ☎ 06.485.528. Mon–Sat 12.30–3.30pm & 7.30–11pm. MAP P.76–77, POCKET MAP H3

Very simple, very popular restaurant serving rustic food from both the Marche region and Rome. Excellent value.

IL CHIANTI

Via del Lavatore 81/82a ☎ 06.678.7550. Mon–Sat noon–2am. MAP P.76–77, POCKET MAP G14

Just metres from the Fontana di Trevi, this Tuscan specialist is a find in a part of town not generally known for its good-value food and drink. Good spreads of Tuscan cheese and cold meats, a selection of meat dishes, and the usual pasta dishes and pizzas. You can sit outside in summer if you can bear the travelling musicians who congregate to entertain the tourists.

CIAMPINI

Viale Trinità dei Monti ☎ 06.678.5678. Daily 8am–midnight. MAP P.76–77, POCKET MAP F3

The best branch of this city-wide chain, with great views from its garden terrace, where you watch the resident turtles in the fountain while choosing from a good selection of pasta dishes – and meat and fish mains from the grill –

chicken, swordfish and the like.

COLLINE EMILIANE

Via degli Avignonesi 22 ☎ 06.481.7538. Tues–Sat 12.45–2.45pm & 7.30–10.45pm, Sun 12.45–2.45pm. MAP P.76–77, POCKET MAP F4

Just down from Piazza Barberini, on a quiet backstreet parallel to Via del Tritone, not far from the Fontana di Trevi, this cosy family-run restaurant serves excellent Emilian food at moderate prices.

IL LEONCINO

Via del Leoncino 28 ☎ 06.687.6306. Mon–Fri 1–2.30pm & 7pm–midnight, Sat 7pm–midnight. MAP P.76–77, POCKET MAP E13

Cheap, hectic and genuine pizzeria – one of the very best for lovers of crispy Roman-style pizza, baked in a wooden oven.

OSTERIA DELLA FREZZA

Via della Frezza 16 ☎ 06.3211.1482. Daily noon–3.30pm & 7pm–midnight. MAP P.76–77, POCKET MAP E3

Part of the *'Gusto* foodie empire, this place has nice snacks such as cheese or salami plates and full meals. There's outside seating and great pasta.

ANTICA BIRRERIA PERONI

L'ENOTECA ANTICA

You can just settle for a plate of salami or cheese for €5–7, or go for dishes like *tonnarelli cacio e pepe* or mains like rabbit or sausage from the hills to the north and south of the city.

PICCOLO ABRUZZO

Via Sicilia 237 ☎ 06.428.0176. Daily noon–4pm & 7pm–1.30am. MAP P.76–77, POCKET MAP H2

A five-minute stroll up the unprepossessing Via Sicilia from Via Veneto, this is a great alternative to the glitzy, mob-run places on the *Dolce Vita* street. No menu, just a seemingly endless parade of Abruzzese and other goodies plonked on to your table at regular intervals – all for around €35 a head. Be sure to come hungry.

ALLA RAMPA

Piazza Mignanelli 18 ☎ 06.678.2621. Mon–Sat noon–2pm, 8–11pm. MAP P.76–77, POCKET MAP G13

An unashamedly touristy joint, but with perhaps the best antipasti buffet in town – a snip for €10 – as well as excellent service and pretty decent food. The outside terrace, just off Piazza di Spagna is large and undeniably appealing. No credit cards.

OTELLO ALLA CONCORDIA

Via della Croce 81 ☎ 06.679.1178. Mon–Sat 12.30–3pm & 7.30–11pm. MAP P.76–77, POCKET MAP E3

This place used to be one of Fellini's favourites – he lived just a few blocks away on Via Margutta – and it remains an elegant yet affordable choice in the heart of Rome. A complete offering of Roman and Italian dishes, but ask for *spaghetti Otello* for a taste of tradition – a delicious combination of fresh tomatoes and basil with garlic.

PALATIUM

Via Frattina 94 ☎ 06.6920.2132. Mon–Sat 11am–11pm. MAP P.76–77, POCKET MAP F13

Cool and sleek, this Spanish Steps-area wine bar-cum-restaurant celebrates the wine and food of the Lazio region around Rome, with a short menu of local specialities and a long list of Lazio wines.

RECAFÉ

Piazza Augusto Imperatore 9 ☎ 06.6813.4730. Daily 12.45pm–3pm & 7.30pm–1am. MAP P.76–77, POCKET MAP E13

The entrance on Via del Corso is a Neapolitan café, while on the Piazza Augusta Imperatore side you can enjoy proper Neapolitan pizzas, good pasta and salad dishes and excellent grilled *secondi* for moderate prices – €9 or so for a *primo*, €12–18 for a *secondo*. Neapolitan sweets and *fritti* too. The ambience is deliberately chic and the large outside terrace always has a buzz about it.

Bars

L'ANTICA ENOTECA

Via della Croce 76b. Daily 11am–1am. MAP P.76–77, POCKET MAP E3

An old Spanish Steps-area wine bar with a cosy interior bar and a selection of hot and cold dishes, including soups and attractive desserts. Intriguing trompe l'oeil decorations inside, majolica-topped tables outside.

'GUSTO WINE BAR

Via della Frezza 16 ☎ 06.322.6273. Daily 10–2am. MAP P.76–77, POCKET MAP E3

This stylish modern bar is part of the 'Gusto empire (see p.85), and serves drinks, sandwiches and Catalan one-bite tapas to Rome's chattering classes. Entrance to the bar is around the corner from the main entrance.

LOCARNO

Via della Penna 22 ☎ 06.361.0841. MAP P.76–77, POCKET MAP E2

The decadent atmosphere graced with hip cocktail-sippers and a clubby back room with cosy fireplace make Locarno Rome's most egalitarian hotel bar. It's frequented by literati, artists, near-paupers, poseurs, fashionistas and just ordinary folk, and the warm weather adds a roof terrace to the mix.

LOWENHAUS

Via della Fontanella 16. Daily noon–2am. MAP P.76–77, POCKET MAP E2

Just off Piazza del Popolo, this bar serves big German beers and the sausage and other snacks to go with them in an authentic bierkeller-style environment. Full meals too, and outside seating in summer.

ROSATI

Piazza del Popolo 5. Daily 8am–midnight. MAP P.76–77, POCKET MAP E2

This was the bar that hosted left-wingers, bohemians and writers in years gone by, though now it's cocktails and food that draw the crowds to the outside terrace.

Clubs

GILDA

Via Mario de' Fiori 97 ☎ 06.678.4838. Ⓦ www .gildabar.it. Metro A Spagna or bus #85 or #850 from Metro B Colosseo, #95 or #116 from Metro A Barberini, or #119 from Piazza Venezia. Thurs–Sun 11pm–5am. MAP P.76–77, POCKET MAP F13

A few blocks from the Spanish Steps, this slick, stylish and expensive club is the focus for the city's minor celebs and wannabes, mainly of the middle-aged variety. Dress smart.

GREGORY'S

Via Gregoriana 54d ☎ 06.679.6386. Tues–Sun 8pm–3am. MAP P.76–77, POCKET MAP G13

Just up the Spanish Steps and to the right, this elegant nightspot pulls in the crowds with its live jazz, improvised by Roman and international musicians.

ROSATI

The Esquiline, Monti and Termini

Monti is named after the two hills it encompasses: the Esquiline, the city's highest and largest, once ancient Rome's most fashionable residential quarter; and the Viminale, the smallest – home to the Interior Ministry and not much else. In recent years Monti has become increasingly gentrified, its cobbled streets lined with cosy bars and restaurants and arty boutiques. The area is also home to key sights like Nero's Domus Aurea (though this has been closed for some time) and the basilica of Santa Maria Maggiore, and is close to Termini station, the focal point of a down-at-heel area that holds much of the city's budget accommodation. Neighbouring San Lorenzo is a hub of studenty nightlife, full of cool bars and restaurants.

SANTA MARIA MAGGIORE

Piazza di Santa Maria Maggiore. Daily
7am–7pm. Museum daily 9am–6.30pm. €4.
MAP P.92–93, POCKET MAP H5

SANTA MARIA MAGGIORE

One of the city's four
patriarchal basilicas, **Santa
Maria Maggiore** includes
one of Rome's best-preserved
Byzantine interiors. It was
originally built during the fifth
century after the Virgin Mary
appeared to Pope Liberius in a
dream on the night of August
4, 352 AD. She told him to
erect a church in her honour
on the Esquiline Hill – the
exact spot would be marked
the next morning by newly
fallen snow outlining the plan
of the church. Despite it being
the height of summer, Liberius
duly found the miraculous
blueprint and the event is
commemorated every year
on August 5, when at midday
Mass white rose petals are
showered on the congregation
from the ceiling, and at night
the fire department operates
an artificial snow machine
in the piazza in front of the
church.

Inside, the **basilica** is fringed
on both sides with well-kept
mosaics, most of which date
from the time of Pope Sixtus
III and recount incidents from
the Old Testament. The chapel
in the right transept holds the
elaborate tomb of Sixtus V –
another, less famous Sistine
hapel, decorated with frescoes
and stucco reliefs showing
events from his reign. Outside
is the tomb of the Bernini
family; opposite, the Pauline
hapel is home to the tombs
of the Borghese pope, Paul V,
and his immediate predecessor
Clement VIII, as well as
that of Pauline Bonaparte,
Napoleon's sister. Between
the two chapels, the *confessio*
contains a kneeling statue of

Pope Pius IX, and, beneath it, a
reliquary that is said to contain
fragments of the crib of Christ.
It's the mosaics of the arch
that really dazzle, a vivid
representation of scenes from
the life of Christ. The **museum**
underneath the basilica sports
what is, even by Roman
standards, a wide variety of
relics, and a **loggia** above the
main entrance (tours daily at
9am & 1pm; book in advance
on ☎06.6988.6802; €5) has
some magnificent mosaics.

SANTA PUDENZIANA

Via Urbana 160. Daily 8.30am–noon & 3–6pm.
MAP P.92–93, POCKET MAP H5

This church was for many years
believed to have been built on
the site where St Peter lived and
worshipped and once housed
two relics: the chair that St
Peter used as his throne and
the table at which he said Mass,
though both have long gone –
to the Vatican and the Lateran
Palace respectively. It still has
one feature of ancient origin
– its superb fifth-century apse
mosaics, fluid and beautiful
works centring on a golden
enthroned Christ surrounded by
the apostles.

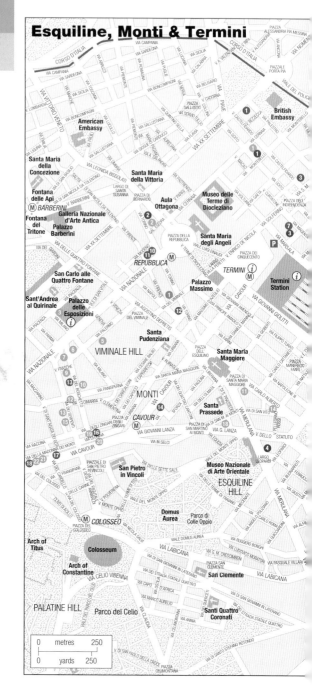

Esquiline, Monti & Termini

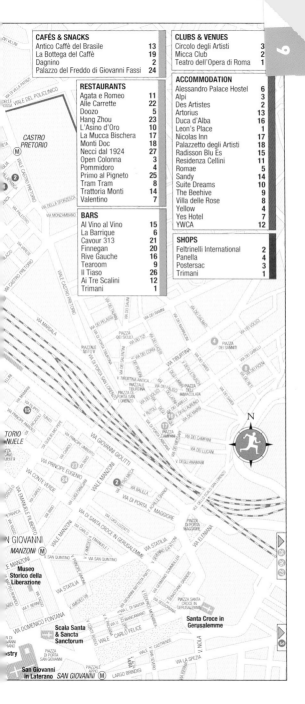

CAFÉS & SNACKS

Antico Caffè del Brasile	13
La Bottega del Caffè	19
Dagnino	2
Palazzo del Freddo di Giovanni Fassi	24

RESTAURANTS

Agata e Romeo	11
Alle Carrette	22
Doozo	5
Hang Zhou	23
L'Asino d'Oro	10
La Mucca Bischera	17
Monti Doc	18
Necci dal 1924	27
Open Colonna	3
Pommidoro	4
Primo al Pigneto	25
Tram Tram	8
Trattoria Monti	14
Valentino	7

BARS

Al Vino al Vino	15
La Barrique	6
Cavour 313	21
Finnegan	20
Rive Gauche	16
Tearoom	9
Il Tiaso	26
Ai Tre Scalini	12
Trimani	1

CLUBS & VENUES

Circolo degli Artisti	3
Micca Club	2
Teatro dell'Opera di Roma	1

ACCOMMODATION

Alessandro Palace Hostel	6
Alpi	3
Des Artistes	2
Artorius	13
Duca d'Alba	16
Leon's Place	1
Nicolas Inn	17
Palazzetto degli Artisti	18
Radisson Blu Es	15
Residenza Cellini	11
Romae	5
Sandy	14
Suite Dreams	10
The Beehive	9
Villa delle Rose	8
Yellow	4
Yes Hotel	7
YWCA	12

SHOPS

Feltrinelli International	2
Panella	4
Postersac	3
Trimani	1

CHAINS AT SAN PIETRO IN VINCOLI

SAN PIETRO IN VINCOLI

Piazza di San Pietro in Vincoli, 4a. Daily 7am–12.30pm & 3–7pm. MAP P.92–93, POCKET MAP G5

San Pietro in Vincoli is one of Rome's most delightfully plain churches. It was built to house an important relic, the two sets of chains (*vincoli*) that bound St Peter when imprisoned in Jerusalem and held him in the Mammertine Prison, which miraculously fused together when they were brought into contact with each other. The chains can still be seen in the *confessio* beneath the high altar, but most people come for the tomb of Pope Julius II at the far end of the southern aisle. The aisle occupied Michelangelo on and off for much of his career and was the cause of many a dispute with Julius and his successors. He reluctantly gave it up to paint the Sistine Chapel – the only statues that he managed to complete are the *Moses*, *Leah* and *Rachel*, which remain here, and two *Dying Slaves*, which are now in the Louvre, Paris. The figures are among the artist's most captivating works, especially *Moses*: because of a medieval mistranslation of

scripture, he is depicted with satyr's horns instead of the "radiance of the Lord" that Exodus tells us shone around his head. Nonetheless this powerful statue is so lifelike that Michelangelo is alleged to have struck its knee with his hammer and shouted "Speak, damn you!"

SANTA PRASSEDE

Via di Santa Prassede 9a. Daily 7.30am–noon & 4–6.30pm. MAP 92–93, POCKET MAP H5

The ninth-century church of **Santa Prassede** occupies an ancient site where it's claimed St Prassede harboured Christians on the run from the Roman persecutions. She apparently collected the blood and remains of the martyrs and placed them in a well where she herself was later buried; a red porphyry disc in the floor of the nave marks the spot. The Byzantine mosaics are the most striking feature, particularly those in the chapel of St Zeno, which make it glitter like a jewel-encrusted box.

MUSEO NAZIONALE DI ARTE ORIENTALE

Via Merulana 248 ☏ 06.469.748. Tues, Wed & Fri 9am–2pm, Thurs, Sat & Sun 9am–7.30pm. €6. MAP P.92–93, POCKET MAP H5

Housed in the imposing Palazzo Brancaccio, the **Museo Nazionale di Arte Orientale** is a first-rate collection of oriental art. Italy's connection with the Far East goes back to Marco Polo in the thirteenth century, and the quality of this collection of Islamic, Chinese, Indian and Southeast Asian art reflects this long relationship. Highlights include finds dating back to 1500 BC from a necropolis in Pakistan; architectural fragments, art works and jewellery from Tibet, Nepal and Pakistan; a solid collection from China, with predictable Buddhas and vases alongside curiosities such as a large Wei-dynasty Buddha with two boddhisatvas.

PIAZZA VITTORIO EMANUELE II

MAP P.92–93, POCKET MAP J6

Piazza Vittorio Emanuele II lies at the centre of a district that became known as the "quartiere piemontese" when the government located many of its major ministries here after Unification. The arcades of the square, certainly, recall central Turin, but it's more recently become the immigrant quarter of Rome, with a heavy concentration of African, Asian and Middle Eastern shops and restaurants. You'll hear a dozen different languages spoken as you pass through, although the morning **market** that used to take place here has moved a few blocks east to Via Giolitti, between Via Ricasoli and Via Lamarmora. Raucous and usually rammed with locals, this is a good place to shop for a picnic.

PIAZZA DELLA REPUBBLICA

MAP P.92–93, POCKET MAP H4

Typical of Rome's nineteenth-century regeneration, **Piazza della Repubblica** is a dignified semicircle of buildings that used to be rather dilapidated but is now – with the help of the very stylish *Hotel Exedra* – once again resurgent. The traffic roars ceaselessly around the centrepiece of the Fontana delle Naiadi, with its languishing nymphs and sea monsters. The piazza's shape follows the outline of the Baths of Diocletian, the remains of which lie across the piazza (see p.96).

PALAZZO DELLE ESPOSIZIONI

Via Nazionale 194 ☎ 06.3996.7500, ⊕ www
.palazzoesposizioni.it. Tues–Thurs & Sun
10am–8pm, Fri & Sat 10am–10.30pm. Approx
€10; joint ticket with Scuderie del Quirinale
€18. MAP P.92–93, POCKET MAP G4

Via Nazionale connects Piazza Venezia and the centre of town with the area around Stazione Termini and the eastern districts beyond. A focus for development after Unification, its overbearing buildings are now occupied by hotels and bland, mid-range shops. It's worth strolling down as far as the imposing **Palazzo delle Esposizioni**, though, which has reopened after a five-year revamp. It hosts large-scale exhibitions and cultural events, and also houses a cinema, café and restaurant (see p.100).

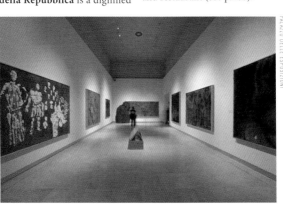

PALAZZO DELLE ESPOSIZIONI

SANTA MARIA DEGLI ANGELI

Piazza della Repubblica. Mon–Sat
7am–6.30pm, Sun 7am–7.30pm. MAP P.92–93,
POCKET MAP H4

The basilica of Santa Maria
degli Angeli was built on the
ruins of the Baths of Diocletian.
Designed by Michelangelo in
1563, a year before his death,
it gives a good impression of
the size and grandeur of the
baths complex: the crescent
shape of the facade remains
from the original caldarium,
the large transept was once
the tepidarium, and eight of
its huge pink-granite pillars
are originals from the baths.
Luigi Vanvitelli rearranged
the interior in 1749, by and
large imitating Michelangelo's
designs. The meridian that
strikes diagonally across the
floor in the south transept,
flanked by representations of
the twelve signs of the zodiac,
was until 1846 the regulator
of time for Romans (now a
cannon shot fires daily at noon
from the Janiculum Hill).

THE AULA OTTAGONA

Via Giuseppe Romita 8 ☎ 06.3996.7700.
Currently closed. MAP P.92–93, POCKET MAP H4

The exit from the church
leaves you behind another
remnant of the baths, the **Aula
Ottagona**, which contains
marble statues taken from
the baths of Caracalla and
Diocletian, and two remarkable
statues of a boxer and athlete
from the Quirinale Hill. It also
holds underground furnaces
for heating water for the baths
and the foundations of another
building from the time of
Diocletian.

MUSEO DELLE TERME DI DIOCLEZIANO

Viale Enrico De Nicola 79 ☎ 06.3996.7700.
Tues–Sun 9am–7.45pm. €7 joint ticket includes
Palazzo Altemps, Palazzo Massimo & Crypta
Balbi, valid 3 days. MAP P.92–93, POCKET MAP H3

Behind the church of Santa
Maria degli Angeli, the huge
halls and courtyards of the
Baths of Diocletian have
been renovated and they now
hold what is probably the
least interesting part of the
Museo Nazionale Romano
– the **Museo delle Terme
di Diocleziano**, the best bit
of which is the large cloister
of the church whose sides
are crammed with statuary,
funerary monuments and
fragments from all over Rome.
The galleries that wrap around
the cloister hold a reasonable
collection of pre-Roman and
Roman finds: terracotta statues,
armour and weapons found in
Roman tombs.

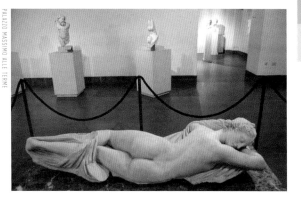

PALAZZO MASSIMO ALLE TERME

Largo di Villa Peretti 1 ☎ 06.3996.7700.
Tues–Sun 9am–7.45pm. €7 joint ticket
includes Palazzo Altemps, Terme di Diocleziano
& Crypta Balbi, valid 3 days. MAP P.92–93,
POCKET MAP H4

The snazzily restored Palazzo
Massimo is home to one
of the two principal parts
of the **Museo Nazionale
Romano** (the other is in the
Palazzo Altemps) – a superb
collection of Greek and Roman
antiquities, second only to
the Vatican's. As one of the
great museums of Rome, there
are too many highlights to
do it justice here, and there
is something worth seeing
on every floor. Start at the
basement, which has displays
of exquisite gold jewellery
from the second century
AD, and – startlingly – the
mummified remains of an
8-year-old girl, along with a
coin collection. The **ground
floor** is devoted to statuary of
the early empire, including a
gallery with an unparalleled
selection of unidentified busts
found all over Rome – amazing
pieces of portraiture, and
as vivid a representation of
patrician Roman life as you'll
find. There are also identifiable
faces from the so-called
imperial family – a bronze

of Germanicus, a marvellous
small bust of Caligula, several
representations of Livia,
Antonia and Drusus and a
hooded statue of Augustus. On
the far side of the **courtyard**
is Greek sculpture, including
bronzes of a Hellenistic prince
holding a spear and a wounded
pugilist at rest.

The gallery on the **first
floor** has groupings of later
imperial dynasties in roughly
chronological order, starting
with the Flavian emperors and
ending with the Severans, with
the fierce-looking Caracalla
looking across past his father
Septimius Severus to his
brother Geta, whom he later
murdered.

The **second floor**, which you
can only visit on an organized
tour, takes in some of the finest
Roman frescoes and mosaics
ever found. There is a stunning
set of frescoes from the Casa
di Livia (see p.73), depicting
an orchard dense with fruit
and flowers and patrolled by
partridges and doves; wall
paintings rescued from what
was perhaps the riverside villa of
Julia and Agrippa; and mosaics
showing naturalistic scenes – sea
creatures, people boating – as
well as four finely crafted chariot
drivers and their horses.

TERMINI STATION

MAP P.92–93, POCKET MAP H4

Named after the nearby Baths (Terme) of Diocletian, **Termini station** is an ambitious piece of architecture that was completed in 1950 and still entirely dominates the streets around with its low-slung, futuristic lines. A huge and sleek renovation has converted part of its cavernous ticket hall to retail and restaurant space. In front of the station, Piazza dei Cinquecento is a terminus for buses and a good place to find a taxi, but otherwise it and the areas around are pretty much low-life territory, and although not especially dangerous, not a great place to linger either.

SAN LORENZO FUORI LE MURA

Piazzale del Verano 3. Daily 8am–noon & 4–6.30pm. MAP P.92–93, POCKET MAP K4

The student neighbourhood of San Lorenzo, behind Termini, is home to **San Lorenzo fuori le Mura**, one of the seven great pilgrimage churches of Rome, and a typical Roman basilica, fronted by a columned portico and with a lovely twelfth-century cloister to its side. The original church was built by Constantine over the site of St Lawrence's martyrdom – the saint was reputedly burned to death on a gridiron, halfway through his ordeal apparently uttering the immortal words, "Turn me, I am done on this side." Because of its proximity to Rome's rail yards, the church was bombed heavily during World War II, but it has been rebuilt with sensitivity, and remains much as it was originally. Inside there are features from all periods, including a Cosmati mosaic floor and thirteenth-century pulpits. The mosaic on the inside of the triumphal arch is a sixth-century depiction of the founder offering his church to Christ. The catacombs below (rarely open) are where St Lawrence was apparently buried – a dank path leads to the pillars of Constantine's original structure. There's also a Romanesque cloister with a well-tended garden.

Shops

FELTRINELLI INTERNATIONAL

Via Emanuele Orlando 84. Mon-Sat
9am-8pm, Sun 10am-1.30pm & 4-8pm. MAP
P.92-93, POCKET MAP G4

This international branch
of the nationwide chain has
an excellent stock of books
in English, as well as in
French, German, Spanish and
Portuguese.

PANELLA

Via Merulana 54. Mon-Fri 8am-midnight,
Sun 8.30am-1.30pm. MAP P.92-93, POCKET MAP H5

Probably the city's priciest
bakery, with fantastic bread
and pastries, delicious pizza
and a small grocery section.
They also do pasta and have
recently added a café, which
does a good happy-hour
buffet.

TRIMANI

POSTERSAC

Via Vicenza 4. Mon-Fri 9.30am-1.30pm &
4.30-6.30pm. MAP P.92-93, POCKET MAP H4

On a nondescript street near
the station, this tiny shop sells
new and vintage Italian film
posters. From reproductions of
classics such as *La Dolce Vita*
for €6.50 to the genuine article
for up to €100, they make great
souvenirs.

TRIMANI

Via Goito 20 ⓦ www.trimani.com. Mon-Sat
9am-8.30pm. MAP P.92-93, POCKET MAP H3

One of the city's best wine
shops, *Trimani* has been in
business since 1876 and is still
run by the same family. It's
close to Termini if you want
to stock up before heading off
to the airport; otherwise, they
can ship anywhere. There's also
a wine bar around the corner
serving decent food (see p.102).

Cafés and snacks

ANTICO CAFFÈ DEL BRASILE

Via dei Serpenti 23. Jan-July & Oct-Dec
Mon-Sat 6am-8.30pm, Sun 7am-2pm, closed
Sun in Aug. MAP P.92-93, POCKET MAP G5

Reliable old Monti stand-by
that has been selling great
coffee, snacks and cakes for
around a century, with a
handful of seats and tables at
the back should you want to
take the weight off your feet.
Light meals are also served.

LA BOTTEGA DEL CAFFÈ

Piazza Madonna dei Monti 5 ☎ 06.474.1578.
Daily 8am-2am. MAP P.92-93, POCKET MAP G5

Right in the heart of Monti,
this is a good place for
breakfast, a lunchtime snack
or an early-evening drink, with
tables outside on a picturesque
square.

DAGNINO

Galleria Esedra, Via E. Orlando 75. Daily
7.30am-10.30pm. MAP P.92-93, POCKET MAP G4

Good for a coffee, snack
or light lunch, this
long-established Sicilian
bakery – ricotta-stuffed *cannoli*
are a speciality – is a peaceful
retreat in the Termini area,
with tables outside in this
small shopping arcade.

PALAZZO DEL FREDDO DI GIOVANNI FASSI

Via Principe Eugenio 65. Tues–Sat noon–midnight, Sun 10am–midnight. MAP P.92–93, POCKET MAP J6

A wonderful, airy 1920s ice cream parlour. Brilliant fruit ice creams and great *frullati*, too.

Restaurants

AGATA E ROMEO

Via Carlo Alberto 45 ⓣ 06.446.6115. Mon–Fri 12.30–2.30pm & 7.30–10.30pm; closed 3 weeks Jan & Aug. MAP P.92–93, POCKET MAP H5

Much-lauded chef Agata Parisella takes classic Roman cuisine to refined heights, in dishes such as her *baccalà* (salt cod) cooked five ways. Pricey for this part of town, but a great place for a blow-the-budget feast. Booking essential.

L'ASINO D'ORO

Via del Boschetto 73 ⓣ 06.4891.3832. Daily 12.30–3pm & 7.30–10.30pm. MAP P.92–93, POCKET MAP G5

The Rome location of legendary chef Lucio Sforza, who blends traditional Roman ingredients in both complex and simple combinations that you won't find anywhere else in the city. Not that expensive.

ALLE CARRETTE

Via Madonna dei Monti 95 ⓣ 06.679.2770. Daily 8pm–midnight. MAP P.92–93, POCKET MAP G5

Inexpensive large pizzeria just up Via Cavour that normally has long queues for the exceptional pizza and phenomenal desserts they serve here.

DOOZO

Via Palermo 51/53 ⓣ 06.481.5655 ⓦ www.doozo.it. Tues–Sat 12.30–3pm & 7.30–11pm, Sun 7.30–11pm. MAP P.92–93, POCKET MAP G4

Arguably the best Japanese restaurant in Monti. Part restaurant, part art gallery and bookshop, *Doozo* serves affordable lunch menus – dinner is a bit pricier. Outdoor seating is in a leafy courtyard with an ancient wall.

HANG ZHOU

Via Principe Eugenio 82 ⓣ 06.487.2732. Daily noon–3pm & 7–midnight. MAP P.92–93, POCKET MAP H5

Rome isn't the best place to get decent Chinese food, but this old Monti favourite is a cut above the rest. Plastered with photos of the sociable owner, it's cheap too.

MONTI DOC

Via G. Lanza 93 ⓣ 06.487.2696. Mon, Sat & Sun 7pm–1am, Tues–Fri 1–3.30pm & 7pm–1am. MAP P.92–93, POCKET MAP H5

Comfortable Santa Maria Maggiore-neighbourhood wine bar, with a comprehensive wine list and nice food: cold cuts and cheese, soups, quiches, salads and pastas, chalked on the blackboard daily.

LA MUCCA BISCHERA

Via degli Equi 56 ⓣ 06.446.9349. Mon–Fri 7.30pm–1am, Sat & Sun 1–3pm & 7.30pm–1am. MAP P.92–93, POCKET MAP K5

This cheap-and-cheerful San Lorenzo restaurant is packed with locals every night.The decor is kitsch – plastic vines,

WINE LIST AT ENOTECA 313

twinkling fairy lights and stuffed cows – but the food is hearty: Tuscan steaks and grilled meats from about €12. And if you overindulge, there's a rickshaw outside to take you back to Termini free of charge.

OPEN COLONNA

Palazzo delle Esposizioni, Via Milano 9a ☎ 06.4782.2641. Tues–Sat noon–midnight, Sun 12.30–3.30pm. MAP P.92–93, POCKET MAP G4

The top floor of the Palazzo delle Esposizioni (see p.95) is the domain of big-shot Italian chef Antonello Colonna. The €15 weekday lunch buffet is a hit with local office workers, while the €28 weekend brunch attracts more of a mixed crowd.

POMMIDORO

Piazza dei Sanniti 44 ☎ 06.445.2692. Mon– Sat 12.30–3pm & 7.30–11pm. MAP P.92–93, POCKET MAP K4

This family-run Roman trattoria has a breezy open veranda in summer and a fireplace in winter, and a great menu: try the tasty *pappardelle* with a wild boar sauce, and *abbacchio allo scottadito*, perfectly grilled lamb.

TRAM TRAM

Via dei Reti 44 ☎ 06.490.416. Tues–Sun noon–3pm & 7.30pm–midnight. MAP P.92–93, POCKET MAP K5

Despite the grungy location, this trendy San Lorenzo restaurant is a cosy spot, and serves good pasta dishes, seafood and unusual salads. Reserve ahead. There's a bar if you want to carry on drinking after dinner.

TRATTORIA MONTI

Via di San Vito 13a ☎ 06.446.6573. Tues–Sat 12.30–3pm & 7.30–11pm, Sun 12.30–3pm. MAP P.92–93, POCKET MAP H5

Small family-run restaurant- specializing in the cuisine of the Marche region, mean ing hearty food from a short

menu. As homely and friendly a restaurant as you could want – something places in this neighbourhood often aren't.

VALENTINO

Via del Boschetto 37 ☎ 06.488.0643. Mon–Sat 12.45–2.45 & 7.30–11.30pm. MAP P.92–93, POCKET MAP G5

With only a faded Peroni sign above the door, this trattoria on an atmospheric street is easy to miss. Inside, it's buzzing, with waiters zipping between the closely packed tables. You'll find grilled meat options, and a *scamorza* (grilled cheese) menu.

Bars

AL VINO AL VINO

Via dei Serpenti 19. Daily 11.30am–2.30pm & 5.30pm–12.30am. MAP P.92–93, POCKET MAP G5

Seriously good wine bar with a choice of over 500 labels, many by the glass. Snacks are generally Sicilian specialities.

LA BARRIQUE

Via del Boschetto 41b ☎ 06.4782.5953. Mon–Fri 1–3.30pm & 6pm–2am, Sat 6pm–2am. MAP P.92–93, POCKET MAP G5

This labyrinthine wine bar is a great spot for an *aperitivo*. French and Italian wines are the main attraction – champagne is a speciality – and there are platters of meats and cheeses. There's occasional live jazz too.

CAVOUR 313

Via Cavour 313. Daily 12.30–3pm & 7.30pm–12.30am; closed Sun in winter. MAP P.92–93, POCKET MAP G5

A lovely old wine bar that makes a handy retreat after seeing the ancient sites. The interior is cosy and wood-panelled, and delicious (though not cheap) snacks are served – cheese platters, salads and the like.

FINNEGAN

Via Leonina 66. Mon–Fri 5pm–2am, Sat & Sun 3pm–2am. MAP P.92–93, POCKET MAP G5

Decent Irish pub with live football on TV, pool, and a friendly expat crowd. There's seating outside, too, on this bustling Monti street.

RIVE GAUCHE

Via dei Sabelli 43. Daily 7pm–2am. MAP P.92–93, POCKET MAP K5

This large San Lorenzo bar is noisy, cavernous and beery – one of the best and longest-established night-time haunts in an area full of them. *Aperitivi* with buffet till 9pm.

MICCA CLUB

TEAROOM

Via del Boschetto 34 ☎ 347.009.5009. Daily 6pm–2am. MAP P.92–93, POCKET MAP G5

This tiny, dimly lit space with an old-world, decadent feel has become hugely popular with the area's discerning trendies. It serves tea and biscuits from 6pm, and there's a DJ from 8pm, when its comfy, overstuffed sofas are in high demand. You have to be a member to enter, but membership is free.

AI TRE SCALINI

Via Panisperna 251 ☎ 06.4890.7495. Mon–Fri noon–3pm & 6pm–midnight, Sat & Sun 6pm–midnight. MAP P.92–93, POCKET MAP G5

Easy-to-miss Monti bar, cosy and comfortable, with a great wine list but beer too if you want it, and decent food – cheese and salami plates, porchetta and other staples.

TRIMANI

Via Cernaia 37b. Mon–Sat 11.30am–3pm & 5.30pm–midnight. MAP P.92–93, POCKET MAP H3

Classy wine bar that's good for a lunchtime tipple. You'll spend around €18 to sample a range of cheeses and cured pork, or soup and salad, with a glass of wine.

Clubs & venues

CIRCOLO DEGLI ARTISTI

Via Casilina Vecchia 42 ☎ 06.7030.5684, ⓦ www.circoloartisti.it. Bus #105. Daily 9pm–3am. Admission from €5. MAP P.92–93, POCKET MAP K7

Alternative live music venue, featuring emerging talent as well as established indie bands, both Italian and international; it also hosts a Friday gay night.

Pigneto

Once a gritty inner-city district, Pigneto has been gentrified in recent years and is now firmly on the radar of Rome's cool set. The area has transformed itself into one of the city's best areas for a night out, with laid-back bars and intimate restaurants, particularly around Via del Pigneto, which is home to a morning market from Monday to Saturday and a bric-a-brac market on the last Sunday of the month. It's a twenty-minute taxi ride from the centre (or tram #14 from Termini), but well worth the trek; below are some of the area's highlights. See Pocket map K6.

Necci dal 1924 Via Fanfulla da Lodi 68 ☎ 06.9760.1552. Daily 8am–1am. Pasolini shot some of his films in Pigneto, and this bar-restaurant was apparently one of his favourite haunts. Now a trendy, buzzing spot throughout the day, it has a lovely shady garden where you can have a drink, snack or a full meal, with its creative dishes chalked afresh on the blackboard each day.

Pigneto Quarantuno Via del Pigneto 41–43 ☎ 06.7039.9483. Tues–Sun 6pm–2am, kitchen opens 8.20pm. Right in the heart of the action, on Via del Pigneto's pedestrianized strip, this excellent-value trattoria with outdoor tables has a short but ever-changing menu, depending on what's in season, though their fantastic *carbonara* (€7) is always on the menu.

Primo al Pigneto Via del Pigneto 46 ☎ 06.701.3827. Tues–Sun 12.30–3pm & 8–11pm. The top Pigneto restaurant, distinguished by its clean, contemporary interior and short menu of unfussy, seasonal dishes made using the freshest of ingredients – the *mezze maniche* pasta with *amatriciana* sauce is a favourite. *Primi* €10–13, *secondi* €16–28. It's a good idea to book for dinner.

Il Tiaso Via Ascoli Piceno 20 ☎ 333.284.5283. Daily 6pm–2am. This relaxed wine bar with free wi-fi has book-lined shelves and lots of wines to try by the glass, accompanied by cheese and salami platters, as well as some more substantial meals. There are often live acoustic sets, too – a great place to kick off an evening out.

MICCA CLUB

Via Pietro Micca 7a ☎ 06.8744.0079. Ⓦ www.miccaclub.com. Ⓜ Manzoni. Mon,Tues & Thurs–Sat 10pm–4am, Sun 6pm–2am; closed June to mid-Sept. MAP P.92–93, POCKET MAP K6

This cavernous underground club, with brick walls and plenty of cosy booths, has a hugely varied programme, with popular themed nights – from swing to funk to burlesque. It also hosts a vintage market every Sunday from 6pm.

TEATRO DELL'OPERA DI ROMA

Piazza Beniamino Gigli 1 ☎ 06.4816.0255. Ⓦ www.operaroma.it. Box office Tues–Sat 9am–5pm, Sun 9am–1.30pm. MAP P.92–93, POCKET MAP H4

Nobody compares it to La Scala, but cheap tickets are a lot easier to come by at Rome's opera and ballet venue – they start at around €20 for opera, less for ballet. If you buy the very cheapest tickets, bring some high-powered binoculars: you'll need them in order to see anything at all.

The Celian Hill and San Giovanni

Just behind the Colosseum, the Celian Hill is the most southerly of Rome's seven hills, and one of its most peaceful, home to a handful of churches and a quiet park. Just to the south and east, are some of Rome's most interesting churches: triple-layered San Clemente and nearby Quattro Coronati, and the complex of San Giovanni in Laterano – which gives its name to the surrounding San Giovanni district – all well worth the walk from the Colosseum. Nearby also is the wartime headquarters of the Nazi SS, now the home of an effective – and affecting – commemorative museum.

VILLA CELIMONTANA

MAP P.106–107, POCKET MAP G7

Much of the Celian Hill is taken up by the park of **Villa Celimontana**, whose shady gardens make a nice spot for a picnic, with lots of leafy walkways and grassy slopes. There are also pony rides and a playground, and outdoor jazz concerts on summer evenings.

SANTA MARIA IN DOMINICA

Daily 8.30am–12.30pm & 4.30–7pm.
MAP P.106–107, POCKET MAP H7

Also known as Santa Maria in Navicella after the ancient Roman stone boat that sits outside, this sixth-century church is just outside the entrance to the Villa Celimontana, and is worth visiting for the ninth-century mosaic above the apse, which shows Paschal I, who restored the church, kneeling at the feet of the Virgin.

SANTO STEFANO ROTONDO

Tues–Sat 9.30am–12.30pm & 3–6pm, Sun 9.30am–12.30pm. MAP P.106–107, POCKET MAP H7

Across Via della Navicella from the Celian Hill proper, this church is an ancient structure, lit by 22 windows – a magnificent and moody circular space, though the feature that really sticks in the mind is the series of stomach-churning frescoes on the walls, showing various saints being martyred in different ways, all in graphic and vividly restored detail.

SANTI GIOVANNI E PAOLO

Daily 8.30am–noon & 3.30–6.30pm.
MAP P.106–107, POCKET MAP G7

Recognized by its colourful campanile, this church is dedicated to two dignitaries in the court of Constantine who were beheaded here in 361 AD after refusing military service. A railed-off tablet in mid-nave marks the shrine where the saints were martyred and buried. The church is best known today as a wedding venue.

CASE ROMANE

Clivio di Scauro. Daily except Tues & Wed 10am–1pm & 3–6pm. €6. MAP P.106–107, POCKET MAP G7

The relics of what is believed to be the residence of the martyrs Giovanni and Paolo (see above) – around twenty rooms in all, patchily frescoed with pagan and Christian subjects. Standouts include the **Casa dei Genii,** frescoed with winged youths and cupids, and the courtyard or nymphaeum, which has a marvellous fresco of a goddess preparing for her marriage to Pluto, sandwiched between cupids in boats, fishing and loading supplies. There's also an interesting antiquarium, with a good haul of finds from the site.

SAN GREGORIO MAGNO

Daily 8.30am–12.30pm & 3–6.30pm; ring the bell marked "portinare" to gain admission.
MAP P.106–107, POCKET MAP G7

This church looks across to the Palatine Hill opposite. **St Gregory the Great** founded the monastery that still exists, and was a monk here before becoming pope in 590 AD. The interior is fairly ordinary, but the lovely Cosmati floor remains intact, and the chapel of the saint at the end of the south aisle has a beautifully carved altar showing scenes from St Gregory's life, along with his marble throne, that actually pre-dates the saint by 500 years.

SANTI QUATTRO CORONATI

Daily 6.15am–8pm; cloister and San Silvestro chapel Mon–Sat 9.30am–noon & 4.30–6pm, Sun 9–10.40am & 4–5.45pm; €1. MAP P.106–107, POCKET MAP H6–H7

Originally built in 1110, the interior feels a world away from the crowds around the nearby Colosseum – an atmosphere that is intensified by the pretty cloister. But its real treasure is the chapel of St Silvestro, whose frescoes, painted in 1248, relate the story of how the fourth-century pope cured the emperor Constantine of leprosy and then baptized him.

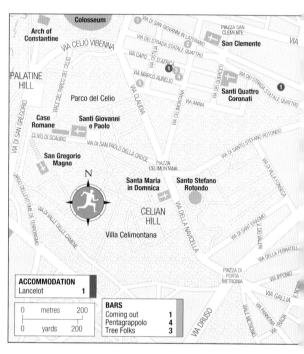

SAN CLEMENTE

Church daily 9am–7pm. Lower church and temple Mon–Sat 9am–12.30pm & 3–6pm, Sun noon–6pm. €5. MAP P.106–107, POCKET MAP H6

This church perhaps encapsulates better than any other the continuity of history in Rome – a conglomeration of three places of worship from three very different eras. The ground-floor church is a superb example of a medieval basilica, with some fine mosaics in the apse and some beautiful and vivid fifteenth-century frescoes. Downstairs there's the nave of an earlier church, dating back to 392 AD, and the **tomb of Pope Clement I**, the saint to whom the church is dedicated. At the eastern end of the fourth-century church, steps lead down to a third level, the remains of a Roman house – a labyrinthine set of rooms that includes a dank Mithraic temple of the late second century.

SAN GIOVANNI IN LATERANO

Daily 7am–6.30pm. Cloisters daily 9am–6pm. €2. MAP P.106–107, POCKET MAP J7

The area immediately south and east of the Esquiline Hill is known as **San Giovanni**, after the great basilica that lies at its heart – the city's cathedral, and the headquarters of the Catholic Church before the creation of the Vatican state. There has been a church on this site since the fourth century, and the present building evokes Rome's staggering wealth of history, with features from different

Celian Hill & San Giovanni

Museo Storico della Liberazione

Scala Santa & Sancta Sanctorum

PIAZZA DI SAN GIOVANNI IN LATERANO

Baptistry

PIAZZA DI PORTA SAN GIOVANNI

San Giovanni in Laterano

PIAZZALE APPIO

❷ SAN GIOVANNI Ⓜ

RESTAURANTS	
Charley's Sauciere	6
Luzzi	2
Taverna dei Quaranta	5

CAFÉ & SNACK	
Valentini	7

SHOPS	
Soul Food	1
Via Sannio	2

periods. The doors to the church were taken from the Roman Curia or Senate House, while the obelisk outside dates from the fifteenth century BC. Inside, the first pillar on the left of the right-hand aisle shows a fragment of Giotto's fresco of Boniface VIII proclaiming the first Holy Year in 1300. On the next pillar, a more recent monument commemorates Sylvester I, and incorporates part of his original tomb, said to sweat and rattle its bones when a pope is about to die. The nave itself is lined with eighteenth-century statues of the apostles: St Matthew, the tax collector, is shown with coins falling out of a sack; St Bartholomew holds a knife

and his own skin (he was flayed alive). The heads of St Peter and St Paul are kept secure behind the altar, while the baldacchino just in front is a splash of Gothic grandeur made by the Tuscan sculptor Giovanni di Stefano in the fourteenth century: it shelters the glassed-over bronze tomb of Martin V, the Colonna pope who was responsible for returning the papacy to Rome from Avignon in 1419. Outside the church, the cloisters are decorated with early thirteenth-century Cosmati work, while next door the Lateran Palace, home of the popes in the Middle Ages, has a small historical museum.

THE BAPTISTRY

San Giovanni in Laterano. Daily
7.30am–12.30pm & 4–6.30pm. Free.
MAP P.106–107, POCKET MAP J7

San Giovanni's **baptistery** is
the oldest surviving in the
Christian world – the octagonal
structure was built during the
fifth century and has been the
model for many such buildings
since. Oddly, it doesn't really
feel its age, although the
mosaics in the side chapels and
the bronze doors to the chapel
on the right, brought here from
the Baths of Caracalla, quickly
remind you where you are.

THE SCALA SANTA AND SANCTA SANCTORUM

Piazza di San Giovanni in Laterano 14.
April–Sept daily 6.15am–noon & 3.30–6.45pm;
Oct–March daily 6.15am–noon & 3–6.15pm.
MAP P.106–107, POCKET MAP J7

The **Scala Santa** is claimed to
be the staircase from Pontius
Pilate's house down which
Christ walked after his trial.
The 28 steps are protected by
boards, and the only way you're
allowed to climb them is on

your knees, which pilgrims
do regularly – although there
are other staircases either side
for the less penitent. At the
top, the Sancta Sanctorum
holds an ancient (sixth- or
seventh-century) painting of
Christ said to be the work of
an angel, hence its name –
acheiropoeton, Greek for "not
done by human hands". You
can't enter the chapel, and,
fittingly perhaps, you can
only really get a view of it by
kneeling and peering through
the grilles.

MUSEO STORICO DELLA LIBERAZIONE

Via Tasso 145. Tues–Sun 9.30am–12.30pm,
Tues, Thurs, Fri also 3.30–7.30pm. Free.
MAP P.106–107, POCKET MAP J6

Occupying two floors of the
building the Nazis used as a
prison during World War II,
this museum incorporates the
prison cells, left deliberately
untouched. It's extremely
well done, and perhaps the
most seriously affecting free
attraction in town.

Shops

SOUL FOOD

Via San Giovanni in Laterano 192. Tues–Sat 10.30am–1.30pm & 3.30–8pm. MAP P.106–107, POCKET MAP H7

Great, mainly vinyl, music store, with lots of rare as well as mainstream rock and punk discs. Flyers and info on gigs and venues too.

VIA SANNIO

Mon–Fri 9am–1pm, Sat 9am–6pm. MAP P.106–107, POCKET MAP J7

Long-standing market that creeps down the Aurelian Wall just beyond San Giovanni. Cheap clothes, luggage shoes...

Café

VALENTINI

Piazza Tuscolo 2 ☎ 06.7720.7427. Daily 8am–6pm. MAP P.106–107, POCKET MAP J8

Café, pastry shop and *tavola calda*, just five minutes' from San Giovanni and a great spot for lunch, with outside seating too.

Restaurants

CHARLEY'S SAUCIERE

Via San Giovanni in Laterano 270 ☎ 06.7049.5666. Mon–Sat 12.30–3pm & 7.30–11pm. MAP P.106–107, POCKET MAP H7

Lots of French classics – including fondues (the owner is Swiss), onion soup and excellent steaks, not to mention a good selection of real French cheeses. Moderate to high prices, but the food, service and overall atmosphere are worth every cent. Best to book.

LUZZI

Via San Giovanni in Laterano 88 ☎ 06.709.6332. Mon, Tues & Thurs–Sun noon–3pm & 7pm–midnight MAP P.106–107, POCKET MAP H6

Midway between San Giovanni in Laterano and the Colosseum, this bustling restaurant sits amid the tourist joints of the neighbourhood. The food is hearty, and there's outside seating. It's extremely cheap – *secondi* go for €6–9. Pizzas, but only in the evening.

TAVERNA DEI QUARANTA

Via Claudia 24 ☎ 06.700.0550. Daily 12.15–3pm & 7.15pm–midnight. MAP P.106–107, POCKET MAP G7

Relaxed locals' joint with moderately priced Roman food – yet only five minutes from the Colosseum.

Bars

COMING OUT

Via San Giovanni in Laterano 8 ☎ 06.700.9871. Daily 11am–2am. MAP P.106–107, POCKET MAP G6

Laid-back gay bar that serves food and hosts karaoke nights.

PENTAGRAPPOLO

Via Celimontana 21b. Tues–Fri noon–3pm & 6pm–1am, Sat & Sun 6pm–1am. MAP P.106–107, POCKET MAP G7

Celio wine bar with lots of good wine bars by the glass, cheese plates and the usual cold cuts, and live piano music several nights a week.

TREE FOLKS

Via Capo d'Africa. Daily 6pm–2am. MAP P.106–107, POCKET MAP G6

Lots of Belgian and German brews, along with their speciality – whisky – with a selection of single malts that must be the city's best. Food served, too.

The Aventine Hill and south

The leafy Aventine Hill – once the heart of plebeian Rome – is now an upscale residential area and one of the city's most pleasant corners. South and west from the hill are two distinct neighbourhoods: Testaccio, a working-class enclave that's become increasingly hip and gentrified (and home to much of the city's nightlife), and the more up-and-coming Ostiense, beyond the ancient city wall, worth a visit for the Centrale Montemartini branch of the Capitoline Museums. Between these districts is Rome's Protestant Cemetery, where the poets Keats and Shelley are buried. Further south lie the magnificent basilica of San Paolo fuori le Mura and the Via Appia Antica with its atmospheric catacombs, and beyond, EUR: Rome's futuristic 1930s experiment in town planning.

CIRCUS MAXIMUS

MAP P.112–113, POCKET MAP F7

The southern side of the Palatine Hill drops down to **Circus Maximus**, a long green expanse that was the ancient city's main venue for chariot races. At one time this arena had a capacity of up to 400,000 spectators, and it still retains something of its original purpose as an occasional venue for festivals and concerts.

THE BATHS OF CARACALLA

Viale Terme di Caracalla 52 ☎ 06.3996.7700. Mon 9am–2pm, Tues–Sun 9am–1 hr before sunset. €7.50 joint ticket includes Tomb of Cecilia Metella & Villa dei Quintili. MAP P.112–113, POCKET MAP H8

The remains of this ancient Roman leisure centre give a far better sense of the monumental scale of Roman architecture than most of the extant ruins in the city – so much so that Shelley was moved to write *Prometheus Unbound* here in 1819. The walls still rise to very nearly their original height and there are many fragments of mosaics – none spectacular, but quite a few bright and well preserved. The complex included gymnasiums, gardens and an open-air swimming pool as well as the hot, tepid and cold series of baths. As for Caracalla, he was one of Rome's worst and shortest-lived rulers, so it's no wonder there's

LATIN PLAQUE ON SANTA SABINA

nothing else in the city built by him. The baths make an atmospheric setting for opera performances during the summer (one of Mussolini's better ideas); for tickets and programme information, see Ⓦ www.operaroma.it.

SANTA SABINA

Piazza Pietro d'Illiria. Daily 7.30am–12.30pm & 3.30–6.30pm. MAP P.112–113, POCKET MAP E7

Crowning the Aventine Hill, **Santa Sabina** is a strong contender for Rome's most beautiful basilica. Look at the main doors, which are contemporary with the church and boast eighteen panels carved with Christian scenes (including one of the oldest representations of the Crucifixion). Santa Sabina is also the principal church of the Dominicans, and inside, just near the doors, a smooth piece of black marble, pitted with holes, was apparently thrown by the devil at St Dominic himself while at prayer, shattering the marble pavement but miraculously not harming the saint. It's also claimed that the orange trees behind, which you can glimpse on your way to a room once occupied by St Dominic himself, are descendants of those planted by the saint. Wherever the truth lies, the views from the park are splendid – across the Tiber to the centre of Rome and St Peter's.

PIAZZA DEI CAVALIERI DI MALTA

MAP P.112–113, POCKET MAP E7

As if to reward those who venture this far up the Aventine Hill, the minuscule **Piazza dei Cavalieri di Malta** holds an intriguing attraction: the imposing doorway to the **Priory of the Knights of Malta** is kept firmly closed to the public, but you can peek through the keyhole for a perfectly framed, dead-ahead view of St Peter's: the work of Giovanni Battista Piranesi.

TESTACCIO

MAP P.112–113, POCKET MAP E9

The working-class neighbourhood of **Testaccio** was for many years synonymous with its slaughterhouse, or *mattatoio*. The area's bustling **market** is a good place to get a flavour of "old" Testaccio, although in recent years the area has become fashionable and the slaughterhouse, once the area's main employer, is now home to the **Villaggio Globale**, a space used for concerts aimed at a studenty crowd (see p.121). The market is due to be moved to a new development of retail and cultural spaces, and currently the only real sight here is a branch of the **Museum of Contemporary Art of Rome** (MACRO Future; ☏ 06.6710.70400, Ⓦ www. macro.roma.museum), home to innovative temporary exhibitions. But the area is home to many excellent restaurants and nightlife spots.

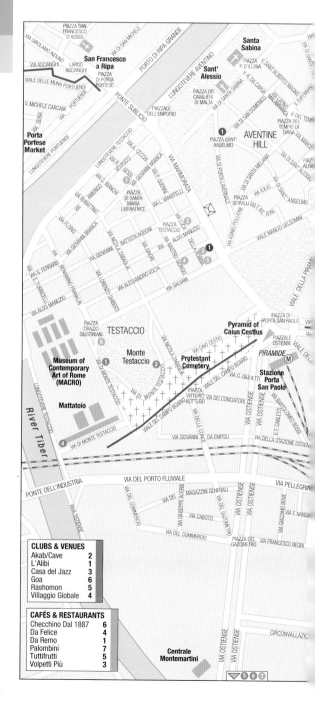

CLUBS & VENUES

Akab/Cave	2
L'Alibi	1
Casa del Jazz	3
Goa	6
Rashomon	5
Villaggio Globale	4

CAFÉS & RESTAURANTS

Checchino Dal 1887	6
Da Felice	4
Da Remo	1
Palombini	7
Tuttifrutti	5
Volpetti Più	3

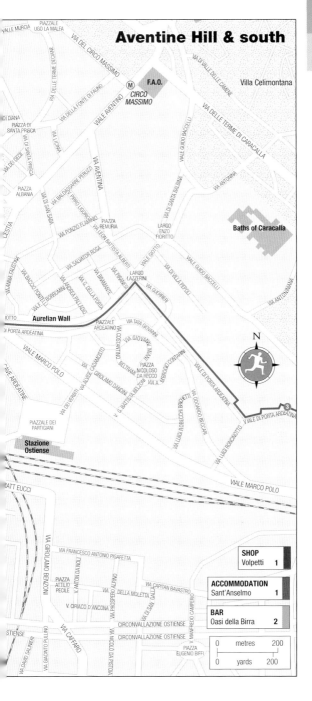

Aventine Hill & south

PIAZZALE
UGO LA MALFA

VALLE MURCIA

VIA DEL CIRCO MASSIMO

VIA DELLE TERME DECIANE

VIA DI VALLE DELLE CAMENE

F.A.O.

M CIRCO
MASSIMO

VIALE AVENTINO

VIA DELLA FONTE DI FAUNO

Villa Celimontana

VIA DELLE TERME DI CARACALLA

VIALE GUIDO BACCELLI

DI DIANA
PIAZZA DI
SANTA PRISCA

VIA LICINIA

VIA DI SANTA PRISCA

VIA DEI CECH

VIA DI SANTA BALBINA

VIA ANTONINA

VIA AVENTINA

PIAZZA
ALBANIA

VIA DI SAN SABA

VIA BALDASSARRE PERUZZI

VIA DI SANTA PRISCA

PIRRO LIGORIO

VIA PONZIO FLAMINIO

PIAZZA
REMURIA

VIA LEON BATTISTA ALBERTI

LARGO
ENZO
FIORITTO

Baths of Caracalla

LESTIA

VIANNA FAUSTINA

VIA BACCIO PONTELLI

VIA SALVATOR ROSA

VIA F.F. BORROMINI

VIA ANDREA PALLADIO

VIA G. DELLA PORTA

VIA BRAMANTE

VIALE GIOTTO

VIA DI VILLA PEPOLI

VIA PIRANESI

LARGO
LAZZERINI

VIA GUERRIERI

VIALE GUIDO BACCELLI

VIA ANTONINIANA

IOTTO

Aurelian Wall

DI PORTA ARDEATINA

PIAZZALE
ARDEATINO

VIA COSTANTINO

VIA TATA GIOVANNI

VIA GIOVANNI

N

VIALE MARCO POLO

VIA LUIGI CADAMOSTO

VIA GIROLAMO DANDINI

BELTRAMI

PIAZZA
NICOLOSO
DA RECCO
VIA A.

VIA AMBROGIO CONTARINI

VIALE DI PORTA ARDEATINA

CAVE ARDEATINE

VIA DEI VERGINI

VIA BALTISTA BELZONI

VIA G.

VIA LUIGI ROBECCHI BRICCHETTI

VIA ODOARDO BECCARI

PIAZZALE DEI
PARTIGIANI

VIALE DI PORTA ARDEATINA

3

Stazione
Ostiense

VIA LUIGI RONCIMOTTO

VIALE MARCO POLO

ATT EUCCI

VIA GIROLAMO BENZONI

VIA FRANCESCO ANTONIO PIGAFETTA

VIA ANTONIO NUNO

PIAZZA
ATTILIO
PECILE

VIA PROSPERO ALPINO

VIA DELLA MOLETTA

VIA CAPITAN BAVASTRO

VIA SAN CALEPO

VIA MANFREDO CAMPERIO

V. CIRIACO D'ANCONA

CIRCONVALLAZIONE OSTIENSE

STIENSE

VIA DAVID SILVERI

VIA GIACINTO PULLINO

VIA CAFFARO

CIRCONVALLAZIONE OSTIENSE

VIA NICOLO DA PISTOIA

PIAZZA
EUGENIO BIFFI

SHOP	
Volpetti	1

ACCOMMODATION	
Sant'Anselmo	1

BAR	
Oasi della Birra	2

0	metres	200
0	yards	200

MONTE TESTACCIO

MAP P.112–113, POCKET MAP E9

Monte Testaccio, which gives the area its name, is a 35-metre-high mound created out of the shards of Roman amphorae that were dumped here over several centuries. It's an odd sight, the ceramic curls clearly visible through the tufts of grass that crown its higher reaches, the bottom layers hollowed out by the workshops of car and bike mechanics – and, now, clubs and bars (see p.120).

THE PROTESTANT CEMETERY

Entrance on Via Caio Cestio 6 ☎ 06.574.1900, ⓦ www.protestantcemetery.it. Mon–Sat 9am–5pm, Sun 9am–1pm; last entrance 30min before closing. €2 donation expected. Bus 23 to Piazzale Ostiense. MAP P.112–113, POCKET MAP E9

The **Protestant Cemetery** isn't in fact a Protestant cemetery at all, but is reserved for non-Roman Catholics of all nationalities. It is nonetheless one of the finest places in the English in Rome, and a fitting conclusion to a visit to the Keats-Shelley Memorial House on Piazza di Spagna (see p.74) since it is here that both poets are buried, along with a handful of other well-known names. Most visitors come to see the grave of Keats, who lies next to his friend, the painter Joseph Severn, in a corner of the old part of the cemetery, his stone inscribed, according to his wishes, with the words "Here lies one whose name was writ in water". Shelley's ashes were brought here at his wife's request and interred, after much obstruction by the papal authorities, in the newer part of the cemetery at the top – the Shelleys had visited several years earlier, the poet praising it as "the most beautiful and solemn cemetery I ever beheld".

THE PYRAMID OF CAIUS CESTIUS

Piazzale Ostiense. MAP P.117–113, POCKET MAP E9 The most distinctive landmark in this part of town is the mossy **pyramidal tomb** of one Caius Cestius, who died in 12 BC. Cestius had spent some time in Egypt, and part of his will decreed that all his slaves should be freed – the white pyramid you see today was thrown up by them in only 330 days of what must have been joyful building. It's open for

1hr visits on the second and fourth Saturday of the month at 11am (book in advance on ☎06.3996.7700; €4.50).

CENTRALE MONTEMARTINI

Via Ostiense 106 ☎06.0608, ✉www
.centralemontemartini.org. Tues–Sun
9am–7pm. €4.50, or €14 for joint ticket
with Capitoline Museums, valid 7 days. MAP
P.112–113, POCKET MAP E11

This former electricity generating is a permanent outpost of the Capitoline Museums, attracting visitors to formerly industrial Ostiense. The huge rooms of the power station are suited to showcasing its ancient sculpture, although the massive turbines and furnaces have a fascination of their own. Among many compelling objects are the head, feet and an arm from a colossal statue, once 8m high, found in Largo Torre Argentina, a large Roman copy of Athena, a fragmented mosaic of hunting scenes, and a lovely naturalistic statue of a girl seated on a stool with her legs crossed, from the third century BC. There's also a figure of Hercules and next to it a soft Muse Polymnia, the former braced for activity, the latter leaning on a rock and staring into the distance.

SAN PAOLO FUORI LE MURA

Via Ostiense 190. Daily 7am–6pm. €3. Metro
B San Paolo. MAP P.112–113, POCKET MAP E12

The basilica of **San Paolo fuori le Mura** (St Paul's Outside the Walls) is one of Rome's five patriarchal basilicas, occupying the site of St Paul's tomb. Victim of a devastating fire in 1823, today its largely a nineteenth-century reconstruction. The huge structure has a powerful and authentic sense of occasion: evidenced by the medallions of the popes fringing the nave and transepts above, starting with St Peter to the right of the apse and ending with Benedict XVI at the top of the south aisle. In the south transept, the paschal candlestick is a remarkable piece of Romanesque carving, supported by half-human beasts and showing scenes from Christ's life; the bronze aisle doors were also rescued from the old basilica and date from 1070, as was the thirteenth-century tabernacle by Arnolfo di Cambio. There's also the cloister, just behind here – probably Rome's finest piece of Cosmatesque work, its spiralling, mosaic-encrusted columns enclosing a peaceful rose garden.

THE AURELIAN WALL

MAP P.112–113, POCKET MAP E10–H9

Built by the Emperor Aurelian in 275 AD to enclose Rome's hills and protect the city from invasion, the Aurelian Wall still surrounds much of the city, but its best-preserved stretch runs 2km between Porta San Paolo and Porta San Sebastiano (which lies a few hundred metres of Largo Terme di Caracalla).

Here, the **Museo delle Mura** at Via di Porta San Sebastiano 18 (06.0608, www.museodellemuraroma.it; Tues–Sun 9am–2pm; €3) occupies two floors of the city gate and has displays showing Aurelian's original plans and lots of photos of the walls past and present. You can climb up to the top of the gate for great views over the Roman countryside beyond, and walk a few hundred metres along the wall itself. From here it's only a short walk up Via di Porta San Sebastiano to the Baths of Caracalla.

VIA APPIA ANTICA

POCKET MAP H10–K12

The **Via Appia Antica**, which starts at the Porta San Sebastiano, is the most famous of the consular roads that used to strike out in each direction from ancient Rome. It was built by one Appio Claudio in 312 BC, and is the only Roman landmark mentioned in the Bible. During classical times the "Appian Way" was the most important of all the Roman trade routes, carrying supplies right down through Campania to the port of Brindisi. It's no longer the main route south out of the city – that's Via Appia Nuova from nearby Porta San Giovanni – but it remains an important part of early Christian Rome, its verges lined with numerous pagan and Christian sites, including, most famously, the underground burial cemeteries, or catacombs, of the first Christians.

THE AURELIAN WALL

Visiting Via Appia Antica and the catacombs

Buses run south along Via Appia Antica and conveniently stop at, or near to, most of the main attractions, starting with Porta San Sebastiano. You can walk it, but bear in mind that much of the Via Appia Antica isn't particularly picturesque, at least until you get down to the Catacombs of San Sebastiano, and the best thing to do is take a bus to San Sebastiano and double back or walk on further for the attractions you want to see. Bus #118 runs from Piazzale Ostiense almost as far as the San Sebastiano catacombs; you can also take bus #218 from Piazza San Giovanni, which goes down Via Ardeatina, or bus #660 from Colli Albani metro station, which goes beyond the Tomb of Cecilia Metella. However, the easiest option is to take the **Archeobus** (www.trambusopen.com), which runs from Termini and Piazza Venezia, among other city-centre locations, every 30min (9am–4.30pm); tickets cost €12 for a 24-hour ticket and you can hop on and off as you wish. Or you could walk from Porta San Sebastiano and take everything in on foot, which allows you to stop off at the Parco Regionale dell'Appia Antica **information office** for the area – it's actually classified as a national park – at Via Appia Antica 58, on the right just before you get to Domine Quo Vadis (Mon–Thurs 9.30am–1.30pm & 2.30–5.30pm, Fri 9am–1.30pm, Sat & Sun closed; 06.513.6314; www.parcoappiaantica.it). You can pick up a good map and other information on the various Appia Antica sights here, as well as hire **bikes** on Sundays and public holidays (€3/hour or €10/day). You can take a tour of the catacombs and nearby sights with Enjoy Rome (see p.183; Sat only; 3hr; €40). Finally, there are a couple of decent **restaurants** down by San Sebastiano: **L'Archeologia** (06.788.0494; closed Tues), just past the church, and the **Cecilia Metella** (06.5136.743; closed Mon) right opposite.

DOMINE QUO VADIS

Via Appia Antica 51. Daily 8am–7pm, 6pm in winter. POCKET MAP J11

About 500m from Porta San Sebastiano, where the road forks, the church of Domine Quo Vadis is the first sight on Via Appia. Legend has this as the place where St Peter saw Christ while fleeing from certain death in Rome and asked "Where goest thou, Lord?", to which Christ replied that he was going to be crucified once more, leading Peter to turn around and accept his fate. The small church is ordinary enough inside, except for its replica of a piece of marble that's said to be marked with the footprints of Christ –

the original is in the church of San Sebastiano (see p.119).

CATACOMBS OF SAN CALLISTO

Via Appia Antica 110/126 ☏ 06.5130.1580, ⓦ www.catacombe.roma.it. Thurs–Tues 9am–noon & 2–5pm. €8. POCKET MAP J12

The largest of Rome's catacombs, the Catacombs of San Callisto were founded in the second century AD and many of the early popes are buried here. There are regular free tours (45min) in English, and the site also features some seventh- and eighth-century frescoes, and the crypt of Santa Cecilia, who was buried here after her martyrdom, before being moved to the church dedicated to her in Trastevere – a copy of Carlo Maderno's famous statue marks the spot.

MAUSOLEO DELLE FOSSE ARDEATINE

Via Ardeatina 174 ☏ 06.513.6742. Mon–Fri 8.15am–3.30pm, Sat & Sun 8.15am–4.30pm. Free. POCKET MAP K12

A ten-minute walk from San Callisto, close by the #218 bus stop, is a site that remembers the **massacre** of over 300 civilians during the Nazi occupation of Rome, after the Resistance had ambushed and killed 32 soldiers in the centre of the city. The Nazis exacted a harsh vengeance, killing ten civilians for every dead German, burying the bodies here and then exploding mines to cover up their crime. The bodies were dug up after the war and reinterred in the mausoleum here.

CATACOMBS OF SAN SEBASTIANO

Via Appia Antica 136 ☏ 06.785.0350, ⓦ www.catacombe.org. Mon–Sat 9am–noon & 2–5pm; closed mid-Nov to mid-Dec. €8. POCKET MAP K12

These **catacombs** sit under a much-renovated basilica that was originally built by Constantine on the spot where the bodies of the apostles Peter and Paul are said to have lain for a time. Half-hour tours take in paintings of doves and fish, a contemporary carved oil lamp and inscriptions dating the tombs themselves. The most striking features are three pagan tombs (one painted, two stuccoed) discovered when archeologists were investigating the floor of the basilica upstairs. Just above here, Constantine reputedly raised his chapel, and although St Peter was later removed to the Vatican and St Paul to San Paolo fuori le Mura, the graffiti records the fact that this was indeed where the two Apostles' remains rested.

TOMB OF CECILIA METELLA

VILLA AND CIRCUS OF MAXENTIUS

Via Appia Antica 153 ☎ 06.0608. ⊚ www
.villadimassenzio.it. Tues–Sun 9am–1.30pm.
€3. POCKET MAP K12

A few hundred metres further
on from the San Sebastiano
catacombs, the group of brick
ruins trailing off into the fields
to the left are the remains
of the Villa and Circus of
Maxentius, a complex built by
the emperor in the early fourth
century AD before his defeat
by Constantine. It's a clear, long
oval of grass, similar to the
Circus Maximus (see p.110),
but slightly better preserved.

THE TOMB OF CECILIA METELLA

Via Appia Antica 161 ☎ 06.780.0093. Tues–
Sun 9am–1hr before sunset. €6 joint ticket
including Terme di Caracalla and Villa dei
Quintili. POCKET MAP K12

Further along the Via Appia,
this circular tomb dates from
the Augustan period, and was
converted into a castle in the
fourteenth century. Known as
"Capo di Bove" for the bulls
on the frieze around it, the
tomb itself, a huge brick-built
drum, is little more than a
large pigeon coop these days;
various fragments and finds are
littered around the adjacent,
later courtyards, and down
below you can see what's left
of an ancient lava flow from
thousands of years earlier.

EUR

Main piazzas at south end of Via Cristoforo
Colombo. Bus #714 from Termini or metro
line B. POCKET MAP E12

The **EUR** district was planned
by Mussolini for the 1942
Esposizione Universale Roma,
but not finished until after
the war. Its monumental
fascist architecture and grand
processional boulevards recall
Imperial Rome (especially
the Palazzo della Civiltà or
"Square Colosseum"). Overall
it's a pretty strange and soulless
place, something of a white
elephant despite the busy
offices and shops. EUR's main
attraction is its museums,
especially the Museo della
Civiltà Romana, Piazza Agnelli
10 (⊚ www.museociviltaromana
.it; Tues–Sun 9am–2pm,
Sun 9am–1.30pm; €8.50, or
€9.50 including planetarium),
which has a large model of the
fourth-century city –perfect
for setting the rest of the city
in context. The museum also
incorporates the Planetario e
Museo Astronomico – no great
shakes, especially if you don't
speak Italian.

Shop

VOLPETTI

Via Marmorata 47. Mon–Sat 8am–2pm &
5–8pm. MAP P.112–113, POCKET MAP E8
It's worth seeking out this
Testaccio deli, truly one of
Rome's very best, with a
fantastic selection of cold meats
and cheeses.

VOLPETTI

Cafés and restaurants

CHECCHINO DAL 1887

Via di Monte Testaccio 30 ☎ 06.574.6318.
Tues–Sat 12.30–3pm & 8–11.30pm. MAP
P.112–113, POCKET MAP E9
A historic symbol of Testaccio
cookery, with an excellent wine
cellar, too. Expensive, but worth
it for its rustic atmosphere and
excellent menu of authentic
Roman meat and offal dishes.

DA FELICE

Via Mastro Giorgio 29 ☎ 06.574.6800.
Daily 12.30–2.45pm & 8–11.30pm. MAP
P.112–113, POCKET MAP E8
This always-buzzing trattoria is
a simple place with brick walls,
a tiled floor and no-nonsense
waiters. The outstanding
bucatini cacio e pepe and,

in winter, artichokes, are
deservedly popular, so it's a
good idea to book.

DA REMO

Piazza Santa Maria Liberatrice 44
☎ 06.574.6270. Mon–Sat 7.30pm–1am;
closed 3wks Aug. MAP P.112–113, POCKET MAP E8
Remo is the best kind of
pizzeria: usually crowded with
locals, very basic, and serving
the thinnest, crispiest Roman
pizza you'll find. It's also worth
trying the heavenly *bruschette*
and other snacks like *suppli*
and *fiori di zucca*. Perfect
pre-clubbing food – and very
cheap.

PALOMBINI

Piazzale Adenauer 12. Mon–Thurs 7am–10pm,
Fri & Sat 7am–1am, Sun 8am–10pm. MAP
P.112–113, POCKET MAP H12
Great EUR café whose outside
terrace and large interior are
a haven amidst EUR's brutal
boulevards. Appropriately
housed on the ground floor
of EUR's official "restaurant
building", it's a café, *tabacchi*
and wine shop all rolled into
one, and serves excellent cakes
and sandwiches.

TUTTIFRUTTI

Via Luca della Robbia 3a ☎ 06.575.7902.
Tues–Sun 7.30–11.30pm. MAP P.112–113,
POCKET MAP E8
This Testaccio favourite
is pretty much the perfect
restaurant – family-run, with
good food and fair prices.
The menu changes daily, and
offers interesting variations on
traditional Roman dishes.

VOLPETTI PIÙ

Via A. Volta 8. Mon–Sat 10.30am–3.30pm &
5.30–9.30pm. MAP P.112–113, POCKET MAP E8
Tavola calda that's attached to
the famous deli a few doors
down. Great pizza, *suppli*,
chicken, deep-fried veg and
much more.

Bar

OASI DELLA BIRRA

Piazza Testaccio 41. Mon–Sat 8am–2.30pm, & 4.30pm–1am, Sun 7.30pm–1am. MAP P.112–113, POCKET MAP E8

Unassumingly situated under a Piazza Testaccio wine bar, the cosy basement rooms here house an international selection of beers that rivals anywhere in the world – 500 in all, and with plenty of wines to choose from as well. You can eat generously assembled plates of cheese and salami, and a great selection of *bruschette* and polenta dishes.

Clubs

AKAB/CAVE

Via di Monte Testaccio 69 ☎ 06.5725.0585. ⓦ www.akabcave.com. Metro B Piramide or bus #23. Tues–Sat 10pm–4am. €10–20, including 1 drink. MAP P.112–113, POCKET MAP E9

Club built into an old carpenter's shop on two floors, one on ground level, the other a cavelike room below. *Akab*'s biggest night is Tuesday's "L-Ektrica" party; Wednesday is retro, Thursday r'n'b, Friday & Saturday house.

L'ALIBI

Via Monte Testaccio 44 ☎ 06.574.3448. ⓦ www.lalibi.it. Metro B Piramide or bus #23. Thurs–Sun midnight–5am. Admission €10–€15, including 1 drink. MAP P.112–113, POCKET MAP E9

Predominantly – but by no means exclusively – male venue that's one of Rome's oldest and best gay clubs. Thursday night's Gloss is ever-popular. Downstairs there's a multi-room cellar disco and upstairs an open-air bar. The big terrace is perfect during the warm months.

CASA DEL JAZZ

Viale di Porta Ardeatina 55 ☎ 06.704.731. ⓦ www.casajazz.it. Metro #B to Piramide or bus #714. Closed Tues & Sun evenings. Admission €10–15. MAP P.112–113, POCKET MAP G9

Sponsored by the city, this converted villa in leafy surroundings is the ultimate jazz-lovers' complex, with a book and CD store and restaurant, recording studios and a 150-seat auditorium that hosts gigs most nights of the week.

GOA

Via Libetta 13 ☎ 06.574.8277. Metro B Garbatella or Bus #29, 769, 770. Tues–Sat 11pm–4am. Admission €10–25, including 1 drink. MAP P.112–113, POCKET MAP E11

Long-running Ostiense club near the Basilica San Paolo, playing techno, house and drum'n'bass. *Goa* has recently had a Gothic makeover, but it's stayed true to its musical roots.

RASHOMON

Via degli Argonauti 16 ⓦ www.rashomonclub .com. Metro B Garbatella. Wed & Thurs 10pm–2am, Fri & Sat 11pm–4am. MAP P.112–113, POCKET MAP F11

A live music performance space which walks the line between underground club and trendy point of reference for Roman indie musicians, artists and DJs. Thursday night's Loaded party draws the biggest crowds.

VILLAGGIO GLOBALE

Lungotevere Testaccio 1 ☎ 347.413.1205. Bus #170, 719. Winter months only; opening hours depend on events. Admission from €5. MAP P.112–113, POCKET MAP D10

Situated in the old slaughterhouse along the river, the "global village" has something on almost every night, whether it's indie rock or avant-garde performance art.

Trastevere and the Janiculum Hill

Across the river from the centre of town, Trastevere (the name means literally "across the Tiber") was the artisan area of the city in classical times, neatly placed for the trade that came upriver from Ostia. Nowadays the area is a long way from its working-class roots, and its many bars and restaurants can be thronged with tourists. But its narrow streets and closeted squares are charming, peaceful in the morning, lively come the evening, with dozens of trattorias setting tables out along the cobbled streets – and still buzzing late at night, when its bars and clubs host one of Rome's most dynamic after-dark scenes.

SAN FRANCESCO A RIPA

Piazza San Francesco d'Assisi. Daily 7am–noon & 4–7pm. MAP P.124–125, POCKET MAP D7–E7

The church of **San Francesco a Ripa** is best known for two things: the fact that St Francis himself once stayed here – you can see the actual room he stayed in if you're lucky enough to find it open – and the writhing, orgasmic statue of a minor saint, the Blessed Ludovica Albertoni, sculpted by Bernini towards the end of his career. As a work of Baroque emotiveness, it's perhaps even more frank in its depiction of an earthly realized divine ecstasy than his more famous *Ecstasy of St Theresa* in the church of Santa Maria della Vittoria (see p.84).

SANTA CECILIA IN TRASTEVERE

Piazza Santa Cecilia 22. Daily 9.30am–1pm & 4–7.15pm. Excavations €3; singing gallery Mon–Sat 10am–12.30pm. €2.50. MAP P.124–125, POCKET MAP E18

In its own quiet piazza off Via Anicia, the church of **Santa Cecilia in Trastevere** was originally built over the site of

the second-century home of St Cecilia, who was – along with her husband – persecuted for her Christian beliefs. The story has it that Cecilia was locked in the caldarium of her own baths for several days but refused to die, singing her way through the ordeal (Cecilia is patron saint of music). Her head was finally half hacked off with an axe, though it took several blows before she died. Below the high altar, under a Gothic baldacchino, Stefano Maderno's statue of the limp saint shows her incorruptible body as it was found when exhumed in 1599, with three deep cuts in her neck. Downstairs, excavations of the baths and the rest of the Roman house are on view in the crypt. But more alluring by far is the singing gallery above the nave of the church (ring the bell to the left of the church door), where Pietro Cavallini's late thirteenth-century fresco of the *Last Judgement* – all that remains of the decoration that once covered the entire church – is a powerful, amazingly naturalistic piece of work for

its time, centring on Christ in quiet majesty, flanked by angels.

SANTA MARIA IN TRASTEVERE

Piazza Santa Maria in Trastevere. Daily 7am–9pm. MAP P.124–125, POCKET MAP C18

In the heart of old Trastevere, Piazza **Santa Maria in Trastevere** is named after the church in its northwest corner. Held to be the first Christian place of worship in Rome, it was built on a site where a fountain of oil is said to have sprung on the day of Christ's birth. The church's mosaics are among the city's most impressive: mostly Byzantine-inspired works depicting a solemn yet sensitive parade of saints thronged around Christ and Mary – the *Coronation of the Virgin* – beneath which are scenes from her life by the Santa Cecilia artist, Pietro Cavallini. Under the high altar on the right, an inscription – "FONS OLEI" – marks the spot where the oil is supposed to have sprung up.

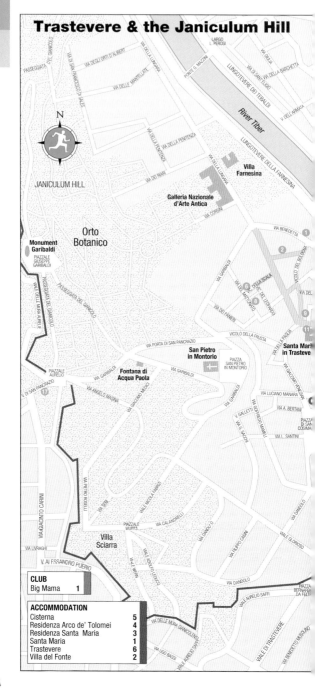

Trastevere & the Janiculum Hill

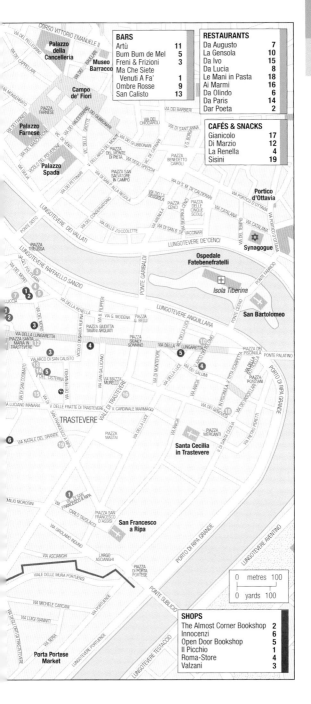

BARS

Artù	11
Bum Bum de Mel	5
Freni & Frizioni	3
Ma Che Siete	
Venuti A Fa'	1
Ombre Rosse	9
San Calisto	13

RESTAURANTS

Da Augusto	7
La Gensola	10
Da Ivo	15
Da Lucia	8
Le Mani in Pasta	18
Ai Marmi	16
Da Olindo	6
Da Paris	14
Dar Poeta	2

CAFÉS & SNACKS

Gianicolo	17
Di Marzio	12
La Renella	4
Sisini	19

SHOPS

The Almost Corner Bookshop	2
Innocenzi	6
Open Door Bookshop	5
Il Picchio	1
Roma-Store	4
Valzani	3

VILLA FARNESINA

Via della Lungara 230 ☎ 06.6802.7268. Mon–Sat & 2nd Sun of the month 9am–1pm. €5. MAP P.124–125. POCKET MAP C16

The early sixteenth-century **Villa Farnesina** was built by Baldassare Peruzzi for the Sienese banker Agostino Chigi. Its opulent rooms are decorated with marvellous frescoes and most people come to view the Raphael-designed painting of *Cupid and Psyche* in the now glassed-in loggia, completed in 1517 by the artist's assistants. The painter and art historian Vasari claims Raphael didn't complete the work because his infatuation with his mistress – "La Fornarina", whose father's bakery was situated nearby – was making it difficult to concentrate. Nonetheless it's very impressive: a flowing, animated work bursting with muscular men and bare-bosomed women, although the only part Raphael is said to have actually completed is the female figure with her back turned on the lunette (to the right of the door leading out to the east). He did, however, apparently manage to finish the Galatea in the room next door. The ceiling illustrates Chigi's horoscope constellations, frescoed by the architect of the building, Peruzzi, who also decorated the upstairs Salone delle Prospettive, where trompe l'oeil balconies give views onto contemporary Rome.

PALAZZO CORSINI

Via della Lungara 10 ☎ 06.32810, ⓦ www .galleriaborghese.it. Tues–Sun 8.30am–7.30pm. €4. MAP P.124–125. POCKET MAP C16–17

Housed in the **Palazzo Corsini**, the **Galleria Nazionale d'Arte Antica** is a relatively small collection that takes up a few rooms of the giant palace. There's a grouping of Flemish paintings, including works by Rubens and Van Dyck; a room full of landscapes, including lush scenes by Dughet and a fanciful depiction of the Pantheon by Charles Clérisseau. Look out for the famous portrayal of *Salome with the Head of St John the Baptist* by Guido Reni and a painting of *Prometheus* by Salvatore Rosa that is one of the most vivid and detailed expositions of human internal anatomy you'll see. You can also visit the bedchamber of Queen Christina, who renounced Protestantism and, with it, the Swedish throne in 1655, and brought her library and fortune to Rome – she died, here in the

PALAZZO CORSINI

palace, in 1689, and is one of only three women to be buried in St Peter's. Also worth a look is the curious Aldobrandini Throne, thought to be a Roman copy of an Etruscan throne of the second or first century.

THE ORTO BOTANICO

Largo Cristina di Svezia 24 ☎ 06.4991.7140. Mon–Sat 9am–6.30pm. €4. MAP P.124–125, POCKET MAP B17

The Orto Botanico occupies the eastern side of the Janicul um Hill. It's a pleasantly neglected expanse these days where you can clamber up to high stands of bamboo and ferns cut by rivulets of water, stroll through a wood of century-old oaks, cedars and conifers, and relax in a grove of acclimatized palm trees. There's also a herbal garden with medicinal plants, a collection of orchids that bloom in springtime and early summer, and a garden of aromatic herbs put together for the blind; the plants can be identified by their smell or touch, and are accompanied by signs in braille. The garden also has the distinction of being home to one of the oldest plane trees in Rome, between 350 and 400 years old, near the rather decrepit monumental staircase.

THE JANICULUM HILL

MAP P.124–125, POCKET MAP A17–B17

It's about a fifteen-minute walk up Via Garibaldi from lively Piazza di Sant'Egidio to the summit of the **Janiculum Hill** – not one of the original seven hills of Rome, but the one with the best and most accessible views of the centre. Follow Vicolo del Cedro from Via della Scala and take the steps up from the end, cross the main road, and continue on the steps that lead up to **San Pietro in Montorio**, best known – and worth stopping off for – the Renaissance architect Bramante's little **Tempietto** in its courtyard. Head up from here to the Passeggiata del Gianicolo and follow the ridge to Piazzale Garibaldi, where there's an equestrian monument to **Garibaldi**. Just below is the spot from which a cannon is fired at noon each day for Romans to check their watches. Further on, the statue of Anita Garibaldi recalls the important part she played in an encounter with the French in 1849 – a fiery, melodramatic work that also marks her grave. Spread out before her are some of the best **views** over the city.

Shops

THE ALMOST CORNER BOOKSHOP

Via del Moro 45. Mon–Sat 10am–1.30pm & 3.30–8pm, Sun 11am–1.30pm & 3.30–8pm; closed Sun in Aug. MAP P.124–125, POCKET MAP D17

Of all Rome's English bookshops, this is the best bet for finding the very latest titles, and staff are helpful too.

THE ALMOST CORNER BOOKSHOP

INNOCENZI

Piazza San Cosimato 66. Mon–Wed, Fri & Sat 7.30am–1.30pm & 4.30–8pm, Thurs 7.30am–1.30pm. MAP P.124–125, POCKET MAP D18

A great dry-goods grocer, with all the usual rice and pasta and Italian goodies, but also a great selection from around the world – tomato ketchup, teas, peanut butter, the works.

OPEN DOOR BOOKSHOP

Via della Lungaretta 23. Mon 4–8.30pm, Tues–Sat 10.30am–8.30pm. July & Aug closed Sat pm. MAP P.124–125, POCKET MAP E18

Although they do have some new titles, especially on Rome and Roman history, used books in English dominate the shelves at this friendly bookshop, where you never know what treasures you might happen upon. They also have books in Italian, German, French and Spanish.

IL PICCHIO

Via del Moro 48. Daily 10.30am–1.30pm & 3.30–8.30pm. MAP P.124–125, POCKET MAP D17

This old-fashioned shop is crammed with children's toys in wood, from xylophones and spinning tops to puzzles.

ROMA-STORE

Via della Lungaretta 63. Mon–Sat 4–8pm, Tues–Sat 9.30am–1.30pm & 4–8pm. MAP P.124–125, POCKET MAP D18

Not a football merchandise store but a shop selling classic perfumes, scented soaps, lotions and candles.

VALZANI

Via del Moro 37a/b. Wed–Sun 10am–8.30pm. MAP P.124–125, POCKET MAP D18

Specializing in the art of confectionary since 1925, this small shop is stuffed full of calorific treats. *Valzani* is most famous for its sublime chocolate, but the traditional Roman treats such as *bigne* and *frappe* are just as hard to resist.

Porta Portese market

On a Sunday it's worth approaching Trastevere from the south, walking over the Ponte Sublicio to Porta Portese; from here the Porta Portese flea market (dawn–2pm) stretches down Via Portuense to Trastevere train station in a congested medley of antiques, old motor spares, cheap and trendy clothing, and assorted junk. Haggling is the rule, and keep a good hold of your wallet or purse. Come early if you want to buy – most of the bargains have gone by 10am, by which time the crush of people can be intense.

Cafés and snacks

GIANICOLO

Piazzale Aurelia 5. Tues–Sat 7am–1am, Sun 7am–9pm. MAP P.124–125, POCKET MAP A18

Quite an ordinary bar, but in a picturesque location and a bit of a hangout for Italian media stars, writers and academics from the nearby Spanish and American academies. Tasty sandwiches, too, and a couple of tables inside as well as out.

DI MARZIO

Piazza di Santa Maria in Trastevere 15. Daily 7am–1am. MAP P.124–125, POCKET MAP D18

This bar isn't much on the inside, but it's a friendly place that does decent sandwiches and whose terrace right on Piazza Santa Maria makes it the best people-watching spot in Trastevere.

LA RENELLA

Via del Moro 15. Daily 9am–9pm. MAP P.124–125, POCKET MAP D17

Arguably the best bakery in Rome, with great foccaccia and superb *pizza al taglio*. Take a number and be prepared to wait at busy times. You can take away or eat on the premises at the long counter.

SISINI

Via di San Francesco a Ripa 137. Mon–Sat 11am–11pm. MAP P.124–125, POCKET MAP D18

Just half a block from Viale Trastevere, there's no sign outside this *pizza al taglio* hole-in-the-wall, but it's worth seeking out, as it has perhaps the best pizza by the slice in Rome. Also roast chicken and potatoes, *supplì* and all the usual *rosticceria* fare. Try their unique spicy green olive pizza.

Restaurants

DA AUGUSTO

Piazza de Renzi 15 ☎ 06.580.3798. Daily 12.30–3pm & 8–11pm. MAP P.124–125, POCKET MAP D17

A Trastevere old-timer serving Roman basics outside on the cobbles in the summer months. You can get a good meal for about €14 here, including a glass of robust house wine. Expect offerings such as pasta and soup starters, and daily meat and fish specials – not haute cuisine, but decent, hearty Roman cooking. No bookings taken.

LA GENSOLA

Piazza della Gensola 15 ☎ 06.5833.2758 & 06.581.6312. Daily 12.30–3pm & 7.30pm–midnight. May 15 to Sept 15 closed Sun. MAP P.124–125, POCKET MAP E18

This place, with charming and simple decor, is a lovely place for a special meal: the Sicilian cuisine is faultless and the atmosphere warm and convivial. The predominantly fishy specialities include tagliolini with tuna and asparagus, and the desserts are excellent too: you can't go wrong with the crumbly apple pie served with deliciously creamy cinnamon ice cream.

DA AUGUSTO

DA IVO

Via di San Francesco a Ripa 158
☎ 06.581.7082. Wed–Mon 7.30pm–1am.
MAP P.124–125, POCKET MAP D18

The Trastevere pizzeria,
almost in danger of becoming
a caricature, but still good
and very reasonable. A nice
assortment of desserts, too –
try the *monte bianco* for the
ultimate chestnut cream and
meringue confection. Arrive
early to avoid a chaotic queue.

DA LUCIA

Vicolo del Mattonato 2 ☎ 06.580.3601. Tues–
Sun 12.30–3pm & 7.30–11.30pm.
MAP P.124–125, POCKET MAP C17

Reliable, moderately priced
old Roman trattoria that is the
best place for summer outdoor
dining in Trastevere. *Spaghetti
cacio e pepe* is the speciality
here – arrive early for one of
the in-demand tables on the
attractive alleyway outside.

LE MANI IN PASTA

Via dei Genovesi 37 ☎ 06.581.6017. Tues–Sat
12.20–3pm & 7.30–11pm. MAP P.124–125,
POCKET MAP E18

Tucked down an alley, this
small and unassuming place
has a tiny kitchen in view and
specializes in pasta and fish
dishes. A full – and excellent
– meal with wine will set
you back around €40–50 per
person. It's deservedly busy, so
be sure to book.

AI MARMI

Viale di Trastevere 53 ☎ 06.580.0919.
Thurs–Tues 6.30pm–2.30am. MAP P.124–125,
POCKET MAP D18

Very reasonably priced
restaurant, nicknamed "the
mortuary" because of its stark
interior and marble tables,
and serving superior *supplì al
telefono* (so named because
of the string of mozzarella it
forms when you take a bite),
fresh *baccalà* and some of
Rome's best pizza.

DA OLINDO

Vicolo della Scala 8 ☎ 06.581.8835.
Mon–Sat 12.30–3pm & 8–11pm. MAP P.124–125,
POCKET MAP C17

With no sign outside, it's easy
to miss this great, family-run
Trastevere trattoria with just a
few tables. There's a small menu
of staples – traditional Roman
fare – and prices are cheap and
easy to remember: primi cost
€7, secondi €9.

DA PARIS

Piazza San Calisto 7a ☎ 06.581.5378.
Tues–Sat 12.30–3pm & 7.30am–11.30pm, Sun
12.30–3pm. MAP P.124–125, POCKET MAP D18

The menu at this moderately
priced Trastevere favourite
is a roll-call of traditional
Roman-Jewish dishes such as
abbacchio (lamb) and *carciofi*
(artichokes). You can either sit
outside, on one of Trastevere's
most atmospheric piazzas, or in
an elegant dining room.

DAR POETA

Vicolo del Bologna 46 ☎ 06.588.0516. Tues–
Sun noon–1am. MAP P.124–125, POCKET MAP C17

A fantastic Trastevere pizzeria,
with a reputation for pizzas
that are a tad thicker than the
traditional Roman variety.
Good beer too, and a lively
atmosphere, especially when a
football match is on. Get there
early, or be prepared to queue.

FRENI & FRIZIONI

Bars

ARTÙ

Largo F. Biondi 5. Tues–Sun 6pm–2am. MAP
P.124–125, POCKET MAP C18

Bar and pub on one of
Trastevere's busiest corners. Its
terrace is great for watching the
world go by, plus there's a full
menu if you're peckish.

BUM BUM DE MEL

Via del Moro 17. Tues–Sun 5pm–2am.
MAP P.124–125, POCKET MAP D17

This tiny, Brazilian-themed
bar – emblazoned with the
county's flag, and staffed by
samba-dancing lovelies – is
great for exotic cocktails, and
can always be relied upon for a
lively night out.

FRENI & FRIZIONI

Via del Politeama 4/6. Daily 6pm–2am. MAP
P.124–125, POCKET MAP D17

Just off Piazza Trilussa, this
former mechanic's workshop
(the name means "Brakes
and clutches") is now home
to one of the city's best
bars. The *aperitivo* buffet
(6.30–10.30pm) is worth
dropping by for, too.

MA CHE SIETE VENUTI A FA'

Via Benedetta 25 ☎ 06.9727.5218. Daily
3pm–2am. MAP P.124–125, POCKET MAP D6

There's an amazing choice of
artisanal beers from all over the
world in this tiny bar. Some of
them can't be found anywhere
else in the city, or even Italy,
and this is a cosy place to work
your way through them.

OMBRE ROSSE

Piazza di Sant'Egidio 12 ☎ 06.588.4155. Daily
8am–2am. MAP P.124–125, POCKET MAP C18

A great place for a morning
cappuccino, with outdoor
seating on one of Trastevere's
most charming piazzas. Light

OMBRE ROSSE

meals are served too, and
there's live jazz and blues on
Tues, Thurs & Sun nights.

SAN CALISTO

Piazza San Calisto 4. Mon–Sat 6am–2am.
MAP P.124–125, POCKET MAP D18

An old-guard Trastevere bar
which attracts a huge, mixed
crowd on late summer nights;
the booze is cheap, and you can
sit at outside tables for no extra
cost. Things are slightly less
demimonde-ish during the day,
when it's simply a great spot
to sip a cappuccino, read and
enjoy the sun.

Club

BIG MAMA

Vicolo San Francesco a Ripa 18
☎ 06.581.2551, ⊛ www.bigmama.it. Tues–Sat
9pm–1am. MAP P.124–125, POCKET MAP D7

Trastevere-based jazz/blues club
of long standing, hosting nightly
acts. A month's membership is
€14, with which entry is free,
except for star attractions (when
it's important to book ahead).
Food is served too.

The Villa Borghese and north

During the Renaissance, the market gardens and olive groves north of the city walls were appropriated as summer estates by Rome's wealthy elite, particularly those affiliated to the papal court. One of the most notable of these, the Villa Borghese, was the summer playground of the Borghese family and is now a public park and home to two of Rome's best museums: the unmissable art collection of the Galleria Borghese, and the Villa Giulia, built by Pope Julius II and now the National Etruscan Museum. North of Villa Borghese stretch Rome's nineteenth- and early twentieth-century residential districts – not of much interest in themselves except perhaps for the Mussolini-era Foro Italico and the new Auditorium.

VILLA BORGHESE

MAP P.134–135, POCKET MAP G2

The vast green expanse of the **Villa Borghese** – accessible by way of the Pincio Gardens, or from entrances at the top of Via Veneto or Via Porta Pinciana – is about as near as you can get to peace in the city centre. The beautiful landscaped grounds and palace were designed for Cardinal Scipione Borghese in 1605 and bought by the city at the turn of the nineteenth century; they now form the city's most central park. There are plenty of attractions for those who want to do more than just stroll or sunbathe, not least a zoo and some of the city's finest museums (see below), but it's full of pockets of interest if you just want to wander. You can rent bikes from the corner of Viale Obelisco and Viale Orologio and other places in the Pincio Gardens (from €4/hr, €12/day), as well as rollerblades and go-karts, but most people take a two- or four-person chariots known as a *risciò*, operated by a mixture of pedal and electrical power, which make for a very relaxed way to see the park (€10–20/hr).

LAKE IN THE GROUNDS OF VILLA BORGHESE

GALLERIA BORGHESE

Piazzale Scipione Borghese ☎ 06.32.810, Ⓦ www.galleriaborghese.it. Tues–Sun 8.30am–7.30pm. €10.50. Pre-book at least a day in advance; pre-booked visits are obligatory. MAP P.134–135, POCKET MAP G2

The collection of Cardinal Scipione Borghese in the **Galleria Borghese** is one of the city's most compelling. The first room has as its centrepiece Canova's infamous statue of the half-naked Pauline Borghese posed as Venus, but otherwise the focus is on Bernini. The face of his marvellous statue of David is a self-portrait, said to have been carved with the help of a mirror held by Scipione Borghese himself. Other highlights include his dramatic, poised *Apollo and Daphne*; *The Rape of Proserpine* from 1622; and a larger-than-life statue of Aeneas, carrying his father, Anchises, out of the burning city of Troy, sculpted by both Bernini and his then 15-year-old son in 1613. There are paintings, too, including notable works such as Caravaggio's *David Holding the Head of Goliath*, and a self-portrait as *Bacchus*, among others, and the upstairs **Pinacoteca** comprises one of the richest collections of paintings in the world, with canvases by Raphael, his teacher Perugino and other masters of the Umbrian school from the late fifteenth and sixteenth centuries. Look for the *Deposition*, *Lady with a Unicorn*, and *Portrait of a Man*, by Raphael, and a copy of the artist's portrait of a tired-out Julius II, painted in 1513. There's also *Venus and Cupid with a Honeycomb* by Cranach, Lorenzo Lotto's touching *Portrait of a Man* and works by the Venetians of the early 1500s, including Titian's *Sacred and Profane Love*, painted in 1514. Check out also the **gallery** at the back of the building, where there are a series of self-portraits done by Bernini at various stages of his life and a bust of Cardinal Scipione executed in 1632, portraying him as the worldly connoisseur of fine art and living that he was.

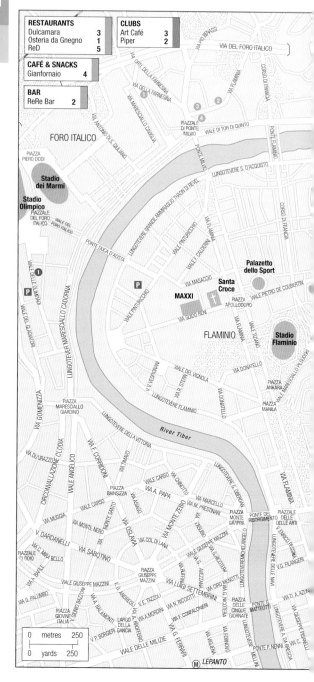

RESTAURANTS
Dulcamara 3
Osteria da Gnegno 1
ReD 5

CAFÉ & SNACKS
Gianfornaio 4

BAR
ReRe Bar 2

CLUBS
Art Café 3
Piper 2

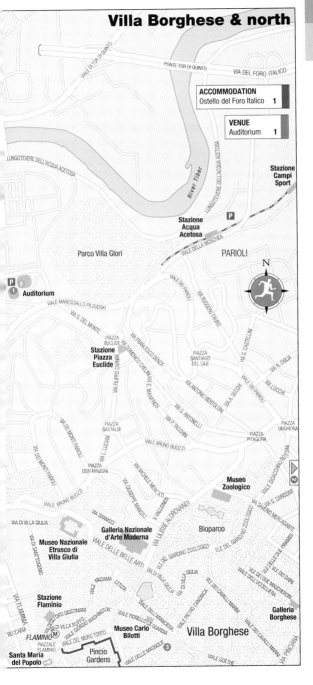

Villa Borghese & north

ACCOMMODATION
Ostello del Foro Italico   1

VENUE
Auditorium   1

BEARS IN THE BIOPARCO

MUSEO CARLO BILOTTI

Viale Fiorello La Guardia. Tues–Sun 9am–7pm.
€8. MAP P.134–135, POCKET MAP F2

Housed in the orangery of the
Villa Borghese, this museum
is, like the Galleria Borghese,
made up of a family bequest,
this time of **Carlo Bilotti** – a
perfume and cosmetics baron
who, until his death in 2006,
collected art and hobnobbed
with the brightest and best in
the international art world.
Good portraits of him by Larry
Rivers, and of his wife and
daughter by Andy Warhol, open
the exhibition and add to the
slightly self-congratulatory air
of the place, but the real reason
for coming is to enjoy the
small collection of high-quality
works by the great modern
Greek-Italian painter, Giorgio
De Chirico, who lived in Rome
for many years (see p.75).

BIOPARCO

Via del Giardino Zoologico, Villa Borghese
☎ 06.360.8211, ⓦ www.bioparco.it. Daily:
Jan–March & Nov–Dec 9.30am–5pm; April–
Oct 9.30am–6pm, open till 7pm Sat & Sun
April–Sept. €12.50 adults, €10.50 children
over 1m tall. MAP P.134–135, POCKET MAP F1

Large, typical city-centre zoo,
much improved and reinvented
as the **"Bioparco"**, focusing on
conservation and education
yet still providing the usual
animals kids are after – tigers,
apes, giraffes, elephants, hippos
and much more – though the
separate Rettilario (Reptile
house) for some reason costs
an extra €2.50, a bit of a rip-off.
The zoological museum next
door – accessible from the
main road (left out of the zoo
and then left again) is less
engaging but worth a visit
– recently revamped, with
displays on different animal
habitats as well as lots of more
traditional stuffed mammals
and birds.

GALLERIA NAZIONALE D'ARTE MODERNA

Via delle Belle Arti 131 ⓦ www.gnam.arti.
beniculturali.it. Tues–Sun 8.30am–7.30pm.
€10. MAP P.134–135, POCKET MAP F1

Rome's **museum of modern
art** is maybe the least enticing
of the Villa Borghese's
museums – a lumbering,
Neoclassical building housing
a collection of nineteenth-
and twentieth-century Italian
(and a few foreign) names.
However, it can make a
refreshing change after several

days of having the senses bombarded with Etruscan, Roman and Renaissance art. The nineteenth-century collection contains a splendid range of paintings by the Tuscan Impressionists (the Macchiaioli school), as well as works by Courbet, Van Gogh and Cézanne, not to mention a giant statue of Hercules by the nineteenth-century Italian sculptor Canova and some mighty battle scenes celebrating Italian Unification. The twentieth-century collection features work by Giacomo Balla (a view of the Villa Borghese divided into 15 panels), his student Boccioni and other Futurists, along with work by Modigliani and De Chirico, whose paintings dominate one room. There are also some postwar canvases by the likes of Rothko, Pollock and Cy Twombly, Rome's own American artist, who has lived in the city for most of his life.

MUSEO NAZIONALE ETRUSCO DI VILLA GIULIA

Piazzale Villa Giulia 9 Ⓦ www.villagiulia. beniculturali.it. Tues–Sun 8.30am–7.30pm. €8. MAP P.134–135, POCKET MAP E1

The Villa Giulia is a lovely collection of courtyards, loggias, gardens and temples put together in a playful Mannerist style for Pope Julius III in the mid-sixteenth century. It now houses the **Museo Nazionale Etrusco di Villa Giulia**, the world's primary collection of Etruscan treasures, along with the Etruscan collection in the Vatican (see p.147). Not much is known about the Etruscans, but the Roman's predecessors were a creative and civilized people, evidenced here by a wealth of sensual sculpture, jewellery and art. They were also deeply religious and much of the collection focuses on preparing for the afterlife. The most famous exhibit is the remarkable *Sarcophagus of the Married Couple* (in the octagonal room in the east wing) – a touchingly lifelike portrayal of a husband and wife lying on a couch. It dates from the sixth century BC and was discovered in the tombs at Cerveteri. Look also at the delicate and beautiful cistae – drum-like objects, engraved and adorned with figures, that were supposed to hold all the things needed for the care of the body after death – and, in the same room, marvellously intricate pieces of gold jewellery, delicately worked into tiny horses, birds, camels and other animals, as well as mirrors, candelabra and religious statues – votive offerings designed to appease the gods. Further on you'll find a drinking horn in the shape of a dog's head that is so lifelike you almost expect it to bark; a *holmos*, or small table, to which the maker attached 24 little pendants around the edge; and a bronze disc breastplate from the seventh century BC decorated with a weird, almost modern abstract pattern of galloping creatures.

(Ple. M. Giardino), 271 (Ple. M. Diaz), ncini), Tram #2 (P. Mancini).

The **Foro Italico** sports complex is one of the few parts of Rome to survive intact pretty much the way Mussolini planned it. The centrepiece is the Ponte Duca d'Aosta, which connects Foro Italico to the town side of the river, and is headed by a white marble obelisk capped with a gold pyramid, engraved MUSSOLINI DUX in beautiful 1930s calligraphy. Beyond the bridge, an avenue patched with mosaics revering the Duce leads up to a fountain surrounded by more mosaics of muscle-bound figures revelling in healthful sporting activities. Either side of the fountain are the two main stadiums: the larger of the two, the Stadio Olimpico on the left, was used for the Olympic Games in 1960 and is still the venue for Rome's two soccer teams; the smaller, the **Stadio dei Marmi** ("stadium of marbles"), is ringed by sixty great male statues, groins modestly hidden by fig leafs, in a variety of elegantly macho poses.

MAXXI

Via Guido Reni 4a ⓦ www.maxxi.beniculturali .it. Tues, Wed, Fri & Sun 11am–7pm, Thurs & Sat 11am–1pm; €11. Tram #2 from Piazzale Fiaminio. MAP P.134–135, POCKET MAP D1

This brand new museum of twenty-first-century art and architecture opened to much fanfare and celebration at the end of 2009, in a landmark building by the Anglo-Iraqi architect Zaha Hadid. It's mainly a venue for temporary exhibitions, but there are small permanent collections, and the building – a jagged, concrete spaceship that looks like it's just landed in this otherwise rather ordinary part of the city – is worth a visit just for itself.

PONTE MILVIO

MAP P.134–135

This footbridge across the Tiber was the site of the battle in which Constantine defeated Maxentius in 312 AD, a victory that brought about the end of Roman paganism. More recently, it has become the home to numerous padlocks, placed here by lovers who then throw the keys into the river – an enactment of a ritual popularized by a best-selling novel.

FORO ITALICO

Café and snacks

GIANFORNAIO

Piazzale Ponte Milvio 35/37. Mon-Sat
7am-2pm & 4.40-9pm. MAP P.134-135.
POCKET MAP D1

Great bakery with pizza and
other goodies, and lots of
seating inside and out.

Restaurants

DULCAMARA

Via Flaminia Vecchia 449 ☏ 06.333.2108.
Tues-Sat 12.15pm-2am. MAP P.134-135.
POCKET MAP D1

Busy place up in the
increasingly hip neighbourhood
across the Ponte Milvio. A
varied menu of good pasta
dishes, soups and salads.

OSTERIA DA GNEGNO

Via Prati della Farnesina 10 ☏ 06.333.6166.
Daily 12.30-3pm & 7.30-11.30pm.
MAP P.134-135. POCKET MAP D1

A classic Roman trattoria,
tucked away behind Piazzale
Ponte Milvio. Good food and
well priced.

RED

Via Pietro de Coubertin 30 ☏ 06.8069.1630.
Daily 8.30-1am. MAP P.134-135. POCKET MAP D1

Part of the Auditorium
complex, this sleek designer
bar-restaurant is good for a
drink or a meal before or after
a performance.

Bar

RERE BAR

Via Flaminia Vecchia 475 ☏ 06334.0483.
Daily 6pm-2am. MAP P.134-135. POCKET MAP D1

Cool, kitsch wine bar, just off
Piazzale Ponte Milvio; it also
serves food and hosts resident
DJs.

Clubs

ART CAFÉ

Via del Galoppatoio 33 ☏ 347.783.5112. Tues-
Sat 9pm-6am. MAP P.134-135. POCKET MAP F2

In the underground car park
in Villa Borghese, this is one of
Rome's trendiest clubs. Expect
to queue, and dress up.

PIPER

Via Tagliamento 9 ☏ 06.855.5398,
Ⓦ www.piperclub.it.Tues-Sat 11pm-4am.
MAP P.134-135. POCKET MAP H1

Established in the Seventies by
cult singer Patty Pravo, Piper
has different nightly events
(fashion shows, screenings,
gigs) and a smart-but-casual
mixed-aged crowd. Music
varies, as do entrance prices.

Venues

AUDITORIUM

Via Pietro de Coubertin 15. Bus #53, 280, 910
or Tram #2, 19. Box office daily 11am-8pm.
Concert tickets €20-30. Buy tickets online,
or in Italy on ☏ 892982 or from abroad on
☏ 06.370.0106. Tours Sat & Sun every hour
11.30am-4.30pm, weekdays groups only;
book in advance on ☏ 06.8024.1281.
Ⓦ www.auditorium.com; €9. MAP P.134-135.
POCKET MAP D1

Designed by Renzo Piano,
this is one of Rome's most
prestigious serious music venue,
home to its premier orchestra,
the Accademia Nazionale di
Santa Cecilia. Two smaller
venues host chamber, choral,
recital and experimental works.
The complex also hosts major
rock and jazz names when they
come to town. And there's a
great book and CD shop and a
decent café too if you just want
to hang out and admire the
building – of which there are
regular organized tours.

The Vatican City

Situated on the west bank of the Tiber, just across from the city centre, the Vatican City has been a sovereign state since 1929, and its 1000 inhabitants have their own radio station, daily newspaper, postal service, and security service, in the colourfully dressed Swiss Guards. It's believed that St Peter was buried in a pagan cemetery on the Vatican hill, giving rise to the building of a basilica to venerate his name and the siting of the headquarters of the Catholic Church here. Stretching north from St Peter's, the Renaissance papal palaces are now home to the Vatican Museums – quite simply, the largest, richest, most compelling and perhaps most exhausting museum complex in the world. The other main Vatican sight worth visiting is the Castel Sant'Angelo on the riverside, a huge fortress which once harboured the popes in times of danger. Apart from visiting the main attractions, you wouldn't know at any point that you had left Rome and entered the Vatican; indeed the area around it, known as the Borgo, is one of the most cosmopolitan districts – full of mid-range hotels, restaurants and scurrying tourists and pilgrims, while the district just beyond, Prati, is a comfortable middle-class district that's home to some of the city's best and often least touristy restaurants.

CASTEL SANT'ANGELO

CASTEL SANT'ANGELO

Lungotevere Castello 50 Ⓦ www.
castelsantangelo.com. Tues–Sun 9am–7.30pm
€8.50. MAP P.142–143, POCKET MAP C13

The great circular hulk of the
Castel Sant'Angelo marks the
edge of the Vatican, designed
and built by Hadrian as his
own mausoleum. It was
renamed in the sixth century,
when Pope Gregory the Great
witnessed a vision of St Michael
here that ended a terrible
plague. The papal authorities
converted the building for
use as a fortress and built a
passageway to link it with the
Vatican as a refuge in times
of siege or invasion. Inside, a
spiral ramp leads up into the
centre of the mausoleum, over
a drawbridge, to the main
level at the top, where a small
palace was built to house the
papal residents in appropriate
splendour. Pope Paul III had
some especially fine renovations
made, including the beautiful
Paolina rooms, where the
gilded ceilings display the
Farnese family arms, and
you'll also notice the pope's
personal motto, *Festina Lenta*
("Make haste slowly"), scattered
throughout the ceilings and
in various corners of all his
rooms. Elsewhere, rooms hold
swords, armour, guns and the
like, while below are dungeons
and storerooms which can be
glimpsed from the spiralling
ramp, testament to the castle's
grisly past as the city's most
notorious Renaissance prison.
Off the Paolina rooms, a
terrace runs around the whole
building and holds a shady
bar for pick-me-up drinks
and sandwiches – and some
great views of Rome, best from
the terrace on the top of the
whole structure – from which
Tosca famously flung herself in
Puccini's eponymous opera.

PIAZZA SAN PIETRO

PIAZZA SAN PIETRO

MAP P.142–143, POCKET MAP A14

Perhaps the most famous of
Rome's many piazzas, Bernini's
Piazza San Pietro doesn't
disappoint, although its size
isn't really apparent until you're
right on top of it, its colonnade
arms symbolically welcoming
the world into the lap of the
Catholic Church. The obelisk
in the centre was brought to
Rome by Caligula in 36 AD,
and was moved here in 1586,
when Sixtus V ordered that
it be erected in front of the
basilica, a task that took four
months and was apparently
done in silence, on pain of
death. The matching fountains
on either side are the work of
Carlo Maderno (on the right)
and Bernini (on the left). In
between the obelisk and each
fountain, a circular stone
set into the pavement marks
the focal points of an ellipse,
from which the four rows of
columns on the perimeter of
the piazza line up perfectly,
making the colonnade appear
to be supported by a single line
of columns.

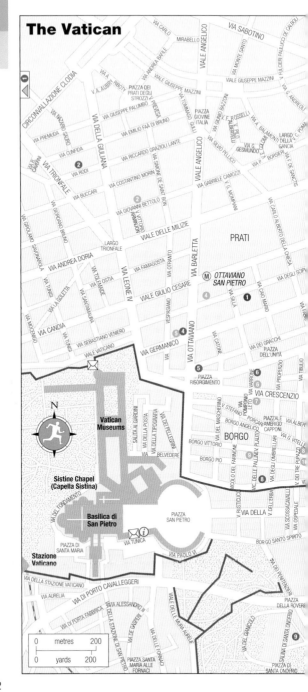

The Vatican

RESTAURANTS

Cacio e Pepe	1
Cantina Tirolese	8
Dal Toscano	5

CAFÉS & SNACKS

Fatamorgana	2
Gran Caffe Borgo	10
Mondo Arancina	3
Non Solo Pizza	4

BARS

Fonclea	6
Nuvolari	9
Passaguai	7

SHOPS

Castroni	2
Colapicchioni	4
Franchi	3
Del Frate	1

ACCOMMODATION

Amalia	4
Bramante	8
Colors	7
Dei Consoli	6
Franklin	2
Giulio Cesare	3
Ottaviano	5
Roma Cavalieri	1
La Rovere	9

ST PETER'S

Daily: April–Sept 7am–7pm; Oct–March 7am–6pm. Strict dress code – no shorts or bare shoulders. MAP P.142–143. POCKET MAP B4

The Basilica di San Pietro, better known to many as **St Peter's**, is the principal shrine of the Catholic Church, built on the site of St Peter's tomb, and worked on by the greatest Italian architects of the sixteenth and seventeenth centuries. Not so long ago you could freely stroll around the piazza and wander into the basilica when you felt like it. Now much of the square is fenced off, and you can only enter St Peter's from the right-hand side (exiting to the left); you also have to go through security first, and the queues can be horrendous unless you get here in early the morning or late afternoon. Once you get close to the basilica, you're channelled through various entrances depending on what you want to see first – all of which is strictly enforced by the unsmiling besuited functionaries that appear at every turn. A carefree experience it is not.

Inside the **basilica**, on the right, is Michelangelo's graceful *Pietà*, completed when he was just 24. Following an attack by a vandal, it sits behind glass, strangely remote from the rest of the building. Further into the church, the dome is breathtakingly imposing, rising high above the supposed site of St Peter's tomb. With a diameter of 41.5m it is Rome's largest dome, supported by four enormous piers, decorated with reliefs depicting the basilica's so-called "major relics": St Veronica's handkerchief, which was used to wipe the face of Christ; the lance of St Longinus, which pierced Christ's side; and a piece of the True Cross. On the right side of the nave is the bronze statue of St Peter, its right foot polished smooth by the attentions of pilgrims. Bronze was also the material used in Bernini's 26-metre high baldacchino, cast out of 927 tonnes of metal removed from the Pantheon roof in 1633. To modern eyes, it's an almost grotesque piece of work, its wild spiralling columns copied from those in the Constantine basilica. Bernini's feverish sculpting decorates the apse too, his bronze *Cattedra* enclosing the supposed chair of St Peter, though his monument to Alexander VII in the south transept is more interesting, its winged skeleton struggling underneath the heavy marble

MICHELANGELO'S PIETÀ

drapes, upon which the Chigi pope is kneeling in prayer.

An entrance off the aisle leads to the steeply priced **Treasury** (daily: summer 9am–6.15pm; winter 9am–5.15pm; €5), while back outside steps lead down to the **Grottoes** (daily: summer 8am–6pm; winter 7am–5pm), where the majority of the popes are buried. Directly beneath St Peter's baldacchino, the **necropolis** contains a row of Roman tombs with inscriptions confirming that the Vatican Hill was a burial ground in classical times.

Whether the tomb claimed as that of St Peter really is the saint's resting place is unclear, although it does tally with some historical descriptions. To be sure of getting a place

on the English-language **tour**, book two or three months in advance via the Scavi office, through the arch to the left of St Peter's (Mon–Sat 9am–3.30pm; ☎06.6988.5318; ✉scavi@fsp.va).

The worthwhile ascent to the **roof and dome** (daily: May–Sept 8am–5.45pm; Oct–April 8am–4.45pm; €7 via lift, €4 using the stairs) – is also outside by the entrance to the church. The views from the gallery around the interior of the dome give you a sense of the vastness of the church, and from there the roof grants views from behind the huge statues onto the piazza below, before the (challenging) climb to the lantern at the top of the dome – the views over the city are as glorious as you'd expect.

THE VATICAN MUSEUMS

Viale Vaticano 13 🚇 www.vatican.va. Mon–
Sat 9am–6pm, last entrance at 4pm, last Sun
of each month 9am–2pm, last entrance at
12.30pm; closed public and religious holidays.
€15, under-18s and under-26s with student
ID €8; audio guides €6; €4 extra for online
booking; last Sun of the month free. MAP
P.142–143, POCKET MAP B3

If you have found any of
Rome's other museums
disappointing, the Vatican is
probably the reason why: so
much booty from the city's
history has ended up here, and
so many of the Renaissance's
finest artists were in the employ
of the pope, that the result
is a set of museums which
put most other European
collections to shame. As its
name suggests, the complex
actually holds a number of
museums on very diverse
subjects – displays of classical
statuary, Renaissance painting,
Etruscan relics and Egyptian
artefacts, not to mention the
furnishings and decoration
of the building itself. There's
no point in trying to see
everything, at least not on one
visit, and the only features
you really shouldn't miss are
the Raphael Rooms and the
Sistine Chapel, and perhaps the
Museo Pio-Clementino and
Pinacoteca. Above all, decide
how long you want to spend
here, and what you want to
see, before you start; it's easy
to collapse from museum
fatigue before you've even got
to your main target of interest.
In high season there may be a
queue to get in, but getting to
the museums late morning or
after lunch can mean a shorter
wait. Try to avoid Monday –
everyone flocks here because
Rome's other big museums are
all closed. Or buy your ticket
in advance online and go to the
front of the queue.

MUSEO PIO-CLEMENTINO

Vatican Museums. MAP P.142–143, POCKET MAP B3

To the left of the entrance, the
Museo Pio-Clementino is
home to some of the Vatican's
best classical statuary, including
two pieces that influenced
Renaissance artists more
than any others – the serene
Apollo Belvedere, a Roman
copy of a fourth-century BC
original, and the first-century
BC *Laocoön*. The former is
generally thought to be a
near-perfect example of male
anatomy and was studied by
Michelangelo; the latter depicts

the prophetic Trojan priest being crushed by a serpent as he warned of the danger of the Trojan horse, and is perhaps the most famous classical statue of all time. Beyond here there are busts of Roman emperors, the statue of *Venus of Cnidos*, the first known representation of the goddess, the so-called *Belvedere Torso*, found in the Campo de' Fiori during the reign of Julius II, and much, much more sublime classical statuary.

MUSEO GREGORIANO EGIZIO

Vatican Museums. MAP P.142–143, POCKET MAP H3

It may not be one of the Vatican's highlights, but the **Museo Gregoriano Egizio** holds a distinguished collection of ancient Egyptian artefacts, including some vividly painted mummy cases (and two mummies), along with canopic jars, the alabaster vessels into which the entrails of the deceased were placed.

GALLERIA DELLE CARTE GEOGRAFICHE

MUSEO GREGORIANO ETRUSCO

Vatican Museums. MAP P.142–143, POCKET MAP XX

The **Museo Gregoriano Etrusco** holds Etruscan sculpture, funerary art and applied art. Especially worth seeing are the finds from the Regolini-Galassi tomb, from the seventh century BC, discovered near Cerveteri, which contained the remains of three Etruscan nobles. There's gold armour, a bronze bedstead, a funeral chariot and a wagon, as well as a great number of enormous storage jars, in which food, oil and wine were contained for use in the afterlife.

GALLERIA DEI CANDELABRI, DEGLI ARAZZI, AND DELLE CARTE GEOGRAFICHE

Vatican Museums. MAP P.142–143, POCKET MAP B3

Outside the Etruscan Museum, a large monumental staircase leads back down to the **Galleria dei Candelabri**, the niches of which are adorned with huge candelabra taken from imperial Roman villas. This gallery is also stuffed with ancient sculpture, its most memorable piece being a copy of the famous statue of *Diana of Ephesus*, whose multiple breasts are according to the Vatican official line in fact bees' eggs. Beyond here the **Galleria degli Arazzi** has Belgian tapestries to designs by the school of Raphael and tapestries made in Rome during the 1600s. The **Galleria delle Carte Geografiche** was decorated in the late sixteenth century with maps of all Italy, the major islands in the Mediterranean, the papal possessions in France, as well as large-scale maps of the maritime republics of Venice and Genoa.

RAPHAEL ROOMS

Vatican Museums. MAP P.142–143, POCKET MAP B3

At the end of the various galleries, the **Raphael Rooms** formed the private apartments of Pope Julius II, and when he moved in here he commissioned Raphael to redecorate them in a style more in tune with the times. Raphael died in 1520 before the scheme was complete, but the two rooms that were painted by him, as well as others completed by pupils, stand as one of the highlights of the Renaissance. The Stanza di Eliodoro, the first room you come to, was painted by three of Raphael's students five years after his death, and is best known for its painting of the *Mass of Bolsena* which relates a miracle that occurred in the town in northern Lazio in the 1260s, and, on the window wall opposite, the *Deliverance of St Peter*. The other main room, the Stanza della Segnatura, or pope's study, was painted between 1508 and 1511, when Raphael first came to Rome, and comes close to the peak of the painter's art. *The School of Athens*, on the near wall as you come in, steals the show, a representation of the triumph of scientific truth in which all the great minds from antiquity are represented. It pairs with the *Disputation of the Sacrament* opposite, which is a reassertion of religious dogma – an allegorical mass of popes, cardinals, bishops, doctors and even the poet Dante.

APPARTAMENTO BORGIA

Vatican Museums. MAP P.142–143, POCKET MAP B3

Outside the Raphael Rooms, the **Appartamento Borgia** was inhabited by Julius II's hated predecessor, Alexander VI, and is host to a large collection of modern religious art, although its ceiling frescoes, the work of Pinturicchio between 1492 and 1495, are really the main reason to visit, especially those of the Sala dei Santi, where the figure of St Catherine is said to be a portrait of Lucrezia Borgia.

SISTINE CHAPEL

Vatican Museums. MAP P.142–143, POCKET MAP B4

Steps lead from the Raphael Rooms to the **Sistine Chapel**, a huge barn-like structure that is the pope's official private chapel and the scene of the conclaves of cardinals for the election of each new pontiff. The walls of the chapel were decorated by several prominent painters of the Renaissance – Pinturicchio, Perugino, Botticelli and

Ghirlandaio. However they are entirely overshadowed by Michelangelo's more famous **ceiling frescoes**, commissioned by Pope Julius II in 1508, and perhaps the most viewed set of paintings in the world. The frescoes were done by **Michelangelo** single-handed over a four year period and depict scenes from the Old Testament, from the *Creation of Light* at the altar end to *The Drunkenness of Noah* over the door. Look also at the pagan sibyls and biblical prophets which Michelangelo incorporated in his scheme – some of the most dramatic figures in the entire work, and all clearly labelled by the painter, from the sensitive figure of the Delphic Sybil to the hag-like Cumaean Sybil and the prophet Jeremiah – a brooding self-portrait of an exhausted-looking Michelangelo. Julius II lived only a few months after the Sistine Chapel ceiling was finished, but the fame of the work he had commissioned spread. It's staggeringly impressive, all the more so for its restoration, which lifted centuries of accumulated soot and candle grime off the paintings to reveal a

much brighter painting. Michaelangelo's other great work here, *The Last Judgement*, is on the altar wall of the chapel, and was painted by the artist more than twenty years later. Michelangelo wasn't especially keen to work on this, but Pope Paul III, an old acquaintance of the artist, was keen to complete the decoration of the chapel. The painting took five years, again single-handed, and is probably the most inspired and most homogeneous large-scale painting you're ever likely to see. The centre is occupied by Christ, turning angrily as he gestures the condemned to the underworld. St Peter, carrying his keys, looks on in astonishment, while Mary averts her eyes from the scene. Below Christ a group of angels blasts their trumpets to summon the dead from their sleep. On the left, the dead awaken from their graves, tombs and sarcophagi, and are levitating into the heavens or being pulled by ropes and the napes of their necks by angels who take them before Christ. At the bottom right, Charon, keeper of the underworld, swings his oar at the damned souls as they fall off the boat into the waiting gates of hell.

MUSEUM OF CHRISTIAN ART AND THE VATICAN LIBRARY

Vatican Museums. MAP P.142–143, POCKET MAP B4

After the Sistine Chapel, you're channelled to the exit by way of the **Museum of Christian Art**, which is not of great interest in itself, but does give access to a small room off to the left that contains a number of ancient Roman frescoes and mosaics, among them the *Aldobrandini Wedding*, a first-century BC Roman fresco that shows the preparations for a wedding in touching detail. Back down the main corridor, the **Vatican Library** is decorated with scenes of Rome and the Vatican, and beyond, the corridor opens out into the dramatic **Library of Sixtus V**, a vast hall built across the courtyard in the late sixteenth century to glorify literature – and of course Sixtus V himself.

BRACCIO NUOVO AND MUSEO CHIARAMONTI

Vatican Museums. MAP P.142–143, POCKET MAP B4

The **Braccio Nuovo** and **Museo Chiaramonti** both hold classical sculpture, although they are the Vatican at its most overwhelming – close on a thousand statues crammed into two long galleries. The Braccio Nuovo was built in the early 1800s and it contains, among other things, probably the most famous extant image of Augustus, and a bizarre-looking statue depicting the Nile. The 300-metre-long Chiaramonti gallery is lined with the chill marble busts of hundreds of nameless ancient Romans, along with the odd deity. It pays to have a leisurely wander, for there are some real characters here: sour, thin-lipped matrons with their hair tortured into pleats, curls and spirals; kids, caught in a sulk or mid-chortle; and ancient old men, their flesh sagging and wrinkling to reveal the skull beneath.

THE PINACOTECA

Vatican Museums. MAP P.142–143, POCKET MAP B4

The **Pinacoteca** is housed in a separate building on the far side of the Vatican Museums' main spine, and is among Rome's picture galleries, with works from the early to high Renaissance and right up to the nineteenth century. Among early works, there is an amazing *Last Judgement* by Nicolò and Giovanni from the twelfth century, the stunning *Simoneschi* triptych by Giotto, painted in the early 1300s for the old St Peter's, and fragments of Melozzo de Forlì's *Musical Angels*, painted for the church of Santi Apostoli. Further on are the rich backdrops and elegantly clad figures of the Umbrian School painters, Perugino and Pinturicchio. Raphael has a room to himself, where you'll find his *Transfiguration*, which he had nearly completed when he died in 1520, *The Coronation of the Virgin*, done when he was only 19 years old, and, on the

THE TRANSFIGURATION

and, on the left, the *Madonna of Foligno*, showing SS John the Baptist, Francis of Assisi and Jerome. Leonardo's *St Jerome*, in the next room, is a remarkable piece of work with Jerome a rake-like ascetic torn between suffering and a good meal, while Caravaggio's *Descent from the Cross*, two rooms on, is a warts-and-all canvas that unusually shows the Virgin Mary as a middle-aged mother grieving over her dead son. Take a look too at the most gruesome painting in the collection, Poussin's *Martyrdom of St Erasmus*, which shows the saint stretched out on a table with his hands bound above him in the process of having his small intestine wound onto a drum – basically being "drawn" prior to "quartering".

MUSEI GREGORIANO PROFANO, PIO CRISTIANO AND MISSIONARIO ETNOLOGICO

Vatican Museums. MAP P.142–143, POCKET MAP B4

Next door to the Pinacoteca, the **Museo Gregoriano Profano** holds more classical sculpture, mounted on scaffolds for all-round viewing,

including mosaics of athletes from the Baths of Caracalla and Roman funerary work, notably the Haterii tomb friezes, which show backdrops of ancient Rome and realistic portrayals of contemporary life. The adjacent **Museo Pio Cristiano** has intricate early Christian sarcophagi and, most famously, an expressive third-century AD statue of the Good Shepherd. The **Museo Missionario Etnologico** displays art and artefacts from all over the world, collected by Catholic missionaries.

VATICAN GARDENS

Daily except Wed & Sun; €30, includes access to the Vatican Museums; visits last about two hours and tickets must be booked in advance on ☎ 06.6988.4476, 🌐 www.vatican.va. MAP P.142–143, POCKET MAP A4

It's possible to visit the lovely **Vatican Gardens** on one guided tour a day – well worth doing for the great views of St Peter's. But you have to be organized and book in advance; you pay when you pick your tickets up on the day. The dress code is as for St Peter's – so no bare knees or shoulders.

Shops

CASTRONI

Via Cola di Rienzo 196. Mon–Sat 7.30am–8pm. MAP P.142–143, POCKET MAP C3

Huge, labyrinthine food store with a large selection of Italian treats as well as hard-to-find international favourites – plus a café with coffee, cakes and sandwiches. There's another branch nearby at Via Ottaviano 55.

COLAPICCHIONI

Via Tacito 76/78; Via Properzio 23/25. Mon–Sat 9am–8pm. MAP P.142–143, POCKET MAP D3

Long-running food store with two branches, the former mainly a bakery, the later incorporating a deli, but both selling the family's excellent *pangiallo* and other foodie goodies.

FRANCHI

Via Cola di Rienzo 200. Mon–Sat 8.30am–8.30pm. MAP P.142–143, POCKET MAP C3

One of the best delis in Rome – a triumph of cheeses and sausages with an ample choice of cold or hot food to go, including delicious *torta rustica* and roast chicken. They'll make up customized lunches for you, and they have the wines to go with it.

DEL FRATE

Via degli Scipioni 118/124 ☎ 06.321.1612. Mon–Sat 8am–1.30pm & 4–8pm. MAP P.142–143, POCKET MAP C3

This large wine and spirits shop is located on a quiet street near the Vatican, and has all the Barolos and Chiantis you could want, alongside shelves full of *grappa* in all shapes and sizes. There's a wine bar/restaurant attached, too.

Cafés and snacks

FATAMORGANA

Via Giovanni Bettolo ☎ 06.8639.1589. Daily 11am–11pm. MAP P.142–143, POCKET MAP B2

Undoubtedly one of the top three *gelaterie* in Rome, *Fatamorgana* serves up perfectly spherical scoops of creative and seasonal flavours, and is just a short walk from the Vatican Museums.

GRAN CAFFE BORGO

Borgo Pio 170/171. Daily 8am–6pm. MAP P.142–143, POCKET MAP B13

The Borgo isn't the best place to get decent food but you have to refuel between sights and this is one of the best places to do it, an unassuming bar that's been in the family for generations and is a cut above the more tourist-targeted places on the same street, with excellent *panini*, *tramezzini* and cakes.

MONDO ARANCINA

Via Marcantonio Colonna 38 ☎ 06.9761.9213. Daily 10am–midnight. MAP P.142–143, POCKFT MAP D2

Great *pizza al taglio* at this Prati Sicilian takeaway, but the real treats are the *arancini* – any number of varieties, from tomato and mozzarella to Bolognese, and cheap too, at €2 each. Just the thing for post-Vatican recovery.

NON SOLO PIZZA

Via degli Scipioni 95/97. Tues–Sun
8.30am–10pm. MAP P.142–143, POCKET MAP B3
Pizza by the slice, as well as
suppli, *olive ascolane*, *fiori
di zucca*, *crocchette*, etc, and
a complete selection of hot
dishes. From 7pm they offer
made-to-order round pizzas,
too. No extra charge to sit,
inside or out.

Restaurants

CACIO E PEPE

Via Avezzana 11 ☏ 06.321.7268. Mon–Fri
12.30pm–3pm & 7.30–11.30pm, Sat
12.30pm–3pm. MAP P.142–143, POCKET MAP D1
Rough-and-ready Prati cheapie
with a menu taped to the wall
but the food can't be beat.
You can't book, and should
expect to wait for a table, but
it's well worth it: great *cacio
e pepe* (naturally), *alla gricia*,
carbonara and other pasta
staples, and good *secondi* too.

CANTINA TIROLESE

Via Vitelleschi 23 ☏ 06.6813.5297. Tues–Fri
& Sun noon–3pm & 7.30pm–midnight, Sat
7.30pm–midnight. MAP P.142–143, POCKET MAP B13
Reputedly the pope's favourite
restaurant while he was still a
cardinal, and no wonder, because
the hearty and wholesome
Austrian and German fare
served at this long-established
Prati standby is excellent, and
there's lots of it. A nice option
if you're craving a change from
Rome's usual offerings.

DAL TOSCANO

Via Germanico 58/60 ☏ 06.3972.5717. Tues–
Sun 12.30–3pm & 8–11.15pm. MAP P.142–143,
POCKET MAP B3
Tuscan food, and very popular,
with great steaks and other
meat dishes, perfectly grilled
on charcoal, delicious *pici*
(thick home-made spaghetti)

DAL TOSCANO

and *ribollita* (veg & bread
soup) – all at moderate prices.
A treat, and very handy for the
Vatican.

Bars

FONCLEA

Via Crescenzio 82a ☏ 06.689.6302. Daily
7pm–2am. MAP P.142–143, POCKET MAP C3
This historic basement joint
is loaded both with devoted
regulars and visitors who have
happily discovered that there is
life in the Vatican's sometimes
somnolent Borgo and Prati
area. Live music every evening
at 9.30pm, and free during the
week.

NUVOLARI

Via degli Ombrellari 10 ☏ 06.6880.3018. Mon–
Sat 6.30pm–2am. MAP 142–143, POCKET MAP A13
Welcoming Borgo wine bar
that has a good choice of wines
by the glass and does a free
buffet (6.30–8.30pm). A local
vibe, quite unexpected in this
part of town.

PASSAGUAI

Via Pomponio Leto 1 ☏ 06.8745.1358. Mon–
Fri 10.30am–2am, Sat & Sun 6pm–2am..MAP
P.142–143, POCKET MAP C3
Busy basement wine bar that
serves great platters of cheese,
meats and salads to go with its
excellent wine. Unusually there's
no cover or bread charge.

ay-trips

You may find there's quite enough in Rome to keep you occupied during your stay. But it can be a hot, oppressive city, and its churches, museums and ruins are sometimes wearing – so if you're around long enough it's worth getting out to see something of the countryside or going to the beach, for which there are lots of options within easy reach. Two of the main attractions close to Rome are among the most compelling attractions in the country, let alone the Rome area: Tivoli, about an hour by bus northeast of Rome, is a small provincial town famous not only for the travertine quarries nearby, but also for two villas – one Renaissance, one Roman, both complete with landscaped gardens and parks; southwest of Rome, Ostia is the city's busiest seaside resort, but more importantly was the site of the port of Rome in classical times, the ruins of which – Ostia Antica – are well preserved and worth seeing.

TIVOLI

Buses leave Rome for Tivoli every 10min from Ponte Mammolo metro station (line B); journey time 30–45min.

Perched high on a hill, with fresh mountain air and a pleasant position on the Aniene River, **Tivoli** has always been a retreat from the city. In classical days it was a retirement town for wealthy Romans; during the Renaissance it again became the playground of the moneyed classes, attracting some of the city's most well-to-do families and their new-built villas. Nowadays the leisured classes have mostly gone, but Tivoli does very nicely on the fruits of its still-thriving travertine business and the relics from its ritzier days. To do justice to the gardens and villas – especially if Villa Adriana is on your list – you'll need the whole day.

THE TEMPLE OF VESTA

VILLA D'ESTE

Jan, Nov, Dec daily 8.30am–4pm, Feb daily 8.30am–4pm, March daily 8.30am–5.15pm, April 8.30am–6.30pm, May–Aug daily 8.30am–6.45pm, Sept daily 8.30am–6.15pm, Oct daily 8.30am–5.30pm; €6.50.

Tivoli's major sight is the **Villa d'Este**, across the main square of Largo Garibaldi. This was the country villa of Cardinal Ippolito d'Este, and has been restored to its original state. Beautiful Mannerist frescoes in its rooms show scenes from the history of the d'Este family in Tivoli, but it's the gardens that most people come to see, peeling away down the hill in a succession of terraces, their carefully tended lawns, shrubs and hedges interrupted by one fountain after another. Among the highlights, the central, almost Gaudí-like Fontana del Bicchierone, by Bernini, is one of the most elegant; to the left of this, the Rometta, or "Little Rome", has reproductions of the city's major buildings and a boat holding an obelisk; while perhaps the best is the Fontana dell'Ovato on the opposite side, fringed with statues, underneath which is a rather dank arcade, in which you can walk.

VILLA GREGORIANA

March & mid-Oct to end-Nov Tues–Sat 10am–2.30pm, Sun 10am–4pm, April to mid-Oct Tues–Sun10am–6.30pm; €5.

Tivoli's other main attraction, the **Villa Gregoriana** was created when Pope Gregory XVI diverted the flow of the river here to ease the periodic flooding of the town in 1831. At least as interesting and beautiful as the d'Este estate, it remains less well known and less visited, and has none of the latter's conceits – its vegetation is lush and overgrown, descending into a gorge over 60m deep. There are two main waterfalls – the larger Grande Cascata on the far side, and a smaller one at the neck of the gorge. Cross the bridge and go in the back entrance, from where the path winds down to the bottom of the canyon, passing a ruined Roman villa. Climb up the other side through hollowed-out rock to where you can get right up to the roaring falls; beyond here the path leads up to the far side to the main entrance and the substantial remains of a **Temple of Vesta**, clinging to the side of the hill.

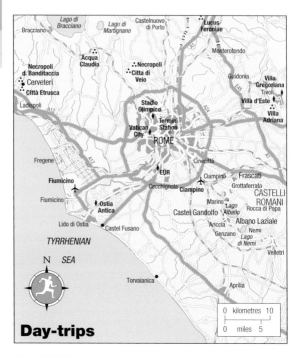

Day-trips

VILLA ADRIANA

Ask the Rome–Tivoli bus to drop you off or take the local CAT #4 bus from Largo Garibaldi in Tivoli. It's a 10min walk from the main road. Daily 9am–1hr before sunset; €10.

Probably the largest and most sumptuous villa in the Roman Empire, **Villa Adriana**, just outside Tivoli, was the retirement home of the Emperor Hadrian for a short while between 135 AD and his death three years later. Hadrian was a great traveller and a keen architect, and parts of the enormous site were inspired by buildings he had seen around the world. The massive Pecile, for instance, through which you enter, is a reproduction of a building in Athens; the Canopus, on the opposite side of the site, is a copy of the sanctuary of Serapis near Alexandria, its

long, elegant channel of water fringed by sporadic columns and statues leading up to a temple of Serapis at the far end. Near the Canopus, a museum displays the latest finds from the ongoing excavations here, though most of the discoveries have found their way to museums in Rome. Back towards the entrance there are the remains of two bath complexes, a fishpond with a cryptoporticus (underground passageway) underneath, marked with the names of the seventeenth- and eighteenth-century artists who visited here, and finally the Teatro Marittimo, with its island in the middle of a circular pond – the place to which it's believed Hadrian would retire for a siesta.

Hitting the beach

There are plenty of places to head for if you fancy a day at the beach – and let's face it, on a hot day in Rome in high summer there's sometimes nothing else for it but to get out of town. Here are some of the best seaside spots.

OSTIA

Lido di Ostia has for years been the number one, or at any rate the closest and most accessible seaside resort for Romans. The beaches are ok, and much cleaner than they used to be, but you have to pay to use them and the town doesn't have a great deal to recommend it apart from its thumping nightlife in summer, and with a little more time you could do better. Ostia is, however, easy to get to, just half an hour by train from Porta San Paolo station, next door to Piramide mero on line #B; get off at Lido Centro or the last stop, Cristoforo Colombo, where the crowds might be thinner.

TORVAIANICA

South of Ostia, the water is cleaner here and the crowds not so thick, plus there are gay and nudist sections of the beach if these are your fancy, and not a lot of development. Buses run from Cristoforo Colombo station in Ostia; take #07 or #061.

FREGENE

Like Ostia, **Fregene,** a little way north, is one of the busier resorts of the Rome area but posher and more family-orientated than Ostia – its beaches are equally crowded and expensive though. Take a train to Maccarese from Rome Trastevere or Ostiense– a roughly twenty-minute journey – and it's a short local bus ride from there to Fregene.

SPERLONGA

SANTA SEVERA

There's not much to sleepy **Santa Severa** but it's easy to get to and has everything you need for a day at the beach, with long stretches of sandy beach – some free, the rest given over to the usual *letti* and *ombrelloni* – and a *tavola calda* right on the seafront; there's also a castle at the southern end of the beach, home to a small municipal museum, if you get bored. The only drawback is the fact that the train station is a 20min walk from town, with erratic connecting buses and no real alternative transport. But trains are regular and quick: hourly from Termini, and the journey takes just under an hour.

The next stop on the train after Santa Severa, **Santa Marinella**, is one of the most popular spots north of the capital. It has a lovely crescent beach, 5min walk from the train station, and although most of it is pay-only the sand is fine and clean and the water shallow – perfect for kids. Trains are hourly from Termini, and take an hour.

CAPALBIO

Just over the border in Tuscany, about 100km northwest of Rome, **Capalbio** is just about possible on a day-trip, and its beaches are worth the journey. The station is a shortish walk from the beach and the village, a little way inland, is an upscale, artsy sort of place, and only a bus-ride from the late Niki St-Phalle's sculpture garden, the **Giardino dei Tarocchi** (April to mid-Oct 2.30–7.30pm; €10.50), which the French artist created over twenty years with her husband, Jean Tinguely.

ANZIO

About 40km south of Rome, and fairly free of the pull of the capital, **Anzio** is worth visiting both for its beaches and its history – much of the town was damaged during a difficult Allied landing here on January 22, 1944, to which two military cemeteries (one British, another, at nearby Nettuno, American), as well as a small museum, bear testimony. It was also a favoured spot of the Roman emperor, the ruins of whose villa spread along the cliffs above and even down onto the beach. Anzio is a good place to eat: it hosts a thriving fishing fleet and some great restaurants down on the harbour. The resort is easy to get to, with trains every hour from Termini; the journey is an hour and from the station it's just a ten-minute walk down to the main square and harbour, with the beaches stretching out north of the centre.

TERRACINA AND SPERLONGA

Both of these are a bit of a schlep compared to the other nearby resorts, and as such you might want to consider staying overnight. But they are do-able for a day-trip and **Terracina** has great sandy beaches and a welcoming small-town feel, as well as a couple of good restaurants. A little further south from Terracina, little **Sperlonga** is a more chi-chi resort, with equally good beaches and an attractive old quarter piled up on the headland just beyond. There are direct trains from Termini to Terracina (1hr 30min).

TERRACINA FROM THE AIR

OSTIA ANTICA

Regular trains from Roma–Porta San Paolo (next door to Piramide metro station, on line B); journey time 30min. March 8.30am–5pm, April–Oct Tues–Sun 8.30am–6pm, Nov–Feb 8.30am–4pm; €6.50.

The excavations of the Roman port of Ostia – **Ostia Antica** – constitute one of the finest ancient Roman sites you'll see anywhere – and easily merits the short journey out of town. Until its harbour silted up and the town was abandoned during the fourth century, Ostia was Rome's principal port and a thriving commercial centre. Over the centuries the sand and mud of the Tiber preserved its buildings incredibly well and the excavations here are an evocative sight: it's much easier to visualize a Roman town here than from any amount of pottering around the Forum – and it even comparies pretty well with far better-known sights like Pompeii.

From the entrance, the Decumanus Maximus, the main street of Ostia, leads west, past the **Baths of Neptune** on the right (where there's an interesting mosaic) to the town's commercial centre, known as the Piazzale delle Corporazioni. On the way, detour down **Via della Fontana**, a wonderfully preserved street which gives a good idea of the typical Roman urban layout: ground-floor shops and upper-floor apartments. There are more shops on Piazzale delle Corporazioni, which specialized in enterprises from all over the ancient world, and the mosaics just in front denote their trade – grain merchants, ship-fitters, ropemakers and the like.

Flanking one side of the square, Ostia's theatre has been much restored and sometimes hosts performances of classical drama during summer. On the left of the square, the **House of Apulius** preserves mosaic floors and, beyond, a dark-aisled Mithraeum with more mosaics illustrating the cult's practices. Behind here, the **House of Diana** is probably the best-preserved private house in Ostia, with a dark, mysterious set of rooms around a central courtyard, and another Mithraeum at the back. You can climb up to its roof for a fine view of the rest of the site, afterwards crossing the road to the Thermopolium – an ancient Roman café, complete with seats outside, a high counter, display shelves and even wall paintings of parts of the menu. North of the House of Diana, the **museum** holds a variety of articles from the site, including wall paintings depicting domestic life in Ostia and some fine sarcophagi and statuary, notably *Mithras Slaying the Bull* from one of Ostia's Mithraeums. Left from here, the Forum centres on the Capitol building, reached by a wide flight of steps, and fringed by the remains of baths and a basilica. Further on, the Porta Occidentale or western gate and the Via delle Foce beyond lead to the **Terme dei Sette Sapienti baths** complex, with a wonderfully intact floor mosaic and atmospheric arcaded passageways that lead to the large **Casa degli Aurighi**. You can climb up to the roof of this, too, and enjoy more marvellous views over the whole site.

OSTIA ANTICA

ACCOMMODATION

Hotels and B&Bs

There's no shortage of places to stay in Rome – but accommodation here tends to be pricier than in other European cities. Location is important: many of the cheaper options are clustered around Termini district, which, despite having improved dramatically in recent years, is not the city's most picturesque. Via Veneto is traditionally home to Rome's fanciest five-stars, and is somewhere to consider if you're looking for some old-world luxury, though much trendier these days are the cobbled lanes of the Monti district, a stone's throw from the Colosseum. You'll feel more in the thick of things in the Tridente area near the Spanish Steps or in the centro storico and around Campo de' Fiori, from where you can walk just about everywhere. Across the river, Prati is a pleasant, well-heeled neighbourhood handy for the Vatican. Trastevere is close to the main sights, quiet by day and lively after dark.

All accommodation prices in this chapter are for the cheapest double room in high season but remember that rates are very much driven by demand – never be afraid to ask for a better rate; they can only say no. Breakfast is included in all but the five-stars, where you can expect to be charged an extra €28–38. Book in advance if you want to snag a bargain, especially when the city is at its busiest (March–July, Sept, Oct and Christmas). If you arrive without a reservation, Enjoy Rome is your best bet (see p.183), while the free Hotel Reservation Service, by platform 24 in Termini train station, can check vacancies for you (daily 7am–10pm, or call ☏ 06.699.1000). It's worth looking online for discounts – try ⓦ www .venere.com (☏ 0845.602.7990).

centro storico

ALBERGO DEL SENATO >
Piazza della Rotonda 73, Bus 116 ☏ 06.678.4343, ⓦ www.albergodel senato.it. MAP P.36–37, POCKET MAP E15. A classy choice next door to the Pantheon, with friendly service and knockout views of the city from the roof and the Pantheon from some of the rooms. €335

CESÀRI >
Via di Pietra 89a, Bus 116 ☏ 06.674.9701, ⓦ www.albergocesari .it. MAP P.36–37, POCKET MAP F14. In a perfect position close to the Pantheon, this has been a hotel since 1787 – as they will be sure to tell you – with the new addition of the Stendhal Room named for their most famous former guest. The quiet, comfortable rooms are elegant and modern, and you can enjoy the roof terrace at breakfast and for drinks on summer evenings. €230

DUE TORRI >
Vicolo del Leonetto 23, Bus 116 ☏ 06.6880.6956, ⓦ www .hotelduetorriroma.com. MAP P.36–37, POCKET MAP E14. Cosy little hotel tucked away in a great location in a warren of streets a couple of minutes from Piazza Navona. Once a residence for cardinals, then a brothel, some rooms are on the small side but have been well renovated, and there's a comfy reception area, though breakfast is on the meagre side. Family rooms available too. €170

NAVONA > Via dei Sediari 8, Bus 492 ☎ 06.6821.1392, ⓦ www.hotelnavona .com. MAP P.36–37, POCKET MAP E15. Constructed on the site of the ancient Baths of Agrippa, this is a moderately priced hotel located between the Pantheon and Piazza Navona – really you couldn't ask for a better location if you want to be in the centre of Rome. Rooms are decently furnished, with their own bathrooms, the welcome is warm, and for the money you can't go wrong. They also rent apartments nearby and have a slightly more upmarket sister hotel, the *Zanardelli* (see below). **€145**

PORTOGHESI > Via dei Portoghesi 1, Bus 116 ☎ 06.686.4231, ⓦ www .hotelportoghesiroma.com. MAP P.36–37, POCKET MAP E14. Decent and well-equipped modern rooms 5min from most centro storico attractions. Breakfast is served on the roof terrace upstairs. It's worth paying a little extra for one of the roomier junior suites (€230). **€200**

RAPHAËL > Largo Febo 2, Bus 64 ☎ 06.682.831, ⓦ www.raphaelhotel .com. MAP P.36–37, POCKET MAP D14. Set on a quiet, picturesque piazza just off Piazza Navona, the *Raphaël* is a mix of plush traditional style – antiques and rich colours – and sleek contemporary furnishings on the second and third floors, designed by American architect Richard Meier (of Ara Pacis fame). There's also a rooftop terrace – one of Rome's loveliest – where you can try to identify the city's domes over a cocktail. **€480**

RESIDENZA CANALI > Via dei Tre Archi 13, Bus 492 ☎ 06.4543.9416, ⓦ www.residenzacanali.com. MAP P.36–37, POCKET MAP D14. Tucked away on a side street just a 3min walk from Piazza Navona, this family-run hotel is hard to beat for location and service. The bright rooms, with wood-beamed ceilings and modern en-suite bathrooms, are great value too, especially rooms 1 and 2, each with their own terrace. Note that there are several flights of stairs – and no lift. **€210**

SANTA CHIARA > Via Santa Chiara 21, Bus 116 ☎ 06.687.2979, ⓦ www .albergosantachiara.com. MAP P.36–37, POCKET MAP E15. Though a rather bland, business-class hotel, the *Santa Chiara*'s location is undeniably superb: on a quiet piazza right behind the Pantheon. Some of the rooms overlook the church of Santa Maria sopra Minerva. **€250**

TEATRO PACE 33 > Via del Teatro Pace 33, Bus 64 ☎ 06.687.9075, ⓦ www.hotelteatropace.com. MAP P.36–37, POCKET MAP D15. This beautifully restored *palazzo*, a few paces from Piazza Navona, was once home to one of the Vatican's most prominent cardinals. Leading off an impressive Baroque spiral staircase (no lift) are four floors of elegant, spacious rooms with original wood beams, floor-sweeping drapes and luxurious bathrooms. **€210**

Apartments and B&Bs

A few hotels rent out apartments, and a number of agencies specialize in short lets. One of the best is At Home, Via Margutta 13 (☎ 06.3212.0102, ⓦ www.at-home-italy.com). Cross-Pollinate (ⓦ www .cross-pollinate.com), run by the owners of *The Beehive* (see p.170), is a good source of budget apartments; ⓦ www.romecityapartments.com and ⓦ www.aplaceinrome.com are also worth a browse. See ⓦ www.b-b.rm.it for a good range of B&Bs all over the city. Prices start relatively low – around €50–60 for a double – with the more upscale options going for up to €140.

ZANARDELLI > Via G. Zanardelli 7, Bus 492 ☎ 06.6821.1392, ⓦ www .hotelnavona.com. MAP P.36–37, POCKET MAP D14. Run by the same family as the *Navona* (see p.165) – this is the very slightly more lavish alternative. Located just north of Piazza Navona, the building used to be a papal residence and has many original fixtures and furnishings. The rooms are elegant, but still decently priced, especially considering the location. €145

Campo de' Fiori and the Ghetto

ARGENTINA RESIDENZA > Via di Torre Argentina 47, Bus 64 ☎ 06.681.35.794, ⓦ www .argentinaresidenza.com. MAP P.52–53, POCKET MAP E16. This former noble carriage house has been converted to a six-room hotel by the people who run *Navona* (see p.165), and it's an elegant affair, with antique ceilings combining with well-chosen modern furnishings and amenitites. It's in a perfect location, too, close to the major transport hub of Largo Argentina. €180

CAMPO DE' FIORI > Via del Biscione 6, Bus 64 ☎ 06.6880.6865, ⓦ www .hotelcampodefiori.com. MAP P.52–53, POCKET MAP D16. A friendly place in a good location just off Campo de' Fiori with 23 individually designed rooms, each a different colour. The sixth-floor roof terrace has great views and the hotel owns a number of recently restored apartments nearby if you're keen to self-cater (from €180 for two, €240 for four). €280

FORTYSEVEN > Via Petroselli 47, Bus H ☎ 06.678.7816, ⓦ www .fortysevenhotel.com. MAP P.52–53, POCKET MAP F17. Tasteful, elegant rooms above the ancient cattle market just outside the Ghetto. Within striking distance of the Forum, Trastevere and the Ghetto, it has a fitness centre and a rooftop bar and restaurant too. €270

RESIDENZA FARNESE > Via del Mascherone 59, Bus 64 ☎ 06.6821.0980, ⓦ www .residenzafarneseroma.it. MAP P.52–53, POCKET MAP D16. Situated on a quiet side street right by the Palazzo Farnese, this hotel has tastefully appointed rooms and helpful staff. The location is excellent too – it's great for both the centro storico and Trastevere, just across the water by way of the Ponte Sisto footbridge. Do ask, though, to see several rooms – they vary a lot and some can be on the small side. €270

ST GEORGE > Via Giulia 62, Bus 40 ☎ 06.686.611, ⓦ www.stgeorgehotel.it. MAP P.36–37, POCKET MAP C15. Modern design, technology and style are the trademarks of this new five-star on one of Rome's most enchanting streets, with ultra-luxurious rooms that may scupper your sightseeing plans. There's a superb spa too. Check the website for off-season deals. €390

TEATRO DI POMPEO > Largo del Pallaro 8, Bus 64 ☎ 06.687.2812, ⓦ www.hotelteatrodipompeo.it. MAP P.52–53, POCKET MAP D16. Built above the remains of Pompey's ancient Roman theatre, this moderately priced hotel has a great location just off the Campo, and comfortable rooms, with high-beamed wooden ceilings, marble-topped furniture and – in some – great views. €210

The Tridente, Trevi and Quirinale

ALEPH > Via di San Basilio 15, Ⓜ Barberini ☎ 06.422.901, ⓦ www .aleph.boscolohotels.com. MAP P.76–77, POCKET MAP G3. The epitome of Rome's recent hotel makeover, the *Aleph* is all unashamed luxury, with over-the-top decor and a suitably fashionable clientele. The best rooms are on the top floor, where there's also a terrace bar and restaurant. €300

BABUINO 181 > Via del Babuino 181 Ⓜ Spagna ☎ 06.322.95295, ⓦ www .romeluxurysuites.com. MAP P.76–77, POCKET MAP E13. *Rome Luxury Suites* operates this and two other locations at Margutta 54 and Mario de'Fiori 37. Decorated with contemporary Italian flair, the accommodation is stylishly comfortable and includes breakfast and concierge service. €360

DEI BORGOGNONI ▸ Via del Bufalo 126, Bus 175 ☎ 06.6994.1505, ⓦ www.hotelborgognoni.it. MAP P.76–77, POCKET MAP F13. Nicely situated four-star that has pleasant, well-renovated rooms. A surprisingly large hotel, considering its location down a side street not far from Piazza di Spagna, and handy for this part of town and for the centro storico. €310

CASA HOWARD ▸ Via Capo le Case 18; Via Sistina 149 ⓜ Spagna ☎ 06.6992.4555, ⓦ www.casahoward. com. MAP P.76–77, POCKET MAP G13. This small boutique hotel offers a series of themed rooms, varying considerably in price, in two locations, one close to Piazza di Spagna, the other just off Piazza Barberini. Rooms are on the small side, but elegantly and stylishly furnished; service is very personal and welcoming and there's free wi-fi in each room. Breakfast is served to you in your room. €200

CASA MONTANI ▸ Piazzale Flaminio 9 ⓜ Flaminio ☎ 06.326.00421, ⓦ www .casamontani.com. MAP P.76–77, POCKET MAP E2. This self-styled "luxury town house" is a boutique hotel with a personal feel. The rooms – all designed by the owners, a friendly French-Italian couple – are decked out in a chic palette of neutrals, with touches of luxury: designer bathrooms, wide-screen TVs and breakfast served on fine porcelain. The five rooms are rightly popular – book well ahead. €220

CONDOTTI ▸ Via Mario de' Fiori 37 ⓜ Spagna ☎ 06.679.4661, ⓦ www .hotelcondotti.com. MAP P.76–77, POCKET MAP E3. This cosy and inviting three-star, with comfortable rooms and cheery, welcoming staff, now has three other locations nearby (reception for all is at the *Condotti*). The most appealing of these is the *Condotti Palace* at Via della Croce 15, whose luxury suites have a refined, elegant feel. €220

DAPHNE ▸ Via di San Basilio 55; Via degli Avignonesi 20 ⓜ Spagna, ☎ 06.8745.0086, ⓦ www.daphne -rome.com. MAP P.76–77, POCKET, MAP F4. Welcoming place in two locations either side of Piazza Barberini, run by an American woman and her Roman husband. Most of the rooms are bright, modern and spacious, and you can choose between shared bathrooms and en-suite. €220

HASSLER ▸ Piazza Trinità dei Monti 6 ⓜ Spagna ☎ 06.699.340, ⓦ www. hotelhasslerroma.com. MAP P.76–77, POCKET MAP F3. You can't get much closer to the heart of Rome than this – and you certainly can't get a much better view. Situated right at the top of the Spanish Steps, this luxury hotel has elegant rooms and every convenience a guest could possibly require. €500

HOMS ▸ Via della Vite 71/72 ⓜ Spagna ☎ 06.679.2976, ⓦ www.hotelhoms .it. MAP P.76–77, POCKET MAP F13. Slap bang in the core of the high-fashion shopping district near the Spanish Steps, this hotel boasts a roof terrace with marvellous views, lovely rooms that have recently been refurbished and a friendly atmosphere – something that's not always guaranteed in the hotels of this neighbourhood. €200

HOTEL ART ▸ Via Margutta 56 ⓜ Spagna ☎ 06.328.711, ⓦ www .hotelart.it. MAP P.76–77, POCKET MAP E3. Tucked away on Via Margutta, this has an impressive bar and lobby fashioned out of a vaulted chapel. Rooms are excellent, too, although oddly for a hotel that strives to be cutting edge, they don't have satellite TV or wi-fi. €310

Our Picks

BUDGET CHOICE The Beehive ⩾ see p.170

CENTRAL HOTEL Navona ⩾ see p.165

BOUTIQUE Casa Montani ⩾ see p.167

ROOM WITH A VIEW Hassler ⩾ see p.167

ROMANCE Casa Howard ⩾ see p.167

CELEBS De Russie ⩾ see p.169

LUXURY Portrait Suites ⩾ see p.169

D'INGHILTERRA ⩾ Via Bocca di Leone 14 Ⓜ Spagna ☏ 06.699.811, Ⓦ www .royaldemeure.com. MAP P.76–77, POCKET MAP F13. This old favourite, formerly the apartments of the princes of Torlonia, has been given a striking makeover, incorporating chic design touches while retaining an old-world elegance. Rooms are furnished with antiques and have Murano glass chandeliers and opulent marble bathrooms. Breakfast is an extra €28. **€320**

LOCARNO ⩾ Via della Penna 22 Ⓜ Flaminio ☏ 06.361.0841, Ⓦ www .hotellocarno.com. MAP P.76–77, POCKET MAP E2. Arguably the most characterful and inviting hotel in central Rome, a quirky and engaging place whose courtyard bar draws a crowd every evening. The rooms aren't the most luxurious or facility-laden but they're comfy and individually furnished. Considering the location, it's well-priced, too and there is a fleet of bikes for guest's use. **€299**

MODIGLIANI ⩾ Via della Purificazione 42 Ⓜ Barberini ☏ 06.4281.5226, Ⓦ www .hotelmodigliani.com. MAP P.76–77, POCKET MAP F3. A young artist couple run this modern hotel on a quiet street just off Piazza Barberini. Rooms are comfortable, and have a/c. Splash out on a superior room – they have views of St Peter's. There's a small garden courtyard. **€200**

IL PALAZZETTO ⩾ Vicolo del Bottino 8 Ⓜ Spagna ☏ 06.6993.41000, Ⓦ www .ilpalazzettoroma.com. MAP P.76–77, POCKET MAP F3. Elegant hotel with just four rooms, all differently designed in chic monochrome. It also runs wine courses in association with the International Wine Academy and has a distinguished restaurant and rooftop bar. Guests can use the facilities of the Hassler too (see p.167). **€260**

PIAZZA DI SPAGNA ⩾ Via Mario de' Fiori 61 Ⓜ Spagna ☏ 06.679.3061, Ⓦ www.hotelpiazzadispagna.it. MAP P.76–77, POCKET MAP F3. This small hotel, just a few minutes' walk from the Spanish Steps, is a good alternative to the opulent palaces that dominate the area. Rooms are comfortable, and all have a/c. Friendly staff too. **€230**

PLAZA ⩾ Via del Corso 126 Ⓜ Spagna ☏ 06.674.95, Ⓦ www.grandhotelplaza .com. MAP P.76–77, POCKET MAP F13. One of the most sumptuous hotels in Rome, with huge rooms furnished with antiques and a fantastic lobby that's worth dropping by to see even if you're not staying here. The rooms have been updated and have everything you might need, including wi-fi. Rates are lower than you would expect for the atmosphere and location. **€330**

PORTRAIT SUITES ⩾ Via Bocca di Leone 23 Ⓜ Spagna ☏ 06.6938.0742, Ⓦ www.lungarnohotels.com. MAP P.76–77, POCKET MAP E3. A relative newcomer to the boutique hotel circuit, this converted town house with 13 rooms, owned and designed by fashion designer Salvatore Ferragamo, is a bastion of luxury and comfort. Prices are high – but the suites are superbly appointed, and there's a lovely rooftop bar. **€480**

LA RESIDENZA ⩾ Via Emilia 22 Ⓜ Barberini ☏ 06.488.0789, Ⓦ www .hotel-la-residenza.com. MAP P.76–77,

POCKET MAP G3. A great option in the expensive Via Veneto area, this place combines the luxuries and atmosphere of a grand hotel with the easy-going comforts and intimacy of a private home. It's set off the busy main drag and is very tranquil. €230

DE RUSSIE > Via del Babuino 9 Ⓜ Flaminio ☏ 06.328.881, Ⓦ www .hotelderussie.it. MAP P.76–77, POCKET MAP E2. Coolly elegant and gorgeously understated, this hotel's emphasis on comfort and quality, not to mention its stellar location just off Piazza del Popolo, make it first choice for the hip traveller spending someone else's money – it's popular among visiting movie stars. €600

VILLA SPALLETTI TRIVELLI > Via Piacenza 4, Bus 64 ☏ 06.4890.7934, Ⓦ www.villaspalletti.it. MAP P.76–77, POCKET MAP G4. In a fantastic location – a five-minute walk from Piazza Venezia – this aristocratic villa is one of Rome's most luxurious accommodation options. The twelve rooms are impeccably furnished with antiques, and the common areas – including a lovely garden – exude an aura of exclusivity. €430

The Esquiline, Monti and Termini

ALPI > Via Castelfidardo 84 Ⓜ Termini ☏ 06.444.1235, Ⓦ www.hotelalpi.com. MAP P.92–93, POCKET MAP J3. One of the more peaceful hotels close to Termini, with pleasant (if somewhat small) rooms, a terrace and a great buffet breakfast – better than you would normally expect from a hotel in this bracket. €185

DES ARTISTES > Via Villafranca 20 Ⓜ Castro Pretorio ☏ 06.445.4365, Ⓦ www.hoteldesartistes.com. MAP P.92–93, POCKET MAP J3. Exceptionally good value, spotlessly clean and with a wide range of rooms, including dorm beds for around €25. Doubles are available with and without en-suite facilities. You can eat breakfast or recover from a long day of sightseeing on the lovely roof terrace. €149

ARTORIUS > Via del Boschetto 13, Bus 64 ☏ 06.482.1196, Ⓦ www .hotelartoriusrome.com. MAP P.92–93, POCKET MAP G5. On a cobbled Monti street and with just ten rooms, the family-run *Artorius* is an appealing mid-range option. The attractive courtyard makes a pleasant spot for breakfast in fine weather, and for drinks after dark. €220

DUCA D'ALBA > Via Leonina 14, Bus 84 ☏ 06.484.471, Ⓦ www .hotelducadalba.com. MAP P.92–93, POCKET MAP G5. A reliable three-star in the heart of Monti, just steps from the district's best restaurants and nightlife. All of the attractively furnished rooms have en-suite bathrooms and a/c, and some have balconies. Rooms are heavily discounted in low season. €250

LEON'S PLACE > Via XX Settembre 90/94 Ⓜ Termini ☏ 06.890.871, Ⓦ www .leonsplace.it. MAP P.92–93, POCKET MAP H3. Walking distance from Termini but on the edge of an upscale residential area. The rooms are on the small side but sleekly modern, all black and white with splashes of colour and trendy design touches. €240

NICOLAS INN > Via Cavour 295 Ⓜ Cavour ☏ 06.9761.8483, Ⓦ www .nicolasinn.com. MAP P.92–93, POCKET MAP G5. A brief stroll from the Colosseum, this B&B is run by a friendly American-Italian couple, who are keen to make guests feel at home. The rooms are a good size, spotless and elegant. Breakfast is served in a nearby bar. €180

PALAZZETTO DEGLI ARTISTI > Via della Madonna dei Monti 108 Ⓜ Cavour ☏ 06.6992.4931, Ⓦ www .palazzettodegliartisti.com. MAP P.92–93, POCKET MAP G5. These mini-apartments, on the edge of the Monti district, are an exercise in pared-down minimalism, but they're practical too: attached kitchens with all mod cons make this a good choice for those who want the option of self-catering, with the comfort and services of a four-star hotel. €130–200

RADISSON BLU ES > Via F. Turati 171 ⓂTermini ☎06.444.841, ⓌWWW .radissonblu.com. MAP P.92–93, POCKET MAP J5. Launched a few years ago as one of Rome's new designer hotels, the rooms here are cool, stylish and minimalist. Though it attracts a largely business clientele, don't be put off: the rates are much lower than you would expect for a hotel of this class. It also has one of Rome's very few swimming pools – on the roof. €290

RESIDENZA CELLINI > Via Modena 5, ⓂRepubblica ☎06.4782.5204, Ⓦwww.residenzacellini.it. MAP P.92–93, POCKET MAP G4. The rooms here are large with a slightly old-fashioned feel; it's worth paying the extra for a spacious junior suite (€280), with hydromassage bath. Staff are extremely friendly. €245

ROMAE > Via Palestro 49 ⓂTermini ☎06.446.3554, Ⓦwww.hotelromae.com. MAP P.92–93, POCKET MAP J3. Rome's self-styled groovy hotel is thoroughly welcoming and extremely comfortable, with thirty contemporary rooms that offer some of the best value in the Termini area. They also run the *Yellow* hostel (see p.173) across the road, where you have breakfast. Free wi-fi and iPads for rent. Great value. €130

SUITE DREAMS > Via Modena 5 ⓂRepubblica ☎06.4891.3907, Ⓦwww .suitedreams.it. MAP P.92–93, POCKET MAP G4. The rooms at this recently opened hotel are simple but stylish, with generous bathrooms, but it's the attention to detail and friendly customer care that really stand out. Services such as a DVD library for guests' use are an unexpected bonus in this price bracket. €180

THE BEEHIVE > Via Marghera 8 ⓂTermini ☎06.4470.4553, Ⓦwww .the-beehive.com. MAP P.92–93, POCKET MAP J4. "Hotel, Café, Art" is the slogan of this ecological – and economical – hotel run by an American couple. The doubles – all of which share bathrooms – are basic but stylishly decorated; more spartan dorms go for €25 a head, and you can also stay in one of three nearby apartments for €35 per person. There is free internet

access, and a restaurant that serves vegetarian breakfast, lunch and dinner daily. €80

VILLA DELLE ROSE > Via Vicenza 5 ⓂTermini ☎06.445.1788, Ⓦwww .villadellerose.it. MAP P.92–93, POCKET MAP J4. This centuries-old villa sits amidst its own tranquil rose gardens, belying the fact that it's only a block from Termini train station. The decor is a little tired, but it has bags of old-world charm, and staff are friendly. Ask for one of the rooms with a terrace. €130

YES HOTEL > Via Magenta 15 ⓂTermini ☎06.4436.3836, Ⓦwww.yeshotelrome .com. MAP P.92–93, POCKET MAP H4. The location – just down the road from Termini – might not be brilliant, but *Yes* is a huge step up from the grotty options that litter the area, and you'll pay considerably less here than for a similar room in the centre. Tailored to the needs of Termini's business travellers – rooms are comfortable but bland. Ten percent discount for cash payments. €170

The Celian and Aventine Hills

LANCELOT > Via Capo d'Africa 47 ⓂColosseo ☎06.7045.0615, Ⓦwww .lancelothotel.com. MAP P.92–93, POCKET MAP H6. Just two minutes from the Colosseum, this friendly family-run hotel has rooms with views of the Colosseum and staff that are well-informed and helpful. Wi-fi is free, as is the lobby internet point. They also have limited parking for €10. €150

SANT'ANSELMO >Piazza Sant'Anselmo 2 ⓂPiramide ☎06.570.057, Ⓦwww .aventinohotels.com. MAP P.92–93, POCKET MAP E8. One of the most peaceful places you could stay, and arguably in Central Rome's most upscale residential neighbourhood, the *Sant'Anselmo*, has beautifully furnished rooms (each with a different theme) that have been fairly recently renovated. Breakfast is good, there's a nice lounge and garden, and parking is free. Deals available outside high season. €215

Trastevere

CISTERNA > Via della Cisterna 7–9, Bus H ☎ 06.581.7212, ⊕ www .cisternahotel.it. MAP P.124–125, POCKET MAP D18. This friendly three-star in an elegant *palazzo* is bang in the middle of Trastevere. The nineteen rooms, some with colourful tiled floors and wooden beamed ceilings, have a homely feel. **€90**

RESIDENZA ARCO DE' TOLOMEI > VIa Arco de' Iolomei 27, Bus H ☎ 06.5832.0819, ⊕ www .arcodeitolomei.com. MAP P.124–125, POCKET MAP E18. In an attractively crumbling *palazzo* on Trastevere's quieter, eastern side, this old-world B&B is full of antiques passed down from generation to generation of the Italian owners' family, but the atmosphere is anything but stuffy. The generous breakfast is served in the conservatory. **€215**

RESIDENZA SANTA MARIA > Via dell'Arco di San Calisto 20, Bus H ☎ 06.5833.5103, ⊕ www .residenzasantamaria.com. MAP P.124–125, POCKET MAP D18. In an eighteenth-century building – which once housed crafts workshops – this intimate hotel has been attractively restored, with features such as brick arches, wood-beamed ceilings and an internal courtyard giving it a welcoming feel. It's especially recommended for families: four of the six rooms are triples or quads. **€230**

SANTA MARIA > Vicolo del Piede 2, Bus H ☎ 06.589.4626, ⊕ www .hotelsantamaria.info. MAP P.124–125, POCKET MAP D18. Just off Piazza Santa Maria in the heart of Trastevere, the rooms of this friendly three-star surround a garden filled with lovely orange trees. There's free internet access, and bikes are provided for guests' use. **€230**

TRASTEVERE > Via Luciano Manara 24a/25, Bus H ☎ 06.581.4713, ⊕ www .hoteltrastevere.net. MAP P.124–125, POCKET MAP C18. A good choice if you want to be in the heart of Trastevere, with nicely decorated – though small –

doubles, and apartments to rent for up to five people. Request a room overlooking the little piazza, rather than the interior courtyard. **€100**

VILLA DELLA FONTE > Via della Fonte d'Olio 8, Bus H ☎ 06.580.3797, ⊕ www.villafonte.com. MAP P.124–125, POCKET MAP C18. This attractive hidden-away place feels almost secret, yet is just a few steps from Piazza Santa Maria in Trastevere. Rooms are cosy and old-fashioned but have free wi-fi. **€170**

Vatican

AMALIA > Via Germanico 66 Ⓜ Ottaviano ☎ 06.3972.3356, ⊕ www .hotelamalia.com. MAP P.142–143, POCKET MAP B3. Located not far from the Vatican, this place has bright, nicely renovated double rooms with generous en-suite bathrooms. Rates can go as low as €99 in low season. Don't be misled by the website – it's nowhere near the Spanish Steps. **€160**

BRAMANTE > Vicolo delle Palline 24, Bus 40 ☎ 06.6880.6426, ⊕ www .hotelbramante.com. MAP P.142–143, POCKET MAP A3. This little hotel, located right next to the ancient wall running from the Vatican to Castel Sant'Angelo, has charming rooms with original wood-beamed ceilings and antiques. **€230**

COLORS > Via Boezio 31 Ⓜ Ottaviano, ☎ 06.687.4030, ⊕ www.colorshotel .com. MAP P.142–143, POCKET MAP C3. This hostel/hotel in a quiet neighbourhood near the Vatican provides kitchen facilities, a lounge with satellite TV and a small roof terrace. Doubles are available both en-suite and with shared facilities, and there are dorm beds (€25) too. **€100**

DEI CONSOLI > Via Varrone 2d, Ⓜ Ottaviano ☎ 06.6889.2972, ⊕ www .hoteldeiconsoli.com. MAP P.142–143, POCKET MAP C3. From the elegantly welcoming entrance to the thoughtfully designed rooms, this is one of the best moderately priced choices in the Vatican area, with a lovely roof terrace and excellent service. **€260**

FRANKLIN > Via Rodi 29 ☎ 06.39030165, ⓦ www.franklinhotelrome.it. MAP P.142–143, POCKET MAP B2. The central theme here is music: don't be surprised to find a snare drum for a night table or a disco ball in the bathroom. Rooms come equipped with Bang & Olufsen stereos and you can choose from a library of hundreds of CDs. **€180**

GIULIO CESARE > Via degli Scipioni 287 ⓜ Lepanto ☎ 06.321.0751, ⓦ www .hotelgiuliocesare.com. MAP P.142–143, POCKET MAP D2. This charming hotel is no longer the Villa Patricia, home of an Italian countess, but you may feel like royalty once you step into the foyer, with its glistening golden ceiling. Friendly staff lead you down mirror-lined hallways to elegant rooms with marble bathrooms. **€210**

ROMA CAVALIERI > Via A Cadlolo 101 ☎ 06.350.91, ⓦ www.romecavalieri .com. MAP P.142–143, POCKET MAP B15. Arguably Rome's best hotel is quite a way out of the city centre, but it is worth staying here once, not only to check out Heinz's Beck's lendary three-Michelin-star rooftop restaurant (although you have to book well in advance for this) but also to enjoy its curious mix of Sixties glamour and old-fashioned style. The rooms are large and comfortable, there are three lovely pools and service that's impeccably gracious and professional. The hotel runs regular free shuttle buses to Piazza Barberini. **€400**

LA ROVERE > Vicolo S. Onofrio 4–5, Bus 64 ☎ 06.6880.6739, ⓦ www .hotellarovere.com. MAP P.142–143, POCKET MAP B15. Just across the bridge from Piazza Navona, this attractive hotel is tucked away from Rome's bustle, and offers a terrace garden and antique-filled setting for its guests to relax in. **€180**

Hostels

There are some privately run hostels alongside the official Hostelling International locations. For dorm accommodation, see also *Des Artistes* (p.169), *The Beehive* (p.170) and *Colors* (p.171).

ALESSANDRO PALACE HOSTEL > Via Vicenza 42, Ⓜ Termini ☏ 06.581.2125, Ⓦ www.sfromana.it. MAP P.92–93, POCKET MAP J3. This place has been voted one of the top hostels in Europe, and it sparkles with creative style. Pluses include no lock-out or curfew, a good bar with free pizza every night, and internet access and satellite TV. Beds cost €15–20; doubles with shared bath are €115. A few blocks away on the other side of Termini, Alessandro Downtown, Via C. Cattaneo 23 (☏ 06.4434.0147), also has dorm beds, from €25.

OSTELLO DEL FORO ITALICO > Viale delle Olimpiadi 61, Bus #32, 224, 280 or 628 ☏ 06.323.6267, Ⓦ www .ostellodiroma.it. MAP P.134–135, POCKET MAP C1. Rome's official youth hostel, though not especially central or easy to reach from Termini. Call ahead to check out availability, but they won't take phone bookings. You can join here if you're not a HI member already (€6). Beds cost €19, including breakfast. Other meals are also served.

OTTAVIANO > Via Ottaviano 6 Ⓜ Ottaviano ☏ 06.3973.8138, Ⓦ www.pensioneottaviano.com. MAP P.142–143, POCKET MAP B3. A simple pensione-cum-hostel near to the Vatican that is very popular with backpackers; book well in advance. Dorm beds €28, doubles €50.

SANDY > Via Cavour 136, Ⓜ Cavour, ☏ 06.488.4585, Ⓦ www.sandyhostel .com. MAP P.92–93, POCKET MAP G5. Good-value hostel near the Colosseum. Dorms €19–27, private en-suite doubles €90.

YELLOW > Via Palestro 44 Ⓜ Termini ☏ 06.498.2682, Ⓦ www.yellowhostel .com. MAP P.92–93, POCKET MAP J4. Friendly youth hostel over the road from grown-up sister *Romae*, and equally well-run. It is self-conciously cool and encourages a lively scene in the downstairs bar, so if you're after somewhere quiet it's probably not for you. Dorms €25, en-suite doubles €55.

YWCA > Via C. Balbo 4 Ⓜ Termini ☏ 06.488.0460, Ⓦ www.ywca-ucdg .it. MAP P.92–93, POCKET MAP H4. Open to women and men, and situated a 10min walk from Termini, although the market outside may get you up earlier than you intended. Small dorms €28, singles from €50, doubles from €80. Curfew midnight. Breakfast included (except on Sun); lunch is available for €12 (booking required).

Arrival

Arriving in Rome is a painless experience if you're travelling by air, by train or even by bus, although negotiating the city's outskirts by car is something you might want to avoid.

By air

Rome has two airports: Leonardo da Vinci, better known simply as Fiumicino, which handles most scheduled flights, and Ciampino, where you'll arrive if you're travelling on a charter or with one of the low-cost European airlines. Information on both airports is available at ☎06.65951, ⓦwww.adr.it.

Fiumicino airport

Fiumicino is connected to the centre of Rome by direct trains, which make the thirty-minute ride to Termini for €15 (€14 from a *tabacchi*); services run at 6min and 36min past the hour (first train at 6.38am, last train at 11.38pm). In the other direction, trains run at 22min and 52min past the hour (first train 5.52am, last train at 10.52pm). Be aware, though, when leaving Rome, that the Fiumicino platform at Termini station is a good five-minute schlep from the main part of the railway station. Alternatively, there are trains every 15min to Ostiense and Tiburtina stations, each on the edge of the city centre; tickets to these stations cost less (€8) and Tiburtina and Ostiense are just a short (€1) metro ride from Termini. You can also catch bus #175 from Ostiense, or #492 or #649 from Tiburtina, to the centre of town (again €1). Taxis for the 30–40min journey to and from the airport cost a fixed-rate €40. Two buses go from the airport to Termini. COTRAL have 6 services a day from 1.15am to 3.30pm (7pm at weekends) to Piazza dei Cinquecento (€4.50 one way; ⓦwww.cotralspa.it), while SIT bus services run every half hour from 7am to 11.30pm to Via Marsala (€4 one way; ⓦwww.sitbusshuttle.it). Both take about 45 minutes.

Ciampino airport

Terravision (ⓦwww.terravision.eu) and SIT bus (ⓦwww.sitbusshuttle.it) run shuttle services to Termini, which leave roughly every 30 minutes and cost €4 one way. They pull up on Via Marsala, right by the station (journey time around 45 minutes). Otherwise ATRAL buses (ⓦwww.atral-lazio.com) run to Via Giolitti, on the south side of Termini, every 50min–1hr (€3.90). If you don't want to get off at Termini, and are staying near a metro stop on the A line (near the Spanish Steps or Via Veneto areas, for example), you could take an ATRAL bus (€1.20) from the airport to Anagnina metro station at the end of metro Line A, and take a metro from there to your destination (€1). Taxis to and from the airport cost a fixed-rate €30 and take 30–40min.

By train

Most Italian and international trains arrive in Rome at Termini station, centrally placed for all parts of the city and the meeting point of the two metro lines and many city bus routes. Tiburtina (see below) is a stop for some north–south intercity trains. For general enquiries about schedules and prices, call ☎892.021 (24hr), or check ⓦwww.trenitalia.it.

By bus

Most national and international services stop at Tiburtina, Rome's second railway terminal after Termini, which is connected to the city centre by metro line B or buses #492 or #649. Other bus stations, mainly serving the Lazio region, include Ponte Mammolo (trains from Tivoli and Subiaco), Lepanto (Cerveteri, Civitavecchia, Bracciano area), EUR Fermi (Nettuno, Anzio, southern Lazio coast) and Anagnina (Castelli Romani); all of these stations are on a metro line.

By car

Driving into Rome can be quite confusing and is best avoided unless you're used to driving in Italy and know where you're going to park (see p.180). Note that non-residents aren't allowed to drive in the centro storico area. It's usually best to get on the Grande Raccordo Anulare (GRA), which circles Rome and is connected with all of the major arteries into the city centre – the Via Cassia from the north, Via Salaria from the northeast, Via Tiburtina or Via Nomentana from the east, Via Prenestina and Via Casilina or Via Cristoforo Colombo from the southeast, Via Appia Nuova and the Pontina from the south, and Via Aurelia from the northwest. From Ciampino, either follow Via Appia Nuova into the centre or join the GRA at junction 23 and follow the signs to the centre. From Fiumicino, just follow the A12 motorway into the city centre; it crosses the river just north of EUR, from where it's a short drive north up Via Cristoforo Colombo to the city walls and, beyond, to the Baths of Caracalla.

Getting around

The best way to get around is to walk – you'll see more and will better appreciate the city. However, you may need to take public transport to get around quickly or reach the more outlying attractions, and the network is good – a largely efficient blend of buses, a two-line metro and a few trams. ATAC runs the city's bus, tram and metro service. There's an information office in the centre of Piazza dei Cinquecento outside Termini station; their website, ⓦ www.atac. roma.it, has information in English and a route planner.

Buses and trams

Buses are cheap, reliable and as quick as the clogged streets allow (see box on p.179 for useful bus routes). Remember to board through the rear doors and punch your ticket as you enter. There is also a small network of electric minibuses that negotiate the narrow backstreets of the old centre and a few trams, mainly serving outlying areas. After midnight, night buses (*bus notturni*) serve most parts of the city through to about 5.30am; some have ticket machines on board but it's best to buy one before boarding.

Tickets and travel cards

Flat-fare **tickets** cost €1 each and are good for any number of bus and tram rides and one metro ride within 75 minutes of validation. Buy them from tobacconists, newsstands and ticket machines located in all metro stations and at major bus stops, and validate them in the yellow machines on buses, trams and at the entrance gates in metro stations. You can also get a **day pass**, valid on all city transport until midnight on the day purchased, for €4, a three-day pass for €11, or a seven-day pass for €16. Alternatively, you can travel on public transport for free with the **Roma Pass** (see p.183). A warning: there are hefty spot fines (€50–100) for fare-dodging, and pleading a foreigner's ignorance will get you nowhere.

Metro

Rome's metro (ⓦ www.metroroma. it) runs from 5.30am to 11.30pm (12.30am Sat), and although its two lines – A (red) and B (blue) – don't cover large parts of the city centre, there are a few useful city-centre stations: Termini is the hub of both lines, and there are stops at the Colosseum, Piazza Barberini, Piazza di Spagna and Ottaviano (for the Vatican). They're working on line C, projected for completion in 2015 at the earliest.

Tourist buses

Many tourist buses circle Rome and its major sights – see the three best options below. All start from outside Termini, and combined tickets are available for the first two.

Bus #110 ⓣ 800.281.281, ⓦ www. trambusopen.com. Good for a quick glance at the sights, this ATAC-run open-top bus has a guided commentary. It leaves from Piazza dei Cinquecento outside Termini station and stops at all the major sights. The trip takes two hours, and in summer departures are every 15min from 8.30am until 8.30pm daily (including hols & Sun). Tickets cost €20 and allow you to get on wherever you like and hop on and off during a 24-hour period. Combined #110 and Archeo-bus (see below) tickets cost €25 for 72 hours. Tickets can be bought on board, or before you get on at Piazza dei Cinquecento.

Archeobus ⓣ 800.281.281, ⓦ www. trambusopen.com. A hop-on-hop-off service, linking the most compelling monuments on and around the Via Appia Antica. It starts at Piazza dei Cinquecento, before heading down to the southern edge of the city via Piazza Venezia, Piazza Bocca della Verità, Circo Massimo and the Porta San Sebastiano. On Via Appia, there

are stops at Domine Quo Vadis, the Catacombs of San Callisto and San Sebastiano, Villa of Maxentius, the Roman aqueducts and the Villa dei Quintili. Buses run daily every thirty minutes between 9am and 4.30pm. Tickets cost €12 (€40 family ticket), and integrated tickets are available, including the #110 bus and various museums, with different lengths of validity. Buy on board, or at Piazza dei Cinquecento.

Roma Cristiana The Vatican's tourist bus service links Rome's major basilicas and other Christian sights, starting in Piazza dei Cinquecento. Services run daily every 30min between 8.40am and 7pm, and tickets cost €13, or €18 for 24 hours; buy on board, at Piazza dei Cinquecento or at PIT information kiosks.

Walking tours

Entrance fees are generally not included in the price of tours, so check costs before booking. Enjoy Rome (see p.183) is the best all-round operator, offering three-hour tours to groups (maximum 25 people). Most popular are the tours of the ancient sights and the highlights of the centro storico (€30). You may prefer the smaller-scale tours of Context Rome (ⓣ 06.9762.5204, ⓦ www. contexttravel.com), who run excellent small-group walking tours (maximum 6 people) of sights and neighbourhoods, led by engaging experts, on subjects ranging from architecture to gastronomic Rome – the city's best choice if you want something both in-depth and personal.

Nightbuses

#N1 follows metro line A; **#N2** calls at all stops along metro line B; and **#N8** runs from Trastevere to Termini station.

Useful bus and tram routes

#3 Tram Stazione Trastevere–Via Marmorata–Piramide–Circo Massimo–Colosseum–San Giovanni–San Lorenzo–Via Nomentana–Parioli–Viale Belle Arti.

#8 Tram Largo Argentina–Via Arenula–Piazza Sonnino–Viale Trastevere–Stazione Trastevere–Casaletto

#23 Piazza Clodio–Piazza Risorgimento–Ponte Vittorio Emanuele II–Ponte Garibaldi–Via Marmorata–Piazzale Ostiense–Centrale Montemartini–Basilica di San Paolo.

#30 Express Piazza Clodio–Piazza Mazzini–Piazza Cavour–Corso Rinascimento–Largo Argentina–Piazza Venezia–Luntotevere Aventino–Via Marmorata–Piramide–Via C.Colombo–EUR.

#40 Express Termini–Via Nazionale–Piazza Venezia–Largo Argentina–Piazza Pia.

#62 Piazza Bologna–Via Nomentana–Porta Pia–Piazza Barberini–Piazza San Silvestro–Via del Corso–Piazza Venezia– Corso V. Emanuele II–Borgo Angelico–Piazza Pio.

#64 Termini–Piazza della Repubblica–Via Nazionale–Piazza Venezia–Largo Argentina–Corso Vittorio Emanuele II–Stazione San Pietro.

#75 Via Poerio (Monteverde)–Via Induno–Porta Portese–Testaccio–Piramide–Circo Massimo–Colosseo–Via Cavour–Termini–Piazza Indipendenza.

#116 Porta Pinciana–Via Veneto–Via del Tritone–Piazza di Spagna–Piazza San Silvestro–Corso Rinascimento–Campo de' Fiori–Piazza Farnese–Lungotevere Sangallo–Terminal Gianicolo.

#117 San Giovanni in Laterano–Piazza Celimontana–Via Due Macelli–Via del Babuino–Piazza del Popolo–Via del Corso–Piazza Venezia–Via Nazionale–Via dei Serpenti–Colosseo–Via Labicana.

#119 Piazza del Popolo–Via del Corso–Piazza Venezia–Largo Argentina–Via del Tritone–Piazza Barberini–Via Veneto–Porta Pinciana–Piazza Barberini–Piazza di Spagna–Via del Babuino–Piazza del Popolo.

#175 Termini–Piazza Barberini–Via del Corso–Piazza Venezia–Colosseo–Circo Massimo–Aventine–Stazione Ostiense.

#271 S. Paolo–Via Ostiense–Piramide–Viale Aventino–Circo Massimo–Colosseo–Piazza Venezia–Ponte Sisto–Castel Sant'Angelo–Via Vitilleschi–Piazza Risorgimento–Ottaviano–Foro Italico.

#492 Stazione Tiburtina–Piazzale Verano–Termini–Piazza Barberini–Via del Corso–Piazza Venezia–Largo Argentina–Corso del Rinascimento–Piazza Cavour–Piazza Risorgimento–Cipro.

#590 Same route as metro line A but with access for disabled; runs every 90min.

#660 Largo Colli Albani–Via Appia Nuova–Via Appia Pignatelli–Via Appia Antica.

#714 Termini–Santa Maria Maggiore–Via Merulana–San Giovanni in Laterano–Viale Terme di Caracalla–EUR.

#910 Termini–Piazza della Repubblica–Via Piemonte–Via Pinciana (Villa Borghese)–Piazza Euclide–Palazzetto dello Sport–Piazza Mancini.

Bikes, mopeds and scooters

Renting a bike, moped or scooter can be the most efficient way of nipping around Rome's clogged city centre, and there are plenty of places offering this facility (see box, below). Some hotels – eg. *Locarno* (see p.168) – have bikes for guest-use or there's Roma-Bike, the city's **bike-sharing** scheme, run by Atac. To use the service, you need to register at an Atac ticket office (in Termini, Spagna and Ottaviano metro stations; Mon–Sat 7am–8pm, Sun 8am–8pm); you will need ID and €5 to pay for an electronic Smartcard; after that it costs €0.50/hr (☏ 06.57003). To pick up a bike, you swipe the Smartcard against the reader of any of the bike stands dotted all over the city. The bike can be returned to any stand, not necessarily the one that you picked it up from; you swipe your card again to lock the bike in place. Bikes can be taken out for a maximum of 24 consecutive hours.

Cycling along Rome's first highway and through the Caffarella Valley on a Sunday is a tranquil way of seeing the area. The visitor centre (see box below) also has good information in English about suggested routes.

Parking

You can park on the street for around €1.20/hr (8am–8pm), or there are parking garages in Villa Borghese (€1.70/hr) and in front of Termini station (€2/hr for the first two hours, then €1.55/hr). There are also car parks next to the terminal metro stations, from where it's easy to get into the city centre.

Taxis

Central taxi stands (*fermata dei taxi*) include Termini, Piazza Venezia, Piazza San Silvestro, Piazza di Spagna, Piazza Navona, Largo Argentina, Piazza San Pietro and Piazza Barberini. Or, call a taxi (☏ 06.3570, ☏ 06.4994, ☏ 06.6645, or ☏ 06.88.177), but note you pay for the time it takes to get to you. Only take licensed white cabs with the "Comune di Roma" insignia on the door, and check the meter is on; a card in every official taxi explains the extra charges for luggage, late-night, Sundays and holidays, and airport journeys. Pick ups from Termini incur a supplement of €2. Journeys from one side of the city to the other should cost around €10 and around €15 on Sunday or at night.

Renting cars, scooters and bicycles

Cars Avis (Termini ☏ 06.481.4273, Ciampino ☏ 06.7934.0368, Fiumicino ☏ 06.6501.1531); Europcar (Termini ☏ 06.488.2854, Ciampino ☏ 06.7934.0387, Fiumicino ☏ 06.6501.0879); Hertz (Termini ☏ 06.474.0389, Ciampino ☏ 06.7934.0616, Fiumicino ☏ 06.6501.1553); Maggiore (Termini ☏ 06.488.0049, Ciampino ☏ 06.7934.0368, Fiumicino ☏ 06.6501.0678); Sixt (Termini ☏ 06.474.0014, Ciampino ☏ 06.7934.0838, Fiumicino ☏ 06.6595.3547).

Scooters Barberini (Via della Purificazione 84 ☏ 06.488.5485, ☏ www.rentscooter.it) for €10/day for bikes, mopeds and scooters from €30/day. Treno e Scooter Rent, near Track 1 in Termini station (☏ 06.4890.5823, ☏ www.trenoescooter.191.it. €10/day for bikes, €34–70/day for mopeds or scooters).

Bicycles Appia Antica Visitor Center (Via Appia Antica 58; ☏ 06.512.6314, ☏ www.parcoappiaantica.org; €3/hr or €10/day for bicycles).

Directory A–Z

For the fire brigade, police or ambulance, call ☎113.

Cinema

Not many cinemas in Rome screen films in their original language, but the Nuovo Olimpia at Via in Lucina 16g (☎06.6861.1068), off Via del Corso, is an exception. Tickets cost around €7; Romac'è (see p.183) has programme details.

Crime

To call the police, dial ☎112. Both the police (Polizia Statale) and the carabinieri (who wear military-style uniforms) have offices in Termini. Otherwise, the questura (main police office) is at Via San Vitale 15, off Via Nazionale; report any thefts to the police here.

Dress

The rules for visiting churches are much as they are all over Italy: dress modestly, which usually means no shorts, short skirts or bare shoulders.

Electricity

220 volts. Both UK and US adaptors are available to buy in Italy, but the latter can be expensive.

Embassies and consulates

Australia Via Bosio 5 ☎06.852.721; **Canada** Via Zara 30 ☎06.85444.3937; **Ireland** Piazza Campitelli 3 ☎06.697.9121; **New Zealand** Via Clitunno 44 ☎06.853.7501; **UK** Via XX Settembre 80a ☎06.4220.000; **US** Via Veneto 119a ☎06.46.741.

Health

AlphaMed, Via Zanardelli 36 (☎06.6830.9493; Mon–Fri 9am–8pm), is a central medical practice with English-speaking doctors; Tobias Wallbrecher at Via Domenico Silveri 30 (☎06.638.0569, Mon–Fri 9am–1pm & 4–7pm) is an English-speaking family doctor close to the Vatican; Absolute Dentistry, Via G. Pisanelli 3, has a 24-hour emergency service (☎06.3600.3837 or 339.250.7016).

The most central hospitals with emergency facilities are: Fatebenefratelli, Isola Tiberina (☎06.683.7299); Rome American Hospital, Via E. Longoni 81 (☎06.22.551), a private multi-speciality hospital with bilingual staff and a 24hr emergency line; San Giovanni at Via A. Aradam 8 (☎06.49.971); Santo Spirito Lungotevere in Sassia 1, near the Vatican (☎6.68.351).

The following pharmacies are open 24hr, year-round: Farmacia della Stazione, Piazza dei Cinquecento 51 ☎06.488.0019; Internazionale, Piazza Barberini 49 ☎06.482.5456; Piram, Via Nazionale 228 ☎06.488.0754.

Internet

Bibli, Via dei Fienaroli 28 (Mon 5.30pm–midnight, Tues–Sun 11am–midnight); Internet Train, Piazza Sant'Andrea delle Valle 3 (Mon–Fri 10am–11pm, Sat 10am–8pm, Sun noon–8pm); Internet Train, Via dei Pastini 21 (same hours). There are also many internet cafés around Termini station. By law, internet cafés will ask you to show ID such as a passport before allowing you to access the internet. There are dozens of free wireless hotspots in the city including the Circus Maximus, Villa Borghese, Piazza Navona, Largo Argentina, Trevi Fountain and the Spanish Steps. See ⓦwww.romawireless.com for other locations.

Left luggage

Termini station (daily 6am–midnight; €4 per piece for 5hr, €0.60 for each additional hour, ☎ 06.474.4777).

Lost property

For property lost on a train call ☎ 06.4730.6682 (daily 7am–11pm); on a bus ☎ 06.581.6040 (Mon & Fri 8.30am–1pm, Tues–Thurs 2.30–6pm); on the metro ☎ 06.487.4309).

Money

You'll find ATMs throughout the city. Nearly all hotels now accept credit cards, though many restaurants are still cash-only. To exchange money, try American Express, Piazza di Spagna 38 (Mon–Fri 9am–5.30pm, Sat 9am–12.30pm); or Travelex, Piazza Barberini 21a (Mon–Sat 9am–8pm, Sun 9.30am–5pm) and Via della Conciliazione 23 (Mon–Sat 9am–7.30pm, Sun 9.30am–5pm). Post offices will exchange American Express travellers' cheques and cash commission-free.

For lost or stolen cards, call: American Express ☎ 800.914.912; MasterCard ☎ 800.870.866; Visa ☎ 800.819.014.

Opening hours

Most museums and galleries are closed on Mondays. Opening hours for state-run museums are generally from 9am until 7pm, Tuesday to Sunday. Most other museums roughly follow this pattern too, although are likely to close for a couple of hours in the afternoon, and have shorter opening hours in winter. Some museums run late-night openings in summer (till 10pm or later Tues–Sat, or 8pm on Sun).

Opening times of ancient sites are more flexible: most are open daily, including Sunday, from 8.30am until the evening – usually one hour before sunset (changes according to the time of year). In winter, times are drastically cut; 4pm is a common closing time.

Most major Roman churches open in the early morning, at around 7am or 8am, and close around noon, opening up again at 4pm and closing at 6pm or 7pm.

Phones

If you have a GSM, dual- or tri-band phone which can be unlocked, consider investing in an Italian SIM card, which can be bought for about €10 from Italian providers TIM, Wind or Vodafone; ask for a "SIM prepagato". To use public telephones, you can buy telephone cards (carta telefonica) from tabacchi and newsstands in denominations of €5 and €10. You always need to dial the local code; ☎ 06 is the code for Rome and around. Numbers beginning ☎ 800 are free, ☎ 170 will get you through to an English-speaking operator, ☎ 176 to international directory enquiries. Any numbers that start with a 3 are mobile numbers. To make long-distance calls, it's cheaper to buy one of the international calling cards, also available from tabacchi for upwards of €5. You can make international reversed-charge or collect calls (chiamata con addebito destinatario) by dialling ☎ 170 and following the recorded instructions.

Post offices

The main post office is at Piazza San Silvestro 12 (☎ 06.6973.7213; Mon–Fri 8am–7pm, Sat 8am–1.15pm).

Smoking

Smoking is banned in all public indoor spaces in Italy, including restaurants, bars and clubs.

Time

Rome is one hour ahead of GMT, six hours ahead of Eastern Standard Time, and nine hours ahead of Pacific Standard Time in North America.

Tourist information and passes

There are tourist information booths in Terminal 2 at Fiumicino (daily 9am–6.30pm; ☎ 060608), in the Arrivals Hall at Ciampino airport (daily 9am–6.30pm) and in Termini station at Via Giolitti 34 (daily 8am–8.30pm; ☎ 060608), although you can also go to **Enjoy Rome** (Via Marghera 8a; Mon–Fri 9am–5.30pm, Sat 8.30am–2pm; ☎ 06.445.1843, ⓦ www.enjoyrome.com), an unofficial but reliable source of information whose English-speaking staff also run a free accommodation-finding service, organize walking and bus tours and can arrange shuttles to the airports. There are also green information kiosks (PIT; open 9.30am–7pm) near key locations around the city, such as Via Nazionale (Palazzo delle Esposizioni), Piazza Navona (Piazza delle Cinque Lune), Castel Sant'Angelo (Piazza Pia) and Trastevere (Piazza Sonnino). Rome's tourist information line ☎ 060608 is open daily 9am–9pm; calls are charged at the local rate. For what's-on information, check out **Romac'è** (€1; Wed), which has details of clubs, restaurants, services and weekly events. The expat bi-weekly, *Wanted in Rome* (€1.50 every other Wed), which is written entirely in English, is useful if you're looking for an apartment or work. If you understand a bit of Italian, the daily arts pages of the Rome newspaper, *Il Messaggero*, lists movies, plays and major musical events, and can be found in most bars, or at news-stands for €1. The newspaper *La Repubblica* (€1.50) also includes the "TrovaRoma" section in its Thursday edition, another handy guide to current offerings.

Rome's main museum and transport pass is the **Roma Pass** (€25; ⓦ www.romapass.it), which gives you free admission to the first two participating museums or archeological sites visited, and discounts on visits elsewhere, plus full access to public transport for three days. Buy it from tourist offices, participating sights or online.Much of Rome's ancient sculpture, alongside other artefacts, has been gathered together into the Museo Nazionale Romano, which operates on five main sites: Palazzo Massimo, the Terme di Diocleziano, the Crypta Balbi, the Aula Ottagona and Palazzo Altemps. You can buy a ticket (at each branch) that grants entry to all five locations for just €7 and is valid for three days. As for the ancient sites, the Colosseum, Roman Forum and Palatine Hill are visitable on a combined ticket.

Travellers with disabilities

Although changes are in the works, Rome can be quite a challenge for those with disabilities. Contact the Cooperative Integrate Onlus (CO.IN), Via Enrico Giglioli 54a (☎ 06.712.9011, toll free in Italy ☎ 800.271.027), who have English-speaking 24-hour information on their phone line, and produce a guide, Roma Accessible, with information on major sites, museums, hotels and restaurants (available in person from their office only). Dynamic Air (ⓔ info@dynamicair.it) offers the free loan of medical equipment to visitors in Italy, including wheelchairs, ventilators and oxygen tanks.

Festivals and events

Public holidays are denoted by **(PH)**; many sights and shops, and some bars and restaurants close.

NEW YEAR'S DAY (PH)

Jan 1

EPIPHANY (PH)

Jan 6
La Befana, or Epiphany, marks the end of a Christmas fair that fills Piazza Navona from mid-December.

CARNEVALE

Mid-Feb 10 days
Roman kids dress up and are paraded round the city by their proud parents, and clubs put on themed nights. Look out for the carnival delicacies sold throughout the city: *frappe* (deep-fried pastry strips) and *castagnole* (bite-sized pastries).

ROME MARATHON

Sunday in mid-March
Ⓦ www.maratondiroma.it
Thousands of runners take to the streets for Rome's annual marathon; the course takes in many of the major sights en route.

EASTER

During Holy Week, Catholics from across the world descend on Rome to witness the pope's address. On Good Friday, a solemn procession moves from the Colosseum to the Capitoline Hill, while on Easter Sunday the main event is the pope's blessing in St Peter's Square.

PASQUETTA (PH)

Easter Monday
Many Romans head out of town, traditionally for a picnic in the countryside.

NATALE DI ROMA

April 21
A spectacular fireworks display set off from the Campidoglio marks Rome's birthday.

FESTA DELLA PRIMAVERA

Late April
The Spanish Steps are lined with thousands of beautiful blooms.

SETTIMANA DELLA CULTURA

April Ⓦ www.beniculturali.it
For one week in April, you can enter all state-owned museums free of charge.

LIBERATION DAY (PH)

April 25

LABOUR DAY (PH)

May 1
"Primo Maggio" is celebrated with a free rock concert in Piazza San Giovanni.

ROME LITERATURE FESTIVAL

Late May–June
Ⓦ www.festivaldelleletterature.it
Readings by well-known authors in one of the city's most atmospheric locations, the Basilica of Maxentius near the Roman Forum.

DAY OF THE REPUBLIC

June 2
The day is marked with a military parade along Via dei Fori Imperiali, and the gardens of the Quirinale palace are open to the public (expect long queues).

ESTATE ROMANA

Early June–late Sept Ⓦ www.estateromana.comune.roma.it

Rome's summer-long cultural extravaganza includes all sorts of events, from open-air film screenings to concerts in atmospheric surroundings. Many events are free.

VILLA CELIMONTANA JAZZ

Mid-June to mid-Sept Ⓦ www.villacelimontanajazz.com

Open-air jazz performances in leafy Villa Celimontana, near the Colosseum. Tickets from just €3.

ROMA INCONTRA IL MONDO

Mid-June to mid-Aug Ⓦ www.villaada.org

An eclectic programme of pop, rock and indie concerts takes place in Villa Ada. Tickets €8–22.

TEATRO DELL'OPERA

Late June to mid-Aug Ⓦ www.operaroma.it

Teatro dell'Opera's summer season takes place in the floodlit setting of the Baths of Caracalla.

CONCERTI DEL TEMPIETTO

June–Oct Ⓦ www.tempietto.org

Classical concerts with dramatic backdrops: the ancient Roman Teatro di Marcello and the Art Nouveau Casina delle Civette.

FESTA DI NOANTRI

Mid-July

Two weeks of street performances and events in Trastevere culminate in a huge fireworks display.

FESTA DELLE CATENE

Aug 1

The chains of St Peter are displayed during a special Mass in the church of San Pietro in Vincoli.

FESTA DELLA MADONNA DELLA NEVE

Aug 5

The miracle of a summer snowfall (see p.91) is remembered in the Basilica of Santa Maria Maggiore with a shower of white petals on the congregation.

FERRAGOSTO (PH)

August 15

On the Feast of the Assumption, Rome empties as locals in search of cooling breezes head for the sea and mountains.

ROMAEUROPA FESTIVAL

Late Sept–Nov Ⓦ www.romaeuropa.net

Rome's performing arts festival showcases international talents in music, theatre and dance, in venues around town.

ROME INTERNATIONAL FILM FESTIVAL

1 week mid-Oct Ⓦ www.romacinemafest.it

Rome's film festival always draws Hollywood talent. The hub of the festival is Rome's Auditorium, but there are venues across town.

OGNISSANTI (PH)

Nov 1

On All Souls' Day, Romans visit family graves in the Verano cemetery in San Lorenzo.

IMMACOLATA CONCEZIONE (PH)

Dec 8

In honour of the Immaculate Conception of the Blessed Virgin Mary, a religious ceremony takes place in the Piazza di Spagna, often attended by the Pope.

NATALE/ SANTO STEFANO (PH)

Dec 25/Dec 26

Chronology

9th century BC > Iron Age village founded on the Palatine Hill.

753 BC > Romulus kills Remus and becomes the city's first ruler.

616–579 BC > Tarquinius Priscus is Rome's first Etruscan king.

509 BC > Tarquinius Superbus, the last Etruscan king, is deposed and the Roman Republic is established.

264–146 BC > Punic Wars against Carthage.

87 BC > Civil war breaks out between Marius and Sulla.

82 BC > Sulla becomes dictator of Rome.

65–63 BC > Marius' nephew, Julius Caesar, establishes a formidable military reputation.

60 BC > Triumvirate of Julius Caesar, Crassus and Pompey rules Rome.

58–51 BC > Caesar colonizes Gaul.

49–45 BC > Caesar marches on Rome, sparking off a civil war between him and Pompey.

44 BC > Caesar is assassinated in Pompey's Theatre on March 15.

43 BC > Leadership is assumed by a triumvirate of Antony, Octavian and Lepidus.

40 BC > Antony marries Octavian's sister, Octavia.

31 BC > Octavian defeats Antony and Cleopatra at the Battle of Actium.

27 BC > Octavian becomes sole ruler as Augustus.

14 AD > Tiberius, Augustus' stepson, assumes power and marries Augustus' daughter, Julia, who gives birth to Caligula, the next emperor.

41 AD > Caligula is assassinated after four years in power. His uncle, Claudius, proves to be a wiser successor.

54 AD > The reign of Claudius' stepson, Nero, is marred by corruption and excess.

69 AD > Emperor Vespasian restores order to Rome and builds the Colosseum in the grounds of Nero's Domus Aurea.

81 AD > Vespasian's son Titus is succeeded by Domitian, who builds the stadium that forms the foundations of today's Piazza Navona.

98 AD > Emperor Trajan expands the empire and Rome grows to a population of around a million.

117 > Trajan is succeeded by Hadrian, a wise and resourceful emperor, who ruled over the empire's golden age.

138–192 > Marcus Aurelius continues to rule a stable city and a rich empire but the Antonine line fizzles out when his son, Commodus, is strangled.

193 > Septimius Severus becomes the first emperor of the Severan dynasty.

211 > Severus' son, Caracalla, murders his brother and assumes power for himself in.

275 > The emperor Aurelian builds a wall around the city to keep it safe from invaders.

284 > Diocletian stabilizes Rome and divides the empire into east and west.

306 > Constantine converts to Christianity and defeats his rival Maxentius to claim the Western Empire.

325 > Constantine shifts the seat of power east to Byzantium, renaming it Constantinople.

410 > Rome is captured by the Visigoths, the first time a foreign invader has held the city for 800 years.

5th century > The city declines to a population of around 30,000.

590 > Gregory I becomes pope, revitalizing the city with new basilicas and converting ancient Roman structures like the Pantheon and the Castel Sant'Angelo.

800 > Charlemagne visits Rome and is crowned ruler of the Holy Roman Empire.

850–1300 > Rome is the focus of struggles between the papacy, Holy Roman emperors and its own aristocracy.

1305 > Clement V transfers the papal court to Avignon, France.

1347 > Cola di Rienzo seizes power and re-establishes Rome's Republic for seven years.

1417 > Martin V consolidates papal power in Rome.

1475 > Pope Sixtus IV commissions the Sistine Chapel.

1503 > Julius II becomes pope and commissions frescoes for the Sistine Chapel from Michelangelo.

1513 > Leo X continues Julius's role as patron of the city's greatest artists and architects.

1527 > Holy Roman Emperor Charles V captures Rome and Clement VII flees to the Castel Sant'Angelo.

1534 > Alessandro Farnese is elected pope as Paul III and Michelangelo completes his Sistine Chapel painting of the *Last Judgement*.

1585 > Sixtus V undertakes widespread construction, creating grand vistas and squares.

1605 > St Peter's is completed under the Borghese pope, Paul V.

1623 > Urban VIII ascends the papal throne and becomes the greatest patron of the Baroque's most dominant figure, Gianlorenzo Bernini.

1700 > The city's population is now 150,000, and Rome becomes an essential stop on any traveller's Grand Tour.

1798 > French forces commanded by Napoleon occupy the city; Pius VI is taken as a prisoner to France.

1815 > Papal rule is restored under Pius VII.

1849 > Giuseppe Mazzini forces

Pope Pius IX to leave Rome but the papacy is restored four months later by Napoleon III.

1859–64 > Unification forces gather strength and Florence becomes the capital of the new kingdom of Italy.

1870 > Italian forces take Rome and declare the city the capital of the new state under Vittorio Emanuele II. Pope Pius IX is confined to the Vatican.

1922–42 > Mussolini oversees the construction of numerous public works.

1929 > The Lateran Pact is signed by Italy and the Vatican, recognizing the sovereignty of the Vatican City.

1946 > King Vittorio Emanuele III is forced to abdicate and a republic is declared under Alcide de Gasperi.

1960 > Fellini releases *La Dolce Vita*, a film that would define the Sixties in Rome.

1970s > The *anni piombi*, or "years of lead", when Rome became a focus for terrorism, culminating in the murder of politician Aldo Moro.

1990s > Corruption scandals lead to a series of trials and the reconfiguration of the entire Italian political landscape.

2001 > Walter Veltroni is elected mayor of Rome, and oversees a series of prestigious public works.

2005 > Pope John Paul II is succeeded by Josef Ratzinger as Pope Benedict XVI.

2008 > Following years of left-leaning mayors, a right-winger, Giovanni Alemanno, is elected.

Italian

Speaking some **Italian**, however tentatively, can mark you out from the hordes of tourists in Rome, and having a little more can open up the city no end. What follows is a brief pronunciation guide, some useful words and phrases, and a food and drink glossary. For more detail, *Italian: The Rough Guide Phrasebook* has a huge and accessible vocabulary, a detailed menu reader and conversational examples to get you through most situations.

Pronunciation

Italian **pronunciation** is very simple – all words are stressed on the penultimate syllable unless an accent (` or ´) denotes otherwise. The only difficulties you're likely to encounter are the few consonants that are different from English:

c before e or i is pronounced as in **ch**urch, while **ch** before the same vowels is hard, as in **c**at.

The same goes with **g** – soft before e or i, as in **g**eranium; hard before h, as in **g**arlic.

sci or **sce** are pronounced as in **sh**eet and **sh**elter respectively.

gn has the ni sound of o**ni**on.

gl in Italian is softened to a sound similar to lyi, as in sta**ll**ion.

h is not aspirated, as in **h**onour.

Words and phrases

BASICS

good morning	buongiorno
good afternoon/ evening	buonasera
good night	buonanotte
hello/goodbye	ciao (informal; to strangers use phrases above)
goodbye	arrivederci
yes	si
no	no

please	per favore
thank you (very much)	grazie (molte/mille grazie)
you're welcome	prego
all right/OK	va bene
how are you? (informal/formal)	come stai/sta?
I'm fine	bene
Do you speak English?	parla inglese?
I don't understand	non ho capito
I don't know	non lo so
excuse me (to get attention)	mi scusi
excuse me (in a crowd)	permesso
I'm sorry	mi dispiace
I'm here on holiday	sono qui in vacanza
I'm English	sono inglese
Scottish	scozzese
Welsh	gallese
Irish	irlandese
American (m/f)	americano/a
Australian (m/f)	australiano/a
a New Zealander	neozelandese
today	oggi
tomorrow	domani
day after tomorrow	dopodomani
Yesterday	Ieri
now	adesso
later	più tardi
tonight	stasera
morning	mattina
afternoon	pomeriggio
evening	sera
wait!	aspetta!
let's go!	andiamo!
here/There	oui/Là
good/bad	buono/cattivo
big/small	grande/piccolo
cheap/Expensive	economico/Caro
early/Late	presto/tardi
hot/cold	caldo/freddo
near/far	vicino/lontano
quickly/Slowly	velocemente/ Lentamente
with/without	con/senza
more/less	più/meno
enough, no more	basta
Mr/Mrs/Miss	signores/signora/ signorina

QUESTIONS AND DIRECTIONS

where?	dove?
Where is/where are...?	Dov'è/Dove sono ... ?
How do I get to ... ?	Per arrivare a ... ?
turn left/right	giri a sinistra/destra
go straight on	vai sempre diritto
How far is it to ... ?	Quant'è lontano a... ?
What time does it open/close?	A che ora apre/chiude?
What time is it?	Che ore sono?
when?	quando?
what? (what is it?)	cosa? (cos'è?)
How much/many?	Quanto/Quanti?
why?	perché?
It is/there is (is it/is there ...)?	C'è ... ?
How much does it/they cost?	Quanto costa/costano?
How do you say it in Italian?	Come si dice in italiano?

TRANSPORT

bus station	autostazione
train station	stazione ferroviaria
a ticket to ...	un biglietto a ...
one-way/return	solo andata/andata e ritorno
Can you tell me when to get off?	Mi può dire dove scendere?
What time does it leave/arrive?	A che ora parte/arriva?
Where does it leave from?	Da dove parte?

SIGNS

aperto	open
bagno/Gabinetto	WC/bathroom
cassa	cash desk
chiuso	closed
chiuso per ferie	closed for holidays
chiuso per restauro	closed for restoration
entrata	entrance
ingresso libero	free entry
signori/Signore	gentlemen/Ladies
spingere	push
tirare	pull
uscita	exit
vietato fumare	no smoking

ACCOMMODATION

Hotel	albergo
Hostel	ostello
I'd like to book a room	Vorrei prenotare una camera
Is there a hotel nearby?	C'è un albergo qui vicino?
I have a booking	Ho una prenotazione
Do you have a room ...	
for one/two night/s	per una/due notte/i
for one/two week/s	per una/due settimana/e
with a double bed	con un letto matrimoniale
with twin beds	con due letti
with a shower/bath	con doccia/bagno
with a balcony	con balcone
with hot/cold water	con acqua calda/fredda
How much is it?	Quanto costa?
It's expensive	È caro
Is breakfast included?	È compresa la colazione?
Do you have anything cheaper?	Ha qualcosa che costa di meno?
Full/half board	Pensione completa/mezza pensione
Can I see the room?	Posso vedere la camera?
I'll take it	La prendo

NUMBERS

uno	1
due	2
tre	3
quattro	4
cinque	5
sei	6
sette	7
otto	8
nove	9
dieci	10
undici	11
dodici	12
tredici	13
quattordici	14
quindici	15
sedici	16
diciassette	17

diciotto	18
diciannove	19
venti	20
ventuno	21
ventidue	22
trenta	30
quaranta	40
cinquanta	50
sessanta	60
settanta	70
ottanta	80
novanta	90
cento	100
centuno	101
centodieci	110
duecento	200
cinquecento	500
mille	1000
cinquemila	5000
diecimila	10,000

Food and drink terms

BASICS AND SNACKS

aceto	vinegar
aglio	garlic
biscotti	biscuits
burro	butter
caramelle	sweets
cioccolato	chocolate
formaggio	cheese
frittata	omelette
marmellata	jam
olio	oil
olive	olives
pane	bread
pepe	pepper
riso	rice
sale	salt
uova	eggs
zucchero	sugar
zuppa	soup

STARTERS (ANTIPASTI) AND FRIED SNACKS (FRITTI)

antipasto misto mixed cold meats and cheese (and a selection of other things in this list)

arancini fried rice balls with mozzarella and tomato

caponata mixed aubergine, olives, tomatoes and celery

caprese tomato and mozzarella salad

insalata di mare seafood salad

insalata di riso rice salad

melanzane alla parmigiana layers of aubergine, tomato and parmesan

mortadella salami-type cured meat

pancetta bacon

peperonata grilled green, red or yellow peppers stewed in olive oil

pomodori ripieni stuffed tomatoes

prosciutto ham

salame salami

supplì fried rice balls with mozzarella

SOUP (ZUPPA)

brodo clear broth

minestrina any light soup

minestrone thick vegetable soup

pasta e fagioli pasta soup with beans

pastina in brodo pasta in clear broth

stracciatella broth with egg

PASTA

bucatini thick, hollow spaghetti-type pasta. Sometimes known as *tonnarelli*

cannelloni large, stuffed pasta tubes

farfalle literally "bow"- shaped pasta; the word also means "butterflies"

fettuccine flat ribbon egg pasta

paccheri large tubes of pasta

pasta al forno pasta baked with minced meat, eggs, tomato and cheese

penne tubed pasta

rigatoni Llrge, curved and ridged tubes of pasta – larger than penne but smaller than paccheri

spaghettini thin spaghettis

strozzapreti literally "strangled priests" – twisted flat noodles

fagliatelle flat ribbon egg noodles, slightly thinner than fettuccine

vermicelli thin strand pasta often served in soup – literally "little worms"

PASTA SAUCES

aglio e olio with garlic and oil

amatriciana With tomato and *guanciale* (similar to bacon)

arrabbiata ("angry") spicy tomato sauce, with chillies

alla carbonara pasta with beaten egg, pan-fried guanciale or bacon, and pecorino cheese

alla gricia with pecorino and guanciale

cacio e pepe pasta with pecorino and ground black pepper

con vongole with clams

panna cream

parmigiano parmesan

pasta alla pajata with calf's intestines – a very Roman dish

peperoncino chilli

pomodoro tomato

puttanesca ("whorish") Tomato, anchovy, olive oil and oregano

ragù (or Bolognese) meat sauce

MEAT (CARNE)

abbacchio milk-fed lamb roasted with rosemary and garlica

agnello lamb

bistecca steak

carpaccio slices of raw beef

cervello brain, usually calves'

cinghiale wild boar

coda alla vaccinara oxtail stewed in a rich sauce of tomato and celery

coniglio rabbit

costolette Cutlet, chop

coratella lamb's heart, liver, lungs and spleen cooked in olive oil with lots of black pepper and onions

fegato liver

guanciale unsmoked bacon made from pigs' cheeks

maiale pork

manzo beef

milza spleen – sometimes served as a pâté on toasted bread

ossobuco shin of veal

pajata the intestines of a unweaned calf

pancetta bacon

pollo chicken

polpette meatballs

porchetta pork stuffed with herbs and roasted on a spit

rognoni kidneys

salsiccia sausage

saltimbocca alla Romana Veal cooked with a slice of prosciutto and sage on top, served plain or with a Marsala sauce

scottadito grilled lamb chops, eaten with the fingers

spezzatino stew

trippa tripe

vitello veal

FISH (PESCE) AND SHELLFISH (CROSTACEI)

acciughe anchovies

anguilla eel

aragosta lobster

baccalà cod, best eaten Jewish-style, deep-fried

calamari squid

cozze mussels

dentice sea bream

gamberetti shrimps

gamberi prawns

granchio crab

merluzzo cod

ostriche oysters

pesce spada swordfish

polpo octopus

rospo monkfish

sampiero John Dory

sarde sardines

sogliola sole

tonno tuna

trota trout

vongole clams

VEGETABLES (CONTORNI) AND SALAD (INSALATA)

carciofi... artichokes

　　...alla Romana stuffed with garlic, mint and parsley and stewed in wine

　　...alla guidea flattened and deep fried in olive oil

carciofini artichoke hearts

cavolfiore cauliflower

cavolo cabbage

cipolla onion

fagioli beans

fagiolini green beans

fiori di zucca batter-fried courgette (zucchini) blossom stuffed with mozzarella and sometimes a sliver of marinated anchovy

finocchio fennel
funghi mushrooms
insalata verde green
  /mista /mixed salad
melanzane aubergine (eggplant)
patate potatoes
peperoni peppers
Piselli peas
pomodori tomatoes
radicchio red salad leaves
spinaci spinach

COOKING TERMS

ai ferri grilled without oil
alla brace barbecued
alla griglia grilled
alla milanese fried in egg and
  breadcrumbs
alla pizzaiola cooked with tomato sauce
allo spiedo on the spit
al dente firm, not overcooked
al forno baked
al sangue rare
arrosto roast
ben cotto well done
bollito/lesso boiled
cotto cooked (not raw)
crudo raw
fritto fried
in umido stewed
ripieno stuffed
stracotto braised, stewed

CHEESE (FORMAGGI)

dolcelatte creamy blue cheese
fontina northern Italian cheese
pecorino strong, hard sheep's cheese
provola/provolone smooth, round mild
  cheese, made from buffalo's or sheep's
  milk, sometimes smoked

FRUIT (FRUTTA) AND NUTS (NOCI)

ananas pineapple
anguria/coccomero watermelon
arance oranges
banane bananas
ciliegie cherries
fichi figs
fichi d'India prickly pears

fragole strawberries
limone lemon
mandorle almonds
mele apples
melone melon
pere pears
pesche peaches
pinoli pine nuts
uva grapes

DESSERTS (DOLCI)

cassata ice-cream cake with candied fruit
crostata pastry tart with fruit, chocolate or
  ricotta topping
gelato ice cream
macedonia fruit salad
Torta cake, tart
zabaglione dessert made with eggs, sugar
  and Marsala wine
zuppa Inglese trifle

DRINKS (BEVANDE)

acqua minerale mineral water
acqua naturale/frizzante still/sparkling
  water
acqua del rubinetto tap water
bicchiere glass
birra beer
bottiglia bottle
caffè coffee
cioccolato caldo hot chocolate
ghiaccio ice
granita lied drink, with coffee or fruit
latte milk
limonata lemonade
spremuta fresh fruit juice
succo concentrated fruit juice with sugar
tè tea
vino wine
vino rosso/bianco/rosato red/white/
  rose wine
vino secco/dolce dry/sweet wine
ltro Litre
mezzo half
quarto quarter
salute! cheers!

PUBLISHING INFORMATION

This second edition published February 2013 by **Rough Guides Ltd**.
80 Strand, London WC2R 0RL
11, Community Centre, Panchsheel Park, New Delhi 110017, India
Distributed by the Penguin Group
Penguin Books Ltd, 80 Strand, London WC2R 0RL
Penguin Group (USA) 375 Hudson Street, NY 10014, USA
Penguin Group (Australia) 250 Camberwell Road, Camberwell, Victoria 3124, Australia
Penguin Group (NZ) 67 Apollo Drive, Mairangi Bay, Auckland 1310, New Zealand
Rough Guides is represented in Canada by
Tourmaline Editions Inc., 662 King Street West, Suite 304, Toronto, Ontario, M5V 1M7
Typeset in Minion and Din to an original design by Henry Iles and Dan May.
Printed and bound in China
© Rough Guides 2013
Maps © Rough Guides
No part of this book may be reproduced in any form without permission from the publisher except for
the quotation of brief passages in reviews.
208pp includes index
A catalogue record for this book is available from the British Library
ISBN 978-1-40936-022-3
The publishers and authors have done their best to ensure the accuracy and currency of all the
information in the **Pocket Rough Guide Rome**, however, they can accept no responsibility for
any loss, injury, or inconvenience sustained by any traveller as a result of information or advice
contained in the guide.
1 3 5 7 9 8 6 4 2

MIX
Paper from
responsible sources
FSC www.fsc.org   FSC™ C018179

ROUGH GUIDES CREDITS

Text editor: Lucy Kane
Layout: Pradeep Thapliyal, Dan May
Photography: James McConnachie, Natascha Sturny
Cartography: Katie Bennett
Picture editor: Mark Thomas
Proofreader: Jennifer Speake
Production: Rebecca Short
Cover design: Nicole Newman, Pradeep Thapliyal

THE AUTHORS

Martin Dunford is the author of Rough Guides to Rome, Italy, Amsterdam and New York, among
others, and is consultant publisher for the series and a freelance writer, editor and publishing
consultant. He lives in London and Norfolk, with his wife Caroline and two daughters.

Natasha Foges packed her bags and moved to Rome on a whim, and stayed for four years. Now
based in London, she misses the food, the sun and the scooter rides, but escapes back to Rome as
often as she can to revisit old haunts and overindulge on ice cream.

ACKNOWLEDGEMENTS

Martin Dunford Thanks to Cory, Lubna, Judy and Katie; to Natasha, who did a fantastic job; to Lucy – typically positive, professional and thorough; and of course to my family, Caroline, Daisy and Lucy: Rome-lovers through-and-through.

Natasha Foges would like to thank Richard, Chiara, Lesley and Antonio for great Roman nights out; and Will, for his map-reading skills and his dedication to finding the perfect plate of *straccetti*.

HELP US UPDATE

We've gone to a lot of effort to ensure that the first edition of the **Pocket Rough Guide Rome** is accurate and up-to-date. However, things change – places get "discovered", opening hours are notoriously fickle, restaurants and rooms raise prices or lower standards. If you feel we've got it wrong or left something out, we'd like to know, and if you can remember the address, the price, the hours, the phone number, so much the better.

Please send your comments with the subject line "**Pocket Rough Guide Rome Update**" to ⓔ mail@roughguides.com. We'll credit all contributions and send a copy of the next edition (or any other Rough Guide if you prefer) for the very best emails.

Have your questions answered and tell others about your trip at ⓦ www.roughguides.com

PHOTO CREDITS

All images © Rough Guides except:
Front cover Colosseum illuminated at dusk © Guy Vanderelst/Getty
Back cover Piazza di Spagna © John Kellerman/Alamy
p.1 View over the domes of Rome © Mark Thomas
p.3 View over St Peters Square © Mark Thomas
p.4 Trevi Fountain © Mark Thomas
p.6 Pantheon and restaurants © Alex Segre/Alamy
p.8 Piazza del Popolo © Mark Thomas
p.10 Spanish Steps © Mark Thomas
p.12–13 The Forum © Mark Thomas
p.15 Galleria Doria Pamphilj © Alinari Archives/Corbis
p.17 View from Spanish Steps © Mark Thomas
p.19 Roman Jewish food © Natasha Foges
p.19 Backstreet Trattoria © Natasha Foges
p.21 Via Condotti © Mark Thomas
p.21 Castroni ©Stephane Gautier/Alamy
p.22 Palazzo Farnese © Gianni Dagli Orti/Alamy
p.26 The Colosseum © Mark Thomas
p.27 Ostia Antica © Mimmo Jodice/Corbis
p.30 Villa Borghese © Mark Thomas
p.31 Via Appia Antica © Eastland/Alamy
p.32–33 Statue in the Pincio Gardens © Mark Thomas
p.39 Marcus Aurelius Column © Werner Dieterich/Alamy
p.42 Via del Governo Vecchio © Cubo Images srl/Alamy

p.45 Specialist tie shop © Pictures Colour Library
p.55 Fontana delle Tartarughe © Natasha Foges
p.63 Capitoline Museums © Adam Eastland/Alamy
p.72 View towards the Colosseum © Mark Thomas © Kevin George/Alamy
p.85 Galleria Alberto Sordi © Kevin George/Alamy
p.95 Palazzo delle Esposizioni Roma, image courtesy of the Palazzo
p.97 Palazzo Massimo © Lanzellotto/Tips Images
p.102 Micca Club © Ursula Persiani/Micca Club
p.118 Tomb of Cecilia Metella © Glyn Thomas Photography
p.119 EUR © Masci/Tips Images
p.126 Corsini Palace © Gaertner/Alamy
p.130 Interior of Freni e Frizioni © Freni e Frizioni
p.144 Michelangelo's Pieta © Reinhard Dirscherl/Photolibrary
p.145 Interior of St Paul's © Mark Thomas
p.149 Sistine Chapel © Russell Mountford/Photolibrary
p.151 Vatican Gardens © Mark Thomas
p.155 Temple of Vesta and Tiburnus © Yannick Luthy/Alamy
p.157 Sperlonga © Juergen Sack/iStock
p.157 Terracina © Iraida Bassi/iStock
p.158 Anzio © Bruce Bean/iStock
p.160 Amphitheatre, Ostia Antica © image-broker/Alamy
p.172–173 View from the Spanish Steps © Mark Thomas

Index

Map entries are in **bold**.

F

G

H

W

SO NOW WE'VE TOLD YOU
ABOUT THE THINGS NOT TO
MISS, THE BEST PLACES TO
STAY, THE TOP RESTAURANTS,
THE LIVELIEST BARS AND THE
MOST SPECTACULAR SIGHTS,
IT ONLY SEEMS FAIR TO
TELL YOU ABOUT THE BEST
TRAVEL INSURANCE AROUND

 WorldNomads.com

keep travelling safely

RECOMMENDED BY ROUGH GUIDES